C000259566

LMS Steam

Uniform with this book

SOUTHERN STEAM

LNER STEAM

London - Glasgow express approaching Shap Summit hauled by Royal Scot class locomotive 6137 *The Prince of Wales Volunteers (South Lancashire)*

LMS STEAM

by

O. S. NOCK, B.Sc., C.Eng.
F.I.C.E., F.I.Mech.E.

DAVID & CHARLES NEWTON ABBOT

ISBN 0 7153 5240 7

Set in eleven point Baskerville
and printed in Great Britain
by Bristol Typesetting Company Limited
for David & Charles (Publishers) Limited
South Devon House Newton Abbot Devon

Contents

Illustrations

Illustrations

Preface

IN writing this companion volume to my previous books *Southern Steam* and *LNER Steam* it has been difficult at times to avoid giving the impression that I was taking sides. The early days of the LMSR were fraught with so much controversy, so much hard feeling on one side or the other, that anyone attempting to do something more than produce a mere statistical account of events is bound to get caught up in some of the fracas himself. And as much of what happened in those early days eventuated directly from many a clash of personalities, the story would be completely bleak and meaningless without some references to the human background. Transcending everything else was the intense rivalry between Derby and Crewe. There were other factions, up and down the country, in this most unnatural of amalgamations; but nothing to compare with the great issue, North Western versus Midland.

It is sometimes assumed that anyone who took an interest in locomotive affairs must be, irreconcilably, on one side or the other. If one looked with any favour upon the products of Crewe one must automatically hate Derby. In writing the story of the early days of the LMS any author with anything but the most rabid partisan outlook must find himself defending Crewe and poking a little mild sarcasm at 'the other place'. But all this arises from the sheer illogicality of what actually took place. That it was inevitable is clear enough from the policy dictated by the high management of the LMS in its earliest days; and the muddle continued while men of medium stature jockeyed for position, until Sir Guy Granet realised he would get nowhere with existing personnel and brought in a complete outsider in Sir Josiah Stamp. Until then the old tag 'The 'ell of a mess' had more truth in it than one likes to contemplate! The subsequent transformation is as much a monument to Stamp's breadth of vision and administrative skill as it is to the distinguished engineers who did the actual work. For Stamp, having no partisan sentiments, was quick to perceive the immense strength and potential of both Crewe and Derby, and at once began to seek means to bring them into a solid alliance. He found the answer in Stanier, not only as a great engineer, but as a man who could build up a strong team that would carry on the tradition. One has only to mention the names of Riddles, Coleman, Ivatt, Bond and Cox, and to recall their subsequent achievements, to appreciate how well Stanier fulfilled his mandate.

This book has been written out of the experience of travel over all parts of the LMS system throughout the twenty-five years of its existence. I am old enough to possess logs of journeys that I made on the London & North Western, Midland, and Furness Railways, and of journeys behind Caledonian and Glasgow and South Western locomotives still bearing their original distinctive liveries. In my earlier days as a student and then a graduate of the Institution of Mechanical Engineers I met young men who were deeply involved in the momentous dynamometer car trials described in Chapter 5. Later, when the privilege of footplate passes began to come my way, I met senior officers, and ultimately I had the great honour of writing Sir William Stanier's biography. Many of the men most intimately concerned in this great saga have become personal friends, and my association with Riddles and Bond in particular has given much background knowledge against which to place the outward evidence of actual construction and working.

I am much indebted to the various running superintendents from whom I received footplate passes, especially R. F. Harvey, and Lieutenant Colonel H. Rudgard. I must also mention particularly Mr D. S. M. Barrie, recently retired from the high office of chairman and general manager of the Eastern Region of British Railways, to whose enthusiasm and drive for publicity in the 1930s, when at Euston House, I am indebted for many facilities on the LMS in those exciting years. I am also deeply grateful to Mr R. W. Crawshaw, public relations and publicity officer of the London Midland Region for putting the fine collection of official photographs at my disposal, with the results that are evident in the illustrated sections of this book.

Preface

As always I am greatly indebted to Olivia, my wife, for typing the manuscript. As a very loyal servant of the LNER she has a way of looking at anything concerning the LMS with a faintly jaundiced eye! And as it turned out her disapproval of the form of streamlining on the Coronation class Pacifics, though in her case purely on aesthetic grounds, was eventually justified for solid practical reasons and led to its removal!

Silver Cedars
High Bannerdown
Batheaston
BATH

O. S. Nock
August 1970

CHAPTER I

The Merger Nobody Wanted

THE title of this opening chapter may be an over-simplification of the state of affairs prevailing on 1 January 1923, when the London Midland & Scottish Railway came into being, because certain high personalities in the directorial and management ranks stood to gain enhanced prestige and power by its accomplishment. But it is no exaggeration to say that of the vast majority of the staff, both salaried and otherwise, those who did not regard the event with indifference were deeply apprehensive regardless of whether they were based in Euston, Derby, Manchester or across the Border. Unlike nationalisation in 1948, the grouping scheme was not the outcome of political pressure. It was a measure of business expediency framed by the 'Chamber of Commerce' Parliament of David Lloyd George resulting from the notorious 'khaki election' of December 1918. While some groupings decreed by the Railways Act of 1921 were effected in relative harmony, if not necessarily enthusiasm, the huge London, Midland & Scottish group brought together some most unlikely bed-fellows. The result was continuous friction which bedevilled many activities of the company for many years.

This is essentially a book about locomotives, but to appreciate the astonishing situation that developed within a very few months of grouping some reference must be made to the higher politics of the amalgamation. The merger only a year earlier of the Lancashire & Yorkshire Railway with the London & North Western would, to all outward appearances, have seemed to put the enlarged London & North Western in a virtually impregnable position, when the larger amalgamation took place. Furthermore the LNW/LYR combination had been achieved in pleasant and friendly circumstances. It is certainly true that LNWR locomotive men received something of a jolt when the chieftainship of the department went to George Hughes; but he was by so many years, and by stature, the senior man that it was an appointment accepted with resignation at Crewe. Furthermore Hughes himself had a charming personality, and the liaison that grew up between the establishments at Horwich and Crewe was cordial to a degree. Against the massive numerical strength of Crewe alone, with 376 superheated express passenger 4–6–0s, whole regiments of hard-slogging, dividend-earning eight-coupled freighters, how conceivably could the precepts of Derby prevail when the best they could put forward for express passenger work were 55 4–4–0s in the Number 4 class, which would be completely eclipsed by the 90 George the Fifth class 4–4–0s of the North Western, not to mention the many Precursors that had been rebuilt with enlarged cylinders, piston valves and superheated boilers. To most outside observers, despite the advent of Hughes, the locomotive situation on the LMS looked like a push-over for Crewe.

Behind locked doors as it were, the men of the enlarged North Western, and no less those of the Scottish companies had, long before that fateful January of 1923, felt the well nigh impregnable strength of the Midland high management, and particularly the personality of Sir Guy Granet. Step by step, inexorably, he virtually dictated the terms of amalgamation and, although he did not become either chairman or deputy chairman of the new company, he dominated the proceedings of the board as surely as Richard Moon had done on the North Western in the critical days of Lord Chandos' chairmanship. The result was that Midland precepts of management were adopted for the new company. Seventeen years earlier Granet had completely overthrown the traditional form of railway organisation which had prevailed on the Midland as firmly as on all other large railways of Great Britain, and now it was the turn of the other constituents of the LMS to experience what the Midland had passed through from 1906 onwards. So far as locomotive working was concerned one fundamental change was made from the very outset, namely the divorcement of responsibility for locomotive running from the chief mechanical engineer. Other changes were to follow later, but the foregoing one was enough to set the heather on fire, as indeed it had done on the Midland in the days of R. M. Deeley.

PRE-GROUPING MISCELLANY

(above) LYR *Hughes 4-cylinder 4–6–0 as rebuilt January 1920;* (centre) *Furness Railway: the last Pettigrew 0–6–0 to retain Furness boiler;* (below) G & SWR: *Peter Drummond superheater 4–4–0 express locomotive*

MIDLAND CLASS 1 VETERANS

(above) *Kirtley 6ft 2in 2–4–0 20002, originally built 1866, withdrawn 1948, and now preserved as* MR *156A;* (centre) *Johnson 7ft 6in 4–2–2 No 631, originally built in 1891 as No 122;* (below) *Johnson 7ft 2–4–0 express engine No 281 formerly No 1501 and built in 1881. This engine still retains its Johnson chimney*

So far as the post of chief mechanical engineer was concerned, Granet was quite prepared to accept Hughes, knowing that he had but few years to go before retirement and that then he would be succeeded by Sir Henry Fowler. Derby would then come as surely into its own as the fountainhead of all mechanical engineering practice, as operating matters were already in process of doing with John H. Follows in the chair as chief general superintendent. In January 1923 another absolutely 'key' position went to a Midland man, that of superintendent of motive power, for the entire LMS system, to J. E. Anderson, formerly deputy chief mechanical engineer of the Midland. Even before Hughes retired it was clearly evident that the influence of Derby was rapidly spreading, and with Follows and Anderson quickly entrenched in their respective and very important spheres, the Midland grip on the whole organisation for running the trains and providing the power was virtually complete at a very early stage in LMS history. To anyone who did not understand the personality of Granet it was a phenomenon as unlikely as it was inexplicable. This is not to suggest that the Midland triumvirate of Follows, Anderson and Fowler were anything but very able men; but they were none of them giants, and giants were needed to get a complex agglomeration like the LMS off to a good start.

The British railway world had been grievously unfortunate in losing two of the ablest of its younger men prior to this great amalgamation, in the persons of Sir Guy Calthrop, general manager of the LNWR who died of influenza in the great epidemic that swept the country at the end of World War I, and Sir Cecil Paget, in pre-war days general superintendent of the Midland. Paget had flourished exceedingly in the first flush of the Granet reorganisation; but during his brilliantly successful command of the Railway Operating Division on the Western Front during the second half of World War I he had so grown in stature and experience, as to find the prospects of a return to the Midland Railway to his old post virtually impossible. So he went into industry. Whether he was ever considered for high office on the LMS is doubtful, because one can well imagine that Granet, like Moon many years before him, no doubt desired to have in the key position of chief general superintendent 'an intelligent executive officer'. A man of Paget's original turn of mind and breadth of outlook—not to mention his unorthodox way of surmounting difficulties—could well have been too much for the railway situation of 1923 onwards which Granet so invincibly influenced. It is nevertheless an interesting field of conjecture to try and imagine how the LMS might have fared if Paget and not Follows had been the first chief general superintendent.

Turning now more particularly to the locomotive departments, apart from Hughes and Fowler three well-known figures were left as mere divisional chiefs: Pickersgill at St Rollox; Robert Whitelegg at Kilmarnock, and above all H. P. M. Beames at Crewe. It must have been disappointing, almost to the point of humiliation, for a man who had held the office of chief mechanical engineer of the London & North Western Railway to find himself in the position that Beames did, but such are the natures of industrial take-overs. It speaks volumes for his devotion to Crewe, and the memory of the LNWR, that he continued and came to render immense service to the enlarged company in a massive modernisation of Crewe works. Whitelegg was for the second time the victim of a take-over, and by the Midland both times! He had succeeded his father as locomotive superintendent of the London Tilbury & Southend Railway, and left after the Midland take-over of 1912; then after succeeding Peter Drummond at Kilmarnock in 1918 he found himself in the same position again. His stay on the LMS was little more than one of weeks for he secured the general managership of Beyer, Peacock & Co Ltd which position he held with distinction for many years. His departure left the Glasgow & South Western Railway wide open and its complete subjugation followed rapidly.

While Beames kept the flag of the North Western flying as bravely as he could at Crewe, the same could not be said of Pickersgill at St Rollox. He was in any case a very retiring type of man. A Whitworth Scholar, a mechanical theorist, but one strangely reluctant to take decisions, he was the very antithesis to the forthright J. F. McIntosh whom he succeeded. With responsibility for running taken from him, the day-to-day control of affairs on the Caledonian passed into the far stronger hands of John Barr, and Whitelegg's departure made it easy for Barr to be given responsibility for all Scotland. No student of Scottish locomotive history needs to be told of the reaction to this situation on the 'Sou' West', though Barr cleverly countered some possible antagonism by initiating some interchange workings whereby Glasgow & South Western 4–6–0s undertook some West Coast turns between Glasgow Central and Carlisle. Pickersgill drops out of the LMS picture almost unobtrusively after the disastrous failure of his big three-cylinder 4–6–0s, and on the works side in Scotland by far the strongest personality came to be David Urie, son of R. W. Urie of the London & South Western, who had succeeded C. Cumming as locomotive superintendent of the Highland Railway in 1922.

Even in the early months of 1923 the pattern of development, not so much in design but in mechanical engineering organisational strategy, could be seen fairly clearly. Hughes was in the chair but behind the amiable and scientific personality of Sir Henry Fowler, his official deputy, there loomed the portentous figure of Sir Guy Granet, determined that at all costs Midland precepts should prevail. Beside Hughes and Fowler only Beames exerted any real influence on constructional and works practice. Whatever Granet may have desired, Crewe was by far the largest manufactory within the new organisation, and must inevitably be used to the full in any new constructional programmes. On the running side, Anderson sought to impose Midland methods throughout. In Scotland he was met by the implacable opposition of John Barr, who upheld Caledonian methods, and by sheer force of personality prevailed for many years. On the North Western the methods dictated by Anderson were met by a certain amount of mild ridicule, particularly in the manner of train loading. I cannot resist retelling the story related some years ago by T. Lovatt Williams, of the driver called 'Fred' at Euston who was quizzed by an ex-Midland traffic inspector: 'One morning,' Williams wrote, 'his engine, a George the Fifth, was standing at the head of a train in No 15 platform, Euston, and Fred was leaning over the side of the cab, surveying the scene on the platform with a cynical eye. A few minutes before starting time a rather pompous Midland official walked up Platform 15 and counted the coaches as he went along. Thirteen coaches, two "diners"—loading equal to "23½". A bit staggered by this he walked up to Fred and said "Good morning, driver, where's your pilot engine?" Fred looked him up and down, removed the dreadful old pipe from beneath his straggling moustache and remarked: "In the shed, where she ought to be. Who do you think we are, the b . . . . Midland?" '

With Hughes in the chair interest centred at first upon ex-Lancashire & Yorkshire designs. With some justification Horwich had derived much satisfaction from the results of rebuilding of the 1500 class four-cylinder 4–6–os. In their original form strong claims could have been laid on their behalf, to the title of 'the world's worst', such was their shocking record of performance and general reliability. The rebuilding turned them into workmanlike and dependable engines, capable of a high output of power; but in overall efficiency they were no more than mediocre. As first tested with the Horwich dynamometer car they gave results that had been highly gratifying to the CME's department of the Lancashire & Yorkshire Railway; but that department, or rather its LMS successors got the shock of their lives when C. B. Collett of the Great Western published, to the World Power Conference of 1924, the results obtained on dynamometer car tests between Swindon and Plymouth from his new 4–6–0 locomotive No 4074 *Caldicot Castle*. For while the rebuilt Horwich 4–6–0 had shown a coal consumption of around 5lb per drawbar horsepower hour, the Great Western figure was less than 3lb!

After the amalgamation of the LYR with the LNWR competitive trials with the dynamometer car were run between Crewe and Carlisle in which one of the Horwich 4–6–os was pitted against LNWR 4–6–os of the Prince of Wales and Claughton classes. No results of these trials were ever published but 'it was generally understood'—to quote a contemporary comment in a technical journal—that the Horwich 4–6–0 had done the most satisfactory work. Who 'generally understood' it was not quoted at the time, but in comparative tests of this kind the locomotives of the reigning management have a way of coming out on top! In support of the 'generally understood' results of these trials of 1922 a further batch of 25 new engines to the same drawings was put in hand and completed at Horwich between December 1922 and August 1923. Of the original 20 engines of 1908-9 only 15 were rebuilt. The remaining 5 were scrapped in their saturated condition in 1925-6, but shortly after the LNWR/LYR merger 10 engines had been built new, in August-November 1921. By August of 1923 therefore there were 50 of these engines in traffic. Another 20 were built in 1924-5. The LMS numbers of those built new ran from 10420 to 10474 while the rebuilds were

10405 to 10419. Many of them were put into regular service between Crewe and Carlisle, working chiefly from the Carlisle end. Despite their reported superiority over the LNWR 4–6–0s they never worked regularly south of Crewe.

There is no doubt they proved an absolute godsend to the running department on the Lancashire & Yorkshire line. The latter had been in a dreadful state in the last years before the amalgamation, and at the end of 1919 there had been not a single 4–6–0 in traffic! Regarding the rebuilt engines, their true place in history so far as working efficiency was concerned was shown in a series of dynamometer car trials run between Preston and Carlisle in 1925. At that time the prime object of the management was to vindicate the Midland compounds, and although the results of these trials were never published officially, I was favoured with a copy of the report many years later and since then have myself published full details of the working; but as these results belong more correctly to a later stage in LMS history, they are withheld to a later chapter (p. 80). At this stage however I may mention that the big Hughes four-cylinder 4–6–0s, far from proving superior to the North Western Claughtons, were consistently and markedly heavier on coal. It is amusing to recall that among North Western men they acquired the nickname of the 'Lanky Claughtons'.

On the L & Y line itself some of the finest work of the day was being performed by the superheated 2–4–2 tank engines, and on certain duties, notably the residential trains working over the northern branch lines from Manchester, they were within measurable distance of being worked all-out over considerable mileages of each journey. It was to provide enhanced engine power on these duties that a tank-engine version of the superheated express passenger 4–6–0 was produced. In view of the success with which the 2–4–2 tanks had been used in the past, and the similarity of many of the L & Y duties to turns being successfully worked by tank engines on the Brighton railway and elsewhere, it was felt that an express tank engine would have a wide application. The first of the new 4–6–4s was completed in March 1924 and a batch of ten was turned out from Horwich works. They were identical in their machinery to the main line 4–6–0s, and had the same boilers. They did good work on the heavily graded lines north of Manchester, but the proposal to build a further twenty was changed, and these engines actually emerged as the final batch of 4–6–0 tender engines. The ten Baltic tanks had a relatively short life; in addition to being non-standard by later LMS ideas they proved generally inferior in all-round performance to the new Derby 2–6–4 tanks of the 2300 class.

Hughes was essentially a 'big-engine' man and, not to be outdone by his confrères on the LNER, he prepared a design for a large four-cylinder 4–6–2 express locomotive for general service on the West Coast route. This had a nominal tractive effort of 33,600lb. Like Sir Nigel Gresley, he had prepared a similar design with the 2–8–2 wheel arrangement for heavy freight. These proposals brought Hughes into mild collision with the newly established operating department. Thinking entirely on Midland lines Follows, ably backed by J. E. Anderson, had in mind a complete recasting of the West Coast services, dispensing entirely with the heavy-load principles of the North Western and running instead a swarm of lightly loaded trains at frequent intervals, which could presumably be operated by Midland compounds. Against such planning a huge Pacific such as that proposed by Hughes would have no place. Hughes was then very near to retirement, and withdrew what would have been the climax of his engine designing achievements. The 2–8–2, which was intended for service on the heavy coal trains of the Midland line between Toton Yard and Cricklewood, was vetoed on account of weight limitations.

One feels that the withdrawal of these great proposals was just as well. The production of an entirely new design almost invariably involves a great deal of nursing when the prototype machines are first placed in traffic. There have been many examples of very large new locomotives placed in service just as the designer was on the point of retirement. A change in management can produce a change of attitude, and a noble project can become 'nobody's baby'. A classic instance of this was the 4–6–4 compound of the Northern Railway of France produced at the end of the Du Bousquet regime, probably one of the finest compound designs in Europe in pre-Chapelon days. Yet it was completely neglected and no more than the two prototype engines built. The Raven Pacifics of the former North Eastern Railway provide another instance, and equally the V4 2–6–2 tender engines of the LNER. Hughes will be remembered as an engineer with a somewhat 'patchy' career. His early work on the Lancashire & Yorkshire Railway was distinguished by some quite advanced thinking on boiler design and superheating, but he seemed to fail completely in appreciating how a valve gear could contribute to the free and economic running of a locomotive. When a commentator once suggested that the outstanding success of his rebuilt and superheated 4–4–0s was due to the use of the Walschaerts valve gear, with a modern setting, he retorted that the valve gear had nothing to do with it, and that the Joy gave just as good a distribution as the Walschaerts. In fact a bad setting of the Joy gear was one of the most crippling handicaps to the original 1500 class 4–6–0s.

There were some curious points in the original organisation set up by Hughes in his capacity as chief mechanical engineer of the LMS. When the LNWR/LYR merger took place the North Western was referred to as the 'A' and the Lancashire & Yorkshire as the 'B' division. Then when the larger amalgamation took place it was rather odd that the Furness section though completely isolated from the former LYR was placed in 'B' division. Presumably it was thought that 'A' division was big enough already without taking in any small constituents. At the time of the amalgamation my home was at Barrow-in-Furness, and when visiting the Furness Railway works one day Mr E. Sharples showed me the new diagram book that had just been issued, and which included line drawings of all the Lancashire & Yorkshire locomotive classes. It was from Sharples that I had many sidelights on the character of Hughes himself. I remember well how Sharples once apostrophised him as a 'dear old man'. In later years too Loughnan Pendred, that great editor of *The Engineer*, showed me a delightful photograph of Hughes in the most informal of gardening clothes, and duly inscribed: 'It's a far cry from "Class 8" to tomatoes!' Class 8 was the official LYR designation of the rebuilt four-cylinder 4–6–0. One feels that Hughes was very glad to be out of the LMS 'rat-race' so soon.

Before he retired however he produced one new class that proved a first class dividend earner. This was the well-known Horwich Mogul, of which no fewer than 245 were eventually built. They were tough, hard-working engines that in their external appearance presented a curious mixture of old-time elegance and modern functionalism. If one took a photograph of one of them and covered the portion from the bottom of the cab windows downward, there was a neat, beautifully proportioned engine, with typical Lancashire & Yorkshire boiler mountings. But then, uncover the 'works', as 'L.B.S.C.' used to call them, and in the steeply inclined cylinders, high, stepped running plate and completely exposed motion one had functionalism in excelsis. Churchward must have shuddered at the sight of those inclined cylinders, but there was good reason for them in that the steam passages could be made very short and direct. When the engines were on the move the effect was most curious. Within weeks the enginemen had nicknamed them 'Crabs', and 'crabs' they were to their dying days! They were powerful engines, having cylinders 21in diameter by 26in stroke; coupled wheels 5ft 6in diameter and a boiler pressure of 180psi. The nominal tractive effort was 26,580lb, little different from one of the Hughes four-cylinder 4–6–0s.

The first engines of the class, completed in 1926 after Hughes had retired, were finished in Midland red, with their five-figure numbers on the tenders in the standard Derby style. Although they were built in the old traditional style, with short lap valves, they had a fine turn of speed and were generally far more reliable engines than the big 4–6–0s, which suffered from many ailments. Although they must be regarded as a wholly LMS product they were equally the ultimate product of the Horwich school of design, before the various constituent sections of the LMS began to draw together and produce a new design policy for the far-flung railway as a whole. The 'crabs' were in every way a most useful addition to the stock, and they came to be used all over the system. I had some excellent runs with them in a variety of circumstances, ranging from my regular train from home to London in the days when I used to travel from Watford Junction or Bushey, to the early morning Highland Mail.

The 8.53am from Watford to Euston rarely had anything but ex-LNWR engines at that time, and two runs with No 13224 remain the only ones I noted with Moguls in all the nine years I was travelling on this service. She was probably put on as a substitute, and was worked by different drivers on the two days. She made fast running on both days, and on the second ran the 17.5 miles from Watford to Euston in 19min 6sec, with a maximum speed of 76½mph at Wembley. Another smart piece of work was on the 9.47am Glasgow and Edinburgh express from Liverpool Exchange in September 1931 when No 13167 had a substantial load of 365 tons. She ran particularly well after leaving Burscough Junction, passing Midge Hall, 8.2 miles, in 9¾min. I am, however, drawing rather ahead of the period in referring to these runs but I have quoted them to show the worth of the final Lancashire & Yorkshire contribution to the LMS stud of the later 1920s.

Before leaving Hughes and the Lancashire & Yorkshire Railway, emphasis must be laid upon the nature of the locomotive workings as it differed so profoundly from that of the Midland. On the LYR the workings were definitely selective, in that picked engines were reserved for the most arduous duties. The cynic may say that such tactics of selection were the only possible means of operation when the running department was saddled with such engines as the original non-superheated four-cylinder 4–6–0s; but it was applied to every class. One certainly could not have taken any superheated 2–4–2 engine and expected to run the 4.25pm residential express from Salford to Colne on time. Similar care was taken in the allocation of the Atlantics, especially when they were carrying the whole weight of the top link express turns in the critical period at the end of the war, when the 4–6–0s were virtually useless. Of course when large numbers of the superheated 4–6–0s became available the position was greatly eased, and for the majority of the L & Y express turns there was ample engine power available.

All the same, during the several years of travelling I had in the north country when the 'Lanky Claughtons' were in their prime, I must confess that I never had a really good run with one of them. One evening in 1931 when I joined the evening Liverpool and Manchester 'Scotsman' at Carnforth to travel to Carlisle, I thought that at last I was in luck, for with engine No 10461 and a 420-ton train we began well to Oxenholme. But there, although the load was reduced by the detaching of the Windermere through carriage, we took a pilot for the ascent to Shap, though conveying a tare load of no more than 375 tons. The pilot was an ex-LNWR Precursor 4–4–2 tank, and with such provision of engine power the running was quite undistinguished.

CHAPTER 2

The Midland Contribution

WITH the retirement of George Hughes the stranglehold of Derby upon LMS locomotive affairs became virtually complete. A future historian, not knowing of the political background and seeking in the record of past achievement for some justification of the situation that developed, could well rub his eyes in wonder. The Midland Railway had not put into service a single *new* express passenger engine since 1907, when the 999 class was introduced. It is true that many small-boilered Johnson 4–4–0s had been twice rebuilt, and that the second of these amounted to the production of engines that were entirely new on every consideration save that of accountancy; but the resulting superheater 4–4–0s, good engines though they were in themselves, were of derisorily small tractive power compared with the modern locomotives of other British railway companies. In the days of 450-500-ton express trains, locomotives that had to be limited to a maximum load of 180 tons were almost beneath consideration. And yet these were the only new class that had appeared since 1907.

If the Midland Railway had built nothing since 1907, so equally had they scrapped very little in the intervening years. Only 36 out of a total of 281 elderly 2–4–0s had been withdrawn by the time of grouping; 12 Johnson small boilered 4–4–0s had gone and 52 of the 4–2–2 singles. The Midland entered the grouping era with the express passenger locomotive stock shown in Table 1.

Even taking the most charitable view this was not a very impressive array of engine power for the dominating partner in the London Midland & Scottish group. It is not generally realised, for example, that at the time of grouping only twenty-four of the compounds had been superheated. It is true that good progress

TABLE I

Power class	Type	Description	Quantity
1	2-4-0	Kirtley classes	121
1	2-4-0	Johnson classes	144
1	4-4-0	Johnson 1876-7 classes un-rebuilt	16
1	4-2-2	Johnson singles	43
2	4-4-0	Non-superheated rebuilds	93
2	4-4-0	Fowler superheater rebuilds	142
3	4-4-0	Johnson Belpaires non-superheated	25
3	4-4-0	Johnson Belpaires superheated	55
4	4-4-0	Deeley 999 class	10
4	4-4-0	Deeley non-superheated compounds	21
4	4-4-0	Superheater compounds including rebuilds of original Smith-Johnson type	24

had been made with the conversion of the Class 2 and Class 3 engines, but with the latter the maximum unpiloted tare load was 205 tons. The Class 4 load at the time of grouping was 230 tons, and yet there were 4-4-0 locomotives within the LMS group—and very many of them—whose drivers would think nothing of taking nearly *double* the latter load without assistance.

Responsibility for the extraordinary state of affairs prevailing on the Midland Railway could not fairly be laid on the doorstep of Sir Henry Fowler. In the days of the Paget reorganisation of the passenger train timetables the guiding principle had been the running of expresses of light formation, and many of them. Locomotives capable of hauling heavy modern loads were not required, and at the outset the aggregate express train mileage caused some embarrassment to the locomotive running department in the sheer number of engines needed. The superheated rebuilt 4-4-0 did not come upon the scene until 1912, and then the running department could not have them fast enough. One thing seems very certain: if Fowler had put forward proposals for entirely new locomotives at that period they would have been vetoed pretty smartly. But the CME was no longer responsible for running on the Midland Railway; his remit was to make-do and mend.

The situation was perhaps even more extraordinary on the freight side, on which the stock on the eve of grouping included 1,598 0–6–0 tender engines in the following five groups:

Class 1, Kirtley, double-framed	440
Class 2, Kirtley, double-framed	31
Class 2, Johnson, small boiler	453
Class 3, Large-boilered, non-superheated	482
Class 4, Fowler, superheated	192

This was the locomotive stud that was operating one of the heaviest mineral traffics in the country. Of course it was necessary for practically every train to be double-headed, usually with a Class 1 or Class 2 engine piloting a Class 3 or Class 4. The last mentioned engines were the only new engines to be built for the Midland Railway since 1912, if one excepts the one and only Lickey 'banker' No 2290. Derby did in fact design and build a bigger freight engine, though this was not for their own line, but for the heavily graded Somerset & Dorset Joint Railway.

Before commenting further it is of interest to study the personality of the chief mechanical engineer himself. Sir Henry Fowler, charming, placid-natured gentleman, was a brilliant scientist; more of a physicist and metallurgist than the usual conception of a railway mechanical engineer. He took the keenest personal interest in the metallurgy of boilers, problems of corrosion, water treatment and so on, and in the physics of evaporation, steam raising and superheating. But he never held any responsibility for running, and seemed to take little interest in it. During World War I he was seconded to the Ministry of Munitions where he did a magnificent job, and returned afterwards duly rewarded with the KBE. For the environment dictated by the Granet régime on the Midland Railway he was an ideal chief mechanical engineer, constantly improving locomotives in details of their equipment, and all within the very modest demands made upon them through the strict loading restrictions laid down. With engines so lightly worked the repair charges were minimal and generations of drivers grew up who had no conception of what it meant to thrash an engine.

If they had the slightest excess over the booked loads they demanded a pilot, and I have had personal experience of trains being quite seriously delayed waiting for a pilot to be found at some intermediate station where an addition had been made to the load.

The Midland philosophy of management on the operating side was to lay down an adequate number of strict regulations for engine working and train loading. There was no question of selecting and reserving engines in good condition for the hardest turns. If, for example, a certain train was booked for a Class 3 engine it was considered that any Class 3 that was in running condition should be able to do the job. The loads were fixed to suit the worst engine. Good bad or indifferent, all that mattered in allocating engines to trains was the figure on the side of the cab. In practice this meant that engines in good condition were grossly under-run on many duties, and it was only the occasional flash of brilliance over a certain section that to some extent gave the show away, and revealed how much was in reserve. Class 3 included both non-superheated and superheated versions of the Johnson Belpaire 4-4-0s; while even more incongruous was the inclusion of both superheated and non-superheated compounds in Class 4. Both varieties were used turn and turn about on important expresses, and the variation in the running intermediately was often farcical. The non-superheated engines would run in some relation to the gradients, bending their backs to the loads uphill, and then flying down on the wings of the wind. The superheater engines would go storming up the banks with almost contemptuous ease, and then have so much time in hand that the drivers would shut off steam altogether, downhill. The farce would sometimes be carried still further when a slight excess of the maximum stipulated load brought out a pilot for a superheater engine in spanking condition!

In my school days I saw a good deal of two very fascinating sections of the Midland Railway, the Settle and Carlisle, and the little North-Western. A five-year spell beginning in 1916 brought me almost to the time of grouping and on those lines we saw practically every type of express passenger engine except the 'singles'. The ten 999 class 4-4-0s were the mainstay of the Anglo-Scottish services, though there were not nearly enough of them to work all the trains. Compounds from Leeds worked some of these turns, but the junior partners were mainly the Class 2 superheater rebuilds. The non-superheater rebuilds, which were so much in evidence in pre-war days had largely been displaced. Separate trains were run from St Pancras to Edinburgh and to Glasgow, and while the Glasgow portions were taken by the 999 class, the superheater Class 2s were often on the Edinburgh trains. The Class 3 4–4–0s were then rarely seen north of Leeds, though I have known one on the up afternoon Glasgow express deputising for a Leeds compound.

The handsome unrebuilt Johnson 4–4–0s were much in evidence at Hellifield. They were used for piloting on the Scotch expresses and also on the Little North-Western line. On the trains to Carnforth and Morecambe were all kinds of engines ranging from Johnson 2–4–0s to superheater Class 2 4–4–0s. I was not able to watch the workings sufficiently to establish the pattern of the locomotive allocations, but to outward appearances the usage of engines seemed entirely indiscriminate. By the period of my school days the Kirtley outside framed 2–4–0s were rare in the north. But withal it was a fascinating picture, yet nevertheless a picture of locomotive action that was already something of an anachronism. The sense of anachronism grew as one travelled south. At the time of grouping there were no compounds stationed at Derby. The largest engines working down the West of England line were the Class 3 superheaters, and at the Bristol and Gloucester sheds there was nothing larger than Class 2 4–4–0s. One found some of the most important turns, like the Bristol—Newcastle mail not infrequently worked by non-superheater engines, and single-wheelers were in constant demand as pilots.

Nowhere was the Midland policy of gentleness to express engines more assiduously practised than at Gloucester where the drivers were past-masters in the art of coal-dodging, and not to the benefit of their timekeeping either. The Derby men, with the Class 3 engine were usually more vigorous, and they shared the working to and from Manchester, over Peak Forest, with the Trafford Park compounds. In pre-war days engines used to work through unchanged between St Pancras and Manchester, and some compounds were stationed at Trafford Park accordingly. After the war, this through working was not revived, though the compounds stayed at their former depot. In Midland days only three sheds had compounds, namely Kentish Town, Trafford Park and Leeds, and they were confined largely to the long through runs. At one time however there was an isolated compound stationed at Carlisle. Everywhere on the line the Class 2 engines were to be seen, and with very few exceptions all passenger engines of whatever class went about their work in the most spotless condition. Occasionally I recall having seen a compound returning from Carlisle in a distinctly travel-stained condition. She had probably gone north on a very stormy night, and there had been no time to spruce her up before returning; but generally there was plenty of time between turns. No one bothered about getting high utilisation out of engines in those days.

This then was the railway whose locomotive department had thrust upon it the responsibility of formulating the future policy of the whole of the LMS. What its men lacked in experience of major weight-haulage, and of the locomotives necessary to do it, they made up for in self-confidence. Midland men were intensely proud of their railway. I recall, not so many years ago, hearing a running superintendent say 'It was a grand firm to work for,' and it is perhaps not surprising that when they saw the way the wind was settling they developed a terrific superiority complex. This was not likely to endear them to their new-found colleagues on the other railways, and on the North Western in particular it was to lead to quite serious friction. Fortunately, after some stormy years, circumstances were to arise that began to smooth over the early antagonisms, and to bring Derby and Crewe together into a formidable *entente*. At the outset however one can sympathise with Fowler's immediate assistants in the unpremeditated circumstances in which they found themselves. From what I have written earlier it will be appreciated that Fowler was no dedicated locomotive engineer, such as Churchward, Bowen-Cooke, or Gresley; he was a man who could readily apply his intensely quick brain and scientific approach to any problem that arose; but so far as locomotive design was concerned his was never a creative attitude. Three men lay behind Fowler's beneficent façade: S. J. Symes, the former Midland Railway chief draughtsman, who eventually became stores superintendent for the LMS; Herbert Chambers, chief draughtsman from 1926, and D. W. Sandford who was in charge of locomotive testing and experimental work.

TABLE 2

ST PANCRAS—LEICESTER

Engine No			562			1008		
Engine Class			2			4		
Load tons tare/full			193/205			229/245		
Distance			Actual		Speed	Actual		Speed
Miles		min	min	sec	mph	min	sec	mph
0.0	ST PANCRAS	0	0	00	–	0	00	–
1.5	Kentish Town	4	5	08	Fog	3	50	–
6.9	Hendon	10	13	45	delay	11	30	–
12.4	Elstree		20	24	47	18	00	46
15.2	Radlett		23	13	66½	20	55	67
19.9	ST ALBANS	25	27	55	46	25	55	46½
24.6	Harpenden		33	45	–	31	30	–
30.2	LUTON	36	39	22	–	37	05	66
32.8	Leagrave		41	53	–	39	30	–
37.3	Harlington		45	57	82	43	35	79
41.8	Ampthill		49	24	76	47	10	–
49.8	BEDFORD	54	55	26	84	53	45	79
56.7	Sharnbrook		61	43	–	60	15	–
59.7	*Milepost 59¾*	65	66	04	37½	64	25	39½
65.0	WELLINGBORO'	70	70	55	75*	69	25	70½*
72.0	KETTERING	77	78	00	–	76	35	–
78.5	*Desborough North*		86	10	45	84	45	44½
82.9	MARKET HARBOROUGH	90	90	39	72*	89	00	70½*
86.3	East Langton		94	44	59	92	25	64½
89.7	*Kibworth North*		98	35	46	96	10	48
95.4	Wigston		104	05	69*	101	40	66*
99.1	LEICESTER	109	108	48	–	106	35	–

* Maximum speeds before observing speed restrictions

At the time of grouping, although few realised it at the time, the Midland locomotive department had one absolutely trump card, in the superheated compound 4–4–0 engines. There were a mere twenty-four of them on New Year's Day 1923. Sandford probably knew something of their magnificent potentialities, but elsewhere on the Midland everyone concerned with train running thought inevitably in terms of 230-ton maximum loads. The difficulty with the loading regulations was that in all three classes, 2, 3 and 4 alike, the same loadings were applied to both super-

MIDLAND 4–4–0 EXPRESS TYPES

bove) *Non-superheater 6ft 6in rebuilt Class 2 No 480; originally No 2588 (Johnson) uilt 1900;* (centre) *Fowler rebuilt and superheated Class 2 No 508;* (below) *Superheater rebuild of Johnson Belpaire Class 3 No 726*

VINTAGE MIDLAND ON THE LICKEY

(above) *West to North express, hauled by 7ft non-superheater Class 2 rebuilt 4–4–0 No 4*[illegible] *with bank engine in rear;* (below) *Bristol to the North express hauled by 7ft 6in sing*[illegible] *No 630 and 7ft 2–4–0 No 197 with bank engine in rear*

heated and non-superheated engines. There was a world of difference between the two, in all three classes, but it was that ominous little number on the side of the cab that governed everything! To indicate the kind of running that prevailed on the Midland at the time of grouping I have chosen a few runs from published records, mainly from logs compiled by the late E. L. Diamond, who was at one time a pupil of Sir Henry Fowler at Derby, and who at one critical moment, as will be told later, exercised a massive influence on future LMS design.

There are first of all two runs on the London road, (Table 2) made when the crack timing of down expresses was 109min for the 99.1 miles between St Pancras and Leicester. On the first of these runs a Class 2 superheater engine was officially overloaded by 13 tons; but 193 tons tare was taken without a pilot. Although the start was hampered by thick fog, this cleared after Mill Hill and a good effort was made to recover the 3¾min that had been lost between St Pancras and Hendon. There was some really fast running down the bank after Luton with average speeds of 79.2mph over the 2 miles between mileposts 38 and 40, and of 81.8mph from milepost 44 to 48. The sharp inclines after Sharnbrook and Kettering naturally took their toll with an overloaded Class 2 engine but the engine was being skilfully and resolutely handled and the train reached Leicester on time. The companion run, on the 9.50am Glasgow express was of some significance. As usual it was worked by Leeds men, on this occasion by driver Heseltine with superheater compound No 1008. The load was just inside the maximum permitted. At that time on the Midland Railway drivers had their own engines, and the combination of Heseltine with No 1008, which continued for some years, was to prove an association that literally turned the course of locomotive history. On this run, while the sharp initial timing to Hendon was not kept, the job was an easy one for an excellent engine and a keen driver, and Leicester was reached 2½min early.

A run with engine No 760, on the 107min schedule from Leicester to St Pancras is equally very much of a period piece, and the idea of a 205-ton load being the maximum for a Class 3 superheater 4-4-0 would have been treated with some derision on the West Coast route. The engine was obviously being treated gently uphill, and allowed to make her own pace where the

TABLE 3
GLOUCESTER—BRISTOL

Load: 137 tons tare, 150 tons full
Engine: 7ft 6in 4–2–2 No 662

Distance Miles		Sch min	Actual min	Actual sec	Speed mph
0.0	GLOUCESTER	0	0	00	–
			sigs		51/31
5.6	Haresfield		10	15	45
6.9	*Standish Junction*	11	12	05	–
8.6	Stonehouse		13	55	61½
10.4	Frocester		15	45	58
12.5	Coaley		17	50	64
14.9	Berkeley Road	19	20	15	60
20.1	Charfield		25	45	–
22.0	Wickwar		28	05	46
26.7	Yate		34	10	60
31.9	MANGOTSFIELD	38	40	05	(slack)
34.0	Fishponds		42	40	–
			sigs		–
37.0	BRISTOL	48	prolonged		–

gradients favoured her. A concluding signal check cost at least a minute, and the net time of 105¾min showed a start-to-stop average speed of 56.3mph.

Some interesting work was to be seen on the West of England main line, between Derby and Bristol. Into the mid-1920s single-wheelers were still to be seen, not only as pilots, but as train engines on certain summer relief trains. The forerunner of the present day 'Devonian' was a case in point, and in Table 3 are set out details of a run on a Saturday relief train worked by engine No 662 with a modest load of 150 tons. This particular engine was one of the old 179 class of 1893-6, with 7ft 6in driving wheels, and 19in by 26in cylinders. The start was hindered by a bad signal check at Naas Crossing; but after passing Standish the engine did well, and the hill-climbing after Berkeley Road, on the long 1 in 281 ascent past Charfield and through Wickwar Tunnel was excellent, with its minimum speed of 46mph. The load for a Class 1 engine on these timings was 150 tons, so that No 662 was not far below her maximum.

TABLE 4

7.20pm BRISTOL—NEWCASTLE MAIL

CHELTENHAM—BIRMINGHAM

Run No	1		2		3	
Engine No	431		521		761	
Engine Class	2*		2†		3	
Load tons, tare/full	240/260		225/245		285/305	
Distance miles	Actual min sec	Speed mph	Actual min sec	Speed mph	Actual min sec	Speed min
0.0 CHELTENHAM	0 00	–	0 00	–	0 00	–
3.8 Cleeve	6 05	–	5 45	–	6 05	–
7.2 ASHCHURCH	9 30	64	9 00	68	9 35	64
9.4 Bredon	11 50	–	11 05	60	11 50	53½
13.2 Defford	15 35	59	14 40	67	15 55	59
18.0 *Abbots Wood Junction*	21 15	50½	19 40	51	21 30	47½
20.4 *Spetchley*	24 05	–	22 30	–	24 30	–
24.6 *Dunhampstead*	28 45	57	26 40	62	29 20	56
31.3 BROMSGROVE	36 45	–	34 25		37 50	–
2.2 Blackwell	7 40	–	7 20	–	7 30	
3.6 Barnt Green	10 20	–	10 00	–	10 05	–
8.7 Kings Norton	16 20	–	15 55	–	16 25	
10.9 Selly Oak	20 00	–	18 40	–	19 45	
14.2 BIRMINGHAM	25 15	–	23 50		25 55	

* 6ft 6in non-superheater   † 7ft 0in superheater

In the reverse direction the section between Cheltenham and Birmingham is always of interest not only through the incidence of the Lickey Incline but also because of the general adverse length that precedes it. The bank itself was always treated with great respect. It seemed usual to employ two 0–6–0 tank engines to assist any passenger train if the special 0–10–0 'Big Bertha' was not available; and if such a train had come from Gloucester double headed it went up the Lickey Incline with four engines! A train that always loaded heavily, by Midland standards, was the 7.20pm Mail from Bristol. Its time allowance was considerably easier than those of the ordinary daytime expresses and it may have come under the 'Limited Load' classification. I mention this because the loads regularly taken without a pilot were considerably above the 'Special Limit' maxima for both the Class 2 and Class 3 engines. Three runs are set out in Table 4 of which the first is without doubt the best I have ever seen with a non-superheated 6ft 6in rebuilt 4–4–0. The 'Special Limit' load for this class was 180 tons, so that by this standard the engine was heavily overloaded. The downhill start to Ashchurch, mostly on a gradient of 1 in 295, makes for a smart initial time, and No 431 had attained 64mph on passing this once busy junction. Up the 1 in 300 gradient to beyond Abbots Wood Junction speed did not fall below 50½mph and attained a maximum of 57mph on the easier gradients beyond.

On the second of the three runs the superheater Class 2 4–4–0 was working the Torquay express, which was allowed 37min to Bromsgrove, against the 40min of the Mail, and her speeds were excellent, as will be seen from the table, and yielded a gain of 2½min on the faster schedule. The Class 3 engine, again on the Mail, had a load of no less than 305 tons—massive for the Midland of those days—but did well to Bromsgrove. All the same, in relation to its power classification, and the fact that it was a superheater engine, the slower times made do not bring this run into the same order of merit as that of the non-superheater Class 2 No 431. All three runs had the assistance of 'Big Bertha' up the Lickey Incline, and all made similar times up the gradient. Not one of the three engines kept strict time afterwards, though in the case of the Mail, while there were important postal connections, to be made with London and North Western trains in Birmingham, the Midland train itself had a long wait in New

Street Station—upwards of three-quarters of an hour—in order to make a neat connection with the West Coast Postal Special at Tamworth. To have left Birmingham earlier would have involved standing for an equal length of time on the main line at Tamworth. This was a time-honoured arrangement that prevailed on the Midland for more than forty years, and continued throughout LMS days.

The section between Derby and Birmingham provided many contrasts in working. The Gloucester men, with superheater Class 2 4-4-0s on the Torquay train, used to lose time almost as a matter of principle. I have before me details of a run with engine No 520 and a load of 255 tons, on which the not very exacting schedule of 51min non-stop for the 41.2 miles from Derby to New Street was increased to an actual time of 56½min without any checks. It is true that the line has a very gradual rising tendency, and by the 'Special Limit' loading regulations the engine had a tare load of 52 tons over the maximum. But speed never exceeded 52mph over the level at Repton, and on the very gradual rise to Kingsbury, never steeper than 1 in 408, speed actually fell to a minimum of 40mph. Yet in the reverse direction the same engine, and probably at that period in Midland history the same driver, worked a tare load of 167 tons from Birmingham to Derby in 44min dead, gaining 5min on a schedule of 49min. One is forced to the conclusion that certain drivers had a standard method of working their engines for the 180-ton maximum load and never varied it. If the train was more heavily loaded they just went slower; it was as simple as that! If it was lighter they went faster, and incidentally seemed to negotiate Burton station much faster than would now be tolerated. The wide island platform between the up and down main lines involved relatively sharp reverse curves at both ends in both directions of running—on what is otherwise a perfectly straight length of main line. The present limit for non-stopping trains is 30mph, but on the run with No 520 they went through at 50mph.

So far as the ever-fascinating Settle and Carlisle line is concerned, I shall have a good deal to say about the performance of Class 4 engines in a later chapter, but the present one may well be concluded by reference to the concluding Midland days, when both morning and mid-day Scotch expresses from St Pancras were run in separate Glasgow and Edinburgh portions throughout. The Edinburgh trains were the lighter of the two, and while the Glasgow sections usually had Class 4 simple engines of the 999 class, the Edinburgh sections had to make do with Class 2. Piloting regulations were normally very strict and a large number of Class 1 and non-superheated Class 2 4–4–0s were available at Hellifield. An unrebuilt Johnson 4–4–0 in front of a 999 used to make a great spectacle climbing the long bank to Blea Moor. At one time the afternoon Edinburgh express used to stop at Hellifield. It made a good connection with a local to Carnforth, and I used it sometimes in travelling from Leeds to Barrow-in-Furness. I remember it as a light and rather crowded train, and against my parent's anxiety in finding seats there was a thrill, for me, of a short ride in a Midland Scotch express. I know there will be purists who will tilt at the use of the term 'Scotch', which seems confined to whisky and certain brands of sticky tape; but on the Midland Railway it was the official description of all express trains that crossed the border, and the name 'Scotch Express' was printed in the public time-table books and the time bills displayed at stations.

This has been rather a long introduction to a good Leeds—Carlisle run, made when the 11.45am from St Pancras to Edinburgh was running non-stop on a schedule of 135min for the 113 miles. With a seven-coach train of M & NB stock including a twelve-wheeled dining car, the engine was overloaded by 13 tons; but this driver was evidently more of a sportsman than some of his contemporaries on the West of England line, and he 'went for it', hard, though once again to the extent of treating some of the permanent speed restrictions with scant respect. Speeds of 40mph round the Shipley curves, and 47mph through Skipton, savoured of the 'one wheel' technique. Nevertheless by these tactics he was less than a minute down at Settle Junction, despite a signal check to 30mph at Saltaire. The uphill timings on this route were, however, very sharp and on the allowance of 22min for the 14 miles from Settle Junction up to Blea Moor—almost entirely at 1 in 100—2min were lost, despite no lower speed than 31½mph on the bank. With a further slight loss on to Aisgill the train was 3min late on crossing the summit in 88min 55sec from Leeds, 64.7 miles. A fast run down to Carlisle regained this lost time, and the arrival was 'on the dot'.

This was certainly an excellent run in itself, but it shows all too clearly how near to the wind the Midland locomotive department was sailing, when reliance had to be placed on such relatively small and moderately powered engines for important Anglo-Scottish express services. The runs mentioned in this chapter represent a typical selection of the kind of performance one could expect on the Midland Railway, and on the Midland Division of the LMS in the early 1920s, and makes one marvel all the more at the role for which the Midland locomotive department was cast.

CHAPTER 3

The Scottish Situation

THE historic prowess of the three great Scottish constituents of the LMS had to a large extent worn itself out by the year 1922. Much of the traditional fire and dash had gone out of Caledonian running; the Glasgow & South Western was caught fairly on the wrong foot, and the Highland had barely begun to recover from the incredible burdens it carried during the war, from the after effects of which some of its leading men were suffering. Nevertheless, through the strong personalities of John Barr and David Urie, Scotland put up a stout and successful fight, at least for partial independence, for many years. It is not in the nature of men like John Barr to blame their tools, but it must be admitted that he would have had some justification with the Caledonian locomotive stock as it was in 1922-3. When I met him many years later, he spoke highly of the Pickersgill 4–4–0s; but such praise was no doubt in recognition of their freedom from mechanical troubles, and low repair costs. In other respects, and taking the most charitable view, they seemed generally inferior in road performance to the McIntosh Dunalastair IV superheated 4–4–0s.

So far as express passenger working was concerned, the Caledonian was then essentially a 4–4–0 line. The days of carefully regulated workings with selected and highly-serviced 4–6–0s on special duties had long passed. The long innings of *Cardean* on the afternoon corridor train from Glasgow to Carlisle and back ended during the war, and although her driver, David Gibson, was afterwards allocated a Pickersgill 60 class 4–6–0 the same regularity of working was never revived. Barr dismissed 4–6–0s generally as express locomotives. Other engines of the Cardean class worked regularly between Perth and Aberdeen but there was barely a handful of them, and they worked turn and turn about with 4–4–0 superheater locomotives. The Pickersgill 60 class 4–6–0s, though massively built and notably light on repair costs, were altogether too sluggish to be regarded as regular express engines by the standards of the old-time Caledonian Railway. In my experience the two original McIntosh large express engines 49 and 50, which became LMS Nos 14750 and 14751, always seemed the fastest and freest running among the 4–6–0s, though they then had no specially allocated duties.

The record of Pickersgill as an engine designer must surely be one of the most curious of any in British railway history. As mentioned in Chapter 1 he had a scientific brain and considerable ingenuity as a designer of machinery; but in applying these undoubted talents to the business of producing powerful and free-running express passenger engines he seems to have failed signally. In my monograph dealing with the Dunalastairs I have discussed at some length the detail design of his superheater 4–4–0s. By all ordinary dimensional characteristics they should have been excellent engines. The frame construction was massive, to an even greater extent than in the Dunalastairs IV class; the bearing surfaces were everywhere even more generous, and the piston valves were far larger in proportion to the cylinder volume than on the preceding 4–4–0 engines. Yet they seemed to lack the freedom and power of the Dunalastair IVs and seemed to be considerably heavier on coal. One can only imagine that the actual valve setting was at fault. I rode on the footplate of some of them when they were still called upon for first-class duties between Glasgow and Aberdeen, and my impression was that they had no 'go' in them. It does not take long to get the 'feel' of a locomotive, and unlike some inside-cylinder 4–4–0s one could name—the Great Western Bulldogs, the rebuilt Glover 4–4–0s on the Great Northern of Ireland, and above all the immortal *City of Truro*—the Pickersgill 4–4–0s seemed dead things. It probably needed nothing more than a few expert adjustments to the valve settings to put them right, but after grouping there was probably no initiative at St Rollox to do other than maintain the stock.

The stand taken by John Barr, that Caledonian locomotives were more than adequate for the needs of Scotland, probably negated any moves there might have been from Derby to investigate any possible improvements; and when in 1924-5 the

Pickersgill 4–4–0s showed up so badly in the Interchange Trials on the Settle and Carlisle line, there were many at Derby who were not displeased. After all it eliminated another competitor, and brought the actual pre-eminence of Derby a little nearer to the complete fulfilment that was the aim of the high management. Even so, in these 4–4–0 locomotives, Pickersgill came nearer to success than in the majority of his ventures into original design. Each of his three 4–6–0 designs was an extraordinary mixture of robust construction, handsome appearance, and ineffective performance on the road. The 60 class was the first and by far the best of this bad lot. They were obviously intended as main line express engines to take over the principal West Coast duties from the ageing McIntosh classes. But like the 4–4–0s they seemed to have absolutely no 'life' in them. They would pound slowly up a hard bank with a heavy train, but once on the easier stretches they would thresh along in the most laboured and ineffective way.

In his later 4–6–0s Pickersgill changed from the Stephenson link motion to Walschaerts gear with no happier results. The special class he built for the Oban line were without any doubt the feeblest things I have ever encountered in the way of locomotives! I had some footplate experience of them. They rode beautifully and seemed quite free-running, but they just would not steam. Why Pickersgill should have made them non-superheated is another of life's little mysteries. I have the most vivid recollections of one of them double-heading the 5.15pm out of Oban in front of an ex-Highland Clan class 4–6–0, with a 375-ton train. On the long and very severe ascent from Dalmally, although the Pickersgill was not being exerted to any great extent, we gradually lost pressure till we topped the summit with no more than 120psi, while behind us the Clan was being well and truly thrashed, doing far more than her fair share of the work, yet showing the white feather from her safety valves all the way up. I had a short run with another of the Oban Pickersgills on the 10.9am from Stirling to Glasgow, with a 235-ton load, on which we barely kept the not very exciting schedule of 46min for the run of 30.2 miles.

To be fair, the 60 class, and the Oban non-superheaters, did a fair amount of revenue earning service, albeit of a not very brilliant kind; but the same could not be said of the big three-cylinder 956 class. They were magnificent-looking engines, and in their mechanical design and construction seemed essentially sound; but all Pickersgill's shortcomings as a valve-gear designer reached a climax in these engines. He wanted to avoid having an inside valve-gear for the middle cylinder. If he had made a straight copy of Gresley's arrangement of conjugated gear all might have been well; but to quote his own words on one memorable occasion, that inside conjugated gear was 'a wee contr-r-raption of m'own'. Contraption indeed! It was David Joy who once referred to the Bryce-Douglas valve gear fitted to one of the Drummond 4-4-os of the Caledonian as a 'birdcage'; the extraordinary complication of links and pin joints that Pickersgill contrived to conceal between the frames of that externally splendid engine was more than a 'birdcage'—it was a nightmare. It was nevertheless not only the valve gear that handicapped the 956 class. In their original condition they steamed very poorly. 'Authority' arranged for the pioneer engine to be put on to the up 'corridor' for Lord Monkswell's benefit, working *Cardean*'s old duty to Carlisle and back; but even with all the preparation and nursing that took place, and John Barr himself on the footplate, they made a thorough mess of it.

Many years later, when Edward Thompson was experiencing much trouble with the LNER three-cylinder engines having Gresley conjugated valve gear, and wished to introduce some drastic modification, he was thinking at one time of putting Stephenson's link motion on to the inside cylinder. Why he should have thought of this curious expedient it is hard to imagine, and in any case history includes the highly unsatisfactory examples of the Drummond 330 class of four-cylinder 4-6-os on the London and South Western which had different forms of valve gear for the inside and outside cylinders. Thompson got to the stage of consulting Sir William Stanier on this step, and Stanier then told him of the experience with the Pickersgill 956 class. There were only four of them, but two were actually rebuilt with Stephenson link motion for the inside cylinder though this proved to be no improvement at all. Stanier confided to Thompson: 'I couldn't do anything with them. They had to be scrapped.' In any event their influence on the general LMS motive power position was entirely negative. In retrospect however, the astonishing thing is that the Pickersgill regime at St Rollox produced such a crop of ineffective 4–6–0 designs when they had, under their very noses as it were, what was probably the finest express passenger locomotive design ever made for a Scottish railway in pre-grouping days, namely the ex-Highland River class.

So far as main line workings to and from Carlisle were concerned the Glasgow & South Western Railway was in very poor shape. Of the nineteen Manson 4–6–0s, only two were superheated, and all of them with increasing age were proving very heavy on repairs through structural defects developing. Timekeeping was at a very low ebb. In his six years at Kilmarnock Peter Drummond found little opportunity to improve matters. During the war the design of a large four-cylinder 4–6–0 had been worked out in detail. This was very far from being a copy of his brother's T14 'Paddleboats' on the London & South Western, but after Drummond's death in 1918, Robert Whitelegg, who succeeded him, concentrated his first attentions on the Clyde Coast services and patched up the Manson 4–6–0s as best he could for the main line services. The result was to bequeath to the LMS organisation a stud of locomotives, the influence of which was virtually nil so far as future practice was concerned. The large 4–6–4 tanks came into service in the last year before amalgamation and, impressive engines though they were, the design again had no future influence. This is not to suggest that all running on the Glasgow & South Western line was devoid of interest or merit. Ironically, however, it was from some of the smallest and oldest engines that most of the sparkle came. I had some splendid runs as late as 1930, with small-boilered Manson 4–4–0s, on short journeys to and from the Clyde Coast, but the Manson 4–6–0s in those days were literally on their last legs. They had, in any case, long been displaced from the Anglo-Scottish workings by the Midland compounds.

On the Clyde Coast services the Whitelegg 4–6–4 tanks were generally disappointing. This was not from any lack of tractive power, but from their tendency to roll badly on certain sections of the line. In these engines were repeated the riding characteristics of the Brighton 4–6–4 tanks when first built, which in this latter case was traced to water surging around in the side tanks. One would have thought that Whitelegg, from his interest in 4–6–4 tank engines and his previous experience on the Tilbury line, would have been aware of the trouble Billinton had with his first engines of this type, but apparently Whitelegg walked into exactly the same trouble on the G & SWR. Furthermore, the coast lines had not the solid formation and permanent way of the main line to the south. Some of it ran on sandy subsoils, and while the roadbed had been adequate for the Manson 4–4–0s it was not equal to such heavy engines as the new 4–6–4 tanks. The 'Sou' West' enginemen were used to rough going, but the wild swaying roll of the new engines was too much for them and they ran cautiously in consequence.

By far the best main line engines possessed by the Glasgow &

TABLE 5

STRAWFRANK JUNCTION—CARLISLE

Load: 343 tons tare, 365 tons full
Engine: Manson superheater 4–6–0 No 14674 (ex-G & SWR)

Distance Miles		Sch min	Actual min	sec	Average speeds mph
0.0	STRAWFRANK BOX	0	0	00	–
6.2	SYMINGTON	10	11	35	32.5
9.9	Lamington		15	45	51.8
15.3	Abington		22	05	51.2
17.8	Crawford		25	25	45.1
20.5	Elvanfoot		28	50	47.4
23.4	*Summit*	32	33	15	39.4
33.4	BEATTOCK	43	43	30	58.5
38.6	Wamphray		48	45	59.5
44.4	Nethercleugh		55	05	55.2
–			sigs		–
47.3	LOCKERBIE	57	58	35	49.7
50.4	*Castlemilk Box*		63	25	38.5
56.4	Kirtlebridge	66	69	30	59.2
60.1	Kirkpatrick		73	10	60.5
64.5	Gretna Junction	75	77	05	52.2
69.0	Rockcliffe		81	10	66.0
71.0	*Kingmoor Box*		83	05	62.7
–			sigs		–
73.1	CARLISLE	86	87	20	–

Net time 84min

South Western Railway were the two Manson superheater 4–6–0s, built in 1912, and originally numbered 128 and 129. Having had a much shorter life than the original Manson 4–6–0s of 1903 they had not become subject to the structural weaknesses manifested in the older engines, and in 1922-3 they seemed about the only engines on the Carlisle road that were capable of putting up consistently reliable performances. In the early days of the LMS management it became a matter of policy to inaugurate a degree of pooling of workings between Glasgow and Carlisle, so that enginemen of both pre-grouping constituents knew both roads. In certain workings the Glasgow & South Western men took their own engines, and a record is available of an excellent run from Carstairs to Carlisle with engine No 14674, formerly No 129 and at one time fitted with the Weir feed water-heater and pump. The log of this run is shown in Table 5. The recorder took no details of maximum and minimum speeds, but the average over the easier part of the climb up Clydesdale, between Lamington and Elvanfoot, was 48.8mph. The last 2.9 miles up to Beattock Summit averaged 39.5mph and indicated a minimum of about 30mph. No very high speeds were achieved afterwards, but the train was running on time, and Carlisle was reached punctually despite the two slight signal checks.

This run makes an interesting contrast with one made about the same time on the same Liverpool and Manchester express, but which then called at Symington to combine the Glasgow and Edinburgh portions. The recorder in this case was Baron Vuillet of Paris, and he was fortunate enough to have one of the big McIntosh 4–6–0s on the job, No 14750, formerly No 49. The load was 360 tons and the average speed up the Clyde Valley only 44.5mph to Elvanfoot. But the Caledonian 4–6–0 did better than the G & SW up the last 2.9 miles to Beattock Summit, not falling below 33mph. There was some much faster running downhill, with a maximum of 72mph near Beattock station, and of 71mph at Gretna. The average speed from Beattock was 61.4mph. This run was thoroughly characteristic of the work of these two McIntosh 4–6–0s in their later years. The drivers seemed to treat them gently uphill, and then let them 'fly' downhill. I had a very similar run with this same engine on the Aberdeen road, but with a much lighter load.

Reverting to the Glasgow & South Western however, the immediate post-war years and the early days of grouping formed a sad conclusion to the locomotive history of a great company. It must have been doubly sad for James Manson, who had done so much for Kilmarnock during his distinguished tenure of office, and who, living to a great old age, saw the short periods of Peter Drummond and Robert Whitelegg pass with so little in the way of constructive progress, and then the whole edifice crumble away under the influence of grouping and of pressure from the Caledonian side. Drummond and Whitelegg stood little chance. The former began strongly enough, and after some early hesitations produced some excellent engines in the superheater 4–4–0s and 2–6–0s; but the war clamped down upon any more ambitious developments. As for Whitelegg, he was the victim of a take-over for the second time in his engineering career. That he made the best of it was typical of his buoyant and exhilarating character, but his vigorous personality was lost to the LMS. One could hardly imagine him settling down to work amicably, as a subordinate, with the Derby of early grouping days, any more than he was prepared to work with the Midland masters who took over the London Tilbury & Southend line in 1912.

Farther north, the Highland Railway was in a state of 'betwixt and between' at the time of grouping. There were locomotives of three successive locomotive superintendents all working side by side. The Lochs and the Jones Goods 4–6–0s were still important main line units, while the 'Skye Bogies' had a complete monopoly of the line between Dingwall and the Kyle of Lochalsh. The Castle class 4–6–0s worked turn and turn about with newer engines on the southern part of the main line, but north of Inverness 4–4–0s predominated. Christopher Cumming, taking over at short notice after the River class fiasco, was responsible for the introduction of three solid workmanlike classes, all with outside cylinders and Walschaerts valve gear. The two 4–4–0s *Snaigow* and *Durn*, built specially for the mail trains between Inverness and Wick, were two of the most handsome engines ever built, while the Clans and the so-called Clan Goods 4–6–0s, retaining the same family likeness, were extraordinarily tough and hard working engines. Cumming may not have been directly involved in their detailed design, but as a good running man he knew what was needed for the arduous conditions of the Highland Railway and secured engines that were ideal for the job.

On the Highland itself most English observers travelled over the line in the height of the summer tourist traffic, when loads were inordinately heavy and there was much piloting. After all, one could not expect engines either of the Castle or the Clan class to take loads of over 400 tons unassisted out of Perth, or southbound from Aviemore—quite apart from the exceptional banks leading to the Druimuachdar, Dava and Slochd summits. So one rarely got the chance of seeing what a Clan or a Castle could do with a maximum load, unassisted. The Clans used to take 350 tons out of Perth on the mid-day express, but I saw the Clans in their 'middle age' on the Oban line of the Caledonian, and they were terrific. There was no finesse, no modern efficiency, nor elegance about their going; just honest-to-goodness hard slogging up the banks, with rock-steady steaming, no matter how hard they were flogged. All eight of the Clans were at Oban in the 1930s. Apart from coming to the rescue of the Caledonian in this way, till Stanier Black-Fives were available in sufficient quantities for some to be spared for this route, the Highland locomotive stud had no influence in the LMS development.

In other circumstances, however, one Highland design could have had an immense influence. I refer, of course, to the ill-fated Rivers. Of all the many might-have-beens in British locomotive history those six magnificent engines provide the greatest question mark, and leave the saddest reflections in the mind. As I have written elsewhere, if F. G. Smith had been as good a diplomatist as he was an engineer, he might one day have been chief mechanical engineer, as his colleague on the Highland, Alexander Newlands, became chief civil engineer. As an engine-designer Smith was head and shoulders above most of his British contemporaries. Comparisons may be odious, but I would place his technical outlook, scientific ability, and sheer railway common sense behind only Churchward, Bowen-Cooke, and Gresley. In the River class 4–6–0s he produced a masterpiece that has nevertheless been little appreciated because of the slur cast upon the manner of its introduction. As a personality Smith seems to have 'got across' his fellow officers at Inverness, and the rather tactless incident of a new turntable for Inverness running shed did not improve relations. One feels that after this there were

SCOTLAND: EARLY GROUPING DAYS

(above) *Caledonian line: Glasgow express leaving Aberdeen hauled by Cardean class 4-6-0 No 14754 (formerly No 905)*; (below) G & SWR *line: Ayr-Glasgow Pullman car express passing Prestwick, hauled by 4-6-4 tank engine*

CALEDONIANS IN VARIETY

(above) *McIntosh superheated express goods 2–6–0 No 37;* (upper centre) *Pickersgill 4–6–* *express tank engine;* (lower centre) *the pioneer McIntosh express passenger 4–6–0 No 4* *depicted in* LMS *plain black and numbered 14750;* (below) *one of the Pickersgill 60 cla* *4–6–0s built after grouping, and painted* LMS *red*

certain individuals who were only waiting for Smith to make another false step, and then to pounce. The introduction of the River class engines gave them their opportunity.

Although he had originally come from the North Eastern Railway, Smith had been long enough at Inverness to realise that the Highland needed engines of much greater capacity than the Drummond Castles. There were many restrictions on the Highland line due to the limitations of weight over underline bridges; but Smith, like Bowen-Cooke on the North Western, realised that dead weight was not the factor that had the greatest influence in causing stresses in the underline structures. It was the hammer-blow effect that mattered, and by skilful design a modern locomotive that had a heavy dead weight per axle, and which by its adhesion weight would be a powerful and reliable hill-climber, could be made far less damaging to the track and bridges than many an older one. Bowen-Cooke, following the principle used on certain Bavarian compound 4–6–0s in having all four cylinders driving on to one axle, completely eliminated hammer blow, and put forward a design for a very large, heavy and powerful new express locomotive for the LNWR. Only a few months later Smith, having succeeded Peter Drummond at Inverness, produced a splendid two cylinder 4–6–0 design, so skilfully balanced that the hammer blow effect was no greater than that produced by the Castle class, although these latter engines weighed 59.9 tons. The dead weight of the new engines was calculated at 72 tons.

Bowen-Cooke on the LNWR, naturally referred his new design to the civil engineer and it was not accepted, on the grounds of dead weight. The Crewe drawing office thereupon had to seek means for reducing the weight, and this was eventually done by using a considerably smaller boiler than that originally proposed. At Inverness it will probably never be known now by what dilatory or cabalistic tactics the situation was allowed to develop as it did. It seems extraordinary that the purchase of six large new locomotives was authorised by the board, and that it was not until the delivery of the first two engines at Perth that the civil engineer was consulted. That there were rival factions among the chief officers of the railway is clear enough, but that events should have been allowed to get as far as they did seems quite incredible. It is perhaps too much to suggest that the affair was allowed to drift deliberately as a means of getting rid of Smith, but the immediate outcome was that the Highland Railway lost one of the best locomotive engineers in the country, and six splendid engines.

One element of comedy in an otherwise dismal affair, was that in selling the engines to the Caledonian the Highland got £500 per engine more than they paid for them, thus making a profit of £3,000 on the deal! The thought of one Scottish concern, in a moment of acute embarrassment, scoring such a financial triumph over another—and moreover of Highlanders, over the traditionally 'canny' Lowlanders—certainly makes one chuckle. The Caledonian indeed profited no more on technical grounds than they did financially by the acquisition of these engines. Despite having, so fortuitously, six outstanding machines under his wing, Pickersgill seems to have completely ignored their design features, and his own ill-starred 4–6–0s cut a sorry figure beside the powerful free-running Rivers. The only slight evidence that they were noticed at all in the St Rollox drawing office could be seen in the arrangement of the driving wheel splashers on the Oban 4–6–0s and on the 956 class. The subsequent history of the River class is referred to in Chapter 6.

In spite of the grouping having struck the Scottish railways at an undistinguished period in their locomotive history, the expected and feared swamping of Scotland by English locomotive designs did not occur. It was not until 1925 that new 6ft 9in Midland compounds were allocated to Kingmoor shed, Carlisle, and began working to Glasgow by both Caledonian and G & SW routes; but the real invasion of Scotland by alien types did not begin in earnest until 1927, when more compounds arrived, accompanied by Midland class 4 0–6–0 goods engines, and towards the close of the year, Royal Scots. For the first three years of grouping however the Scottish lines were virtually on their own, and the introduction of the new locomotive livery was relatively slow.

CHAPTER 4

Crewe

IN sheer weight of numbers the contribution of the London & North Western Railway to the 'pool' of LMS motive power was massive and potentially overwhelming. I am referring now to the original North Western, not the enlarged company formed by the merger with the Lancashire & Yorkshire in 1921. Against the rather shaky contingent north of the Border, the far from puissant Midland stud and the Horwich contribution, which at 31 December 1922 could muster no more than 28 rebuilt four-cylinder 4–6–0s that could be called modern main line engines, Crewe had, for express passenger service alone:

90 Superheater 4–4–0s:	George the Fifth class
40 Superheater 4–4–0s:	Precursor class rebuilt with superheater boilers and piston valves
245 Superheater 4–6–0s:	Prince of Wales class
130 Superheater 4–6–0s:	Claughton class

This made an impressive total of 505 superheater express passenger engines, any of which, on current form, could apparently knock the proverbial spots off the best the Midland could then put forward; while it needed no more than the Crewe superheater 4–4–0s to provide more than a match for anything that was then being done on the Caledonian and G & SW lines

South of Preston I believe the official load limits were 400 tons for a George the Fifth or a Prince of Wales, and 440 tons for a Claughton. Certainly in the years 1921-2, when I began travelling regularly to Euston, trains of this magnitude were frequently taken. Over the mountain section circumstances seem to alter cases, and when double-heading occurred it was sometimes a case of pilot engines working home rather than the train engine actually needing assistance. Within my observations—and I saw a good deal of the line in the years 1921-4—Claughtons were taking loads up to 420 tons tare up Grayrigg bank without assistance, though they probably took rear-end banking help from Tebay up to Shap Summit. In the early days of the Claughton class, 420 tons was the scheduled load as far north as Tebay, and throughout from Carlisle on the southbound run. The North Western certainly made their locomotives work, and in this respect the pre-grouping policy was precisely the opposite to that of the Midland.

Until the merger with the Lancashire & Yorkshire Railway, the North Western, like the great majority of British companies, still kept the responsibility for locomotive running within the chief mechanical engineer's department. Both Bowen-Cooke and Whale before him, had been divisional officers responsible for the running as well as the maintenance of locomotive stock; the link between headquarters and those responsible for the running of the trains was close and effective. This had begun to change even before the Grouping, because one result of the merger with the Lancashire & Yorkshire Railway was to set up the running superintendents as independent officers. The death of Bowen-Cooke in the autumn of 1920 at the relatively early age of 62 was a grievous blow to the locomotive department of the LNWR, though it is a little difficult to imagine what might have happened had he survived to the time of the merger with the Lancashire & Yorkshire. Although the status of the North Western chief was far greater, Hughes had actually been chief mechanical engineer longer than Bowen-Cooke, having been appointed in 1904; but it is hard to imagine either man being content to serve as subordinate to the other. Probably one or other of them would have been offered, and accepted the 'golden handshake', as Colonel Billinton of the LBSCR did when Maunsell was preferred to him as chief mechanical engineer of the Southern. But however much one cares to speculate, the death of Bowen-Cooke removed an immense personality from the scene, and left Crewe wide open for alien influences to infiltrate at will.

This is not to belittle in the slightest degree the personality or influence of H. P. M. Beames. Cheerfully, tactfully, and always vigorously he strove to uphold the honour of the old LNWR, and although he was constantly subject to much outside direction and interference, he was, over the years, able to do a great job at Crewe. In the extensive reorganisation carried out in the late 1920s he kept the works in the very forefront of British locomotive constructional and repair practice—Swindon notwithstanding! Crewe was far more fortunate in the long run than any of the other major works within the LMS system, in having a senior officer of the pre-grouping company permanently in residence; and once all the confusion and frustration of the early grouping days had subsided, Beames, drawing upon the vast experience accumulated at Crewe over the years, was able to integrate the best of it with newer techniques to the benefit of the LMS as a whole. Beames never forgot that he had been a North Western man, and no one else on the LMS was allowed to forget it either!

The North Western locomotive stock, as it affected the immediate fortunes of the LMS in the first ten or a dozen years of amalgamation, can be divided quite clearly into three sections:

1 The Precursor family
2 The eight-coupled freight engines
3 The Claughtons

So far as outside influences are concerned, only the superheated versions of the Precursor family need be considered at this stage, namely the 130 4–4–0s of the George the Fifth class, which included 40 rebuilt Precursors which, with superheaters, extended smokeboxes and piston valves, were fully equal to the George the Fifth class proper; and the grand muster of 245 superheated 4–6–0s of the Prince of Wales class. This impressive array of 375 express passenger locomotives was derived from the Whale era, with the addition of superheating, and all entirely the work of J. N. Jackson, the chief draughtsman who had served three chief mechanical engineers in succession. It is important to appreciate that they were not merely Whale engines to which superheating had been applied. Both 4–4–0s and 4–6–0s alike had greatly improved front ends which made them capable of a much enhanced power output. This in turn was to some extent their undoing, because they proved capable of sustained power outputs much in advance of what their frames had originally been designed to transmit, and in consequence they suffered later from cracked frames and other structural defects. In falling into this difficulty Bowen-Cooke and Jackson were in good company! In later years one of the greatest locomotive designers of all time, André Chapelon of the PO-Midi Railway in France, did precisely the same in rebuilding the old 4–6–2s of the Orleans as extremely puissant 4–8–0s.

At their best the 'Georges' and 'Princes' were amazing engines, capable of prodigies of hard work. They required totally different methods on the footplate. The 'Georges' had a deep narrow firebox in which a thick firebed could be readily used. A Derby man once said scathingly that a 'George' drew its fire into such a furnace that it would steam under the efforts of a navvy. Exactly! They were anyone's engines, and consequently immense favourites with footplate men and running staff alike. When they began to build up mileages, after heavy repair, they deteriorated in two ways: they became very rough through weakness in the frame structure, and their coal consumption rose rapidly due to leakage developing past the broad rings of the Schmidt patent piston valves. With the selective diagramming of engines, keeping newly repaired units for the heaviest duties, all was well because the defects that developed in high mileage engines were of less consequence on light duties. But under the Midland system of any engine to any job, the West Coast route was soon in trouble. Supporters of the North Western were up in arms when the George the Fifth 4–4–0s were placed in Class 3, and thus immediately stigmatised as inferior to the Midland compounds. But while a good 'George' with a keen North Western crew could give a compound points and a beating on most scores, an average 'George' was probably no better than Class 3, and the controversial classification was to this extent justified.

The Prince of Wales class, although suffering from the same piston-valve troubles, did not seem to get so rough with age. They had a slightly higher tractive effort, and they came into Class 4. From the fireman's point of view they needed quite different treatment. They had an unusually shallow grate, and the technique of firing had to be mastered. Their firebox design was the same as that of the Experiments, and when these latter engines first came out, even the top link men found considerable difficulty in maintaining a satisfactory firebed. They got the reputation of being sluggish on the level and poor hill-climbers, yet downhill they ran like stags. As the technique was mastered their hill-climbing work greatly improved. It was a case of feeding the coal well forward, and taking care not to feed some of it on to the top of the brick arch, so relatively narrow was the headroom between the underside of the arch and the firebars. By the time the Prince of Wales class was introduced in 1911, the men had thoroughly got the knack of firing that box, and the superheater engines never suffered from steaming troubles. In ordinary working, enginemen switched from 'Georges' to 'Princes' without any trouble. At the time of grouping both classes were taking tare loads of 400 tons between Euston and Crewe, and on the Chester and Holyhead line with the Irish Mails. On the Carlisle road loads of 350 and 370 tons were taken unassisted over Shap in both directions.

At the time of the grouping the freight engine position, so far as the eight-coupled engines were concerned, was as shown in Table 6.

TABLE 6

Class	Type	Description	No at Grouping
B	0–8–0	4-cylinder compound	53
C	0–8–0	19½in small boiler	15
C1	0–8–0	18½in small boiler	24
D	0–8–0	19½in large boiler	63
G	0–8–0	20½in large boiler	89
G1	0–8–0	20½in large boiler superheated	241
G2	0–8–0	20½in large boiler superheated	60
E & F	2–8–0	4-cylinder compound	16

Of the above, the B class were the Webb four-cylinder compounds in their original conditions; while the 2–8–0s were all four-cylinder compounds, some retaining their original boilers, but others had been rebuilt with non-superheated large boilers similar to the D class. The superheater G1 class was the backbone of the freight service, and for many years engines of the C, C1, D and G classes were being converted to G1. These latter engines carried 165lb pressure, while the G2 class introduced in 1921 had 175lb pressure. The superheated 0–8–0s went by the enginemen's nickname of 'Super D'. They were excellent engines in every way, though not exactly comfortable to ride upon, as I learned to my cost when I spent a day on one of them working freight between Bescot and Wichnor Junction.

Another important class that was responsible for a great deal of intermediate freight working was the so-called '19 inch' goods, a small wheeled variant of the Whale Experiment class 4–6–0, with 5ft diameter coupled wheels. There were 170 of these useful engines. They were non-superheated, and they worked all over the LNWR system. By the time of grouping the Webb four-cylinder compound mixed traffic 4–6–0s of the 1400 class (Bill Baileys) had all gone to the scrap-heap—and I can hear many an old LNWR man saying 'a good job too'. At the beginning of 1923 the LNWR still had some of the ex-ROD 2–8–0s of the Great Central design. Thirty of these engines were on the strength at the time of grouping. They were, of course, excellent engines, and were a great help to Crewe in the difficult years just after the war when there was such an acute shortage of engines. All the large-boilered 0–8–0s, non-superheated and superheated alike, were at first placed in Class 5 by the Midland system. This was entirely in keeping with their own practice for the Class 2, 3 and 4 passenger engines, and on the LNWR the non-superheated Precursors, George the Fifths and Experiments were all lumped into Class 3. The '19 inch' Goods 4–6–0s were Class 4, and the ex-ROD 2–8–0s were Class 5. The London North Western thus contributed 453 Class 5 0–8–0s, many of which were later upgraded to Class 7.

The last group of Crewe locomotives to make a major contribution to the LMS was a single class, the famous four-cylinder 4–6–0 Claughtons. These engines have been discussed to a remarkable extent, and sometimes referred to as controversial; but much of the comment extended to them has arisen from a lack of understanding of the circumstances surrounding their working, and certain detail features of their design. As originally introduced in 1913 they had very large superheaters, and although the boiler barrel was of relatively small diameter, the free-flow gas area through the tubes in relation to the grate area, which is generally considered the yardstick of a locomotive's ability to steam, was almost exactly the same as that of the Great Western Stars. But so high a proportion of the total tube cross-sectional area was represented by the superheater flues—giving rise to the comment I once heard that 'they were all-superheater'—that they were inclined to drop their pressure in the early stages of a run. Then the technique was to close, or almost close the superheater damper, and so divert practically all the exhaust gases through the small tubes. This usually had the immediate effect of rallying the boiler pressure, and once this was done the damper was opened stage by stage until conditions were stabilised. The engines were originally fitted with pyrometers to indicate the superheat temperature, and by watching this, in relation to the boiler pressure gauge, a skilful driver could obtain absolutely first class results.

The first three batches of Claughtons, ten in each, turned out in 1913, 1914 and 1915 respectively, were very carefully regulated in their workings and generally confined to no more than two crews. The top link men concerned grew expert in managing the superheater damper controls, and some magnificent performances were recorded, quite apart from the record-breaking dynamometer car test runs with No 1159 *Ralph Brocklebank* in the late autumn of 1913. The Liverpool engines had a particularly fine record of service in those early days, and on the Carlisle road *Sir Gilbert Claughton, Rupert Guinness, E. Tootal Broadhurst*, and *Frederick Baynes* all have splendid runs to their credit. In those days the firemen also contributed to a major degree to this good work. Bowen-Cooke had adopted one feature of the Great Western Star in the Claughtons, namely the floor of the grate, with the rearward portion level, and the front sloping downwards. High quality Welsh coal was used on the majority of top link workings from Crewe North shed where most of the Claughtons were at first stationed, and this form of firebox 'floor' was very well suited to the thick fires necessary with soft coal. The Camden engines usually had hard coal, but only a few Claughtons were stationed there in the early days, and as they were confined to crews of the highest calibre, no trouble was experienced in the firing.

In the stress of wartime conditions, when the enormously increased traffic led to the authorisation of thirty more Claughtons in 1916-17, the superheater dampers were omitted, and at the same time a slightly reduced superheating surface was adopted. There was no change in the arrangement of the tubes, but the elements were reduced in length to lessen any risk of burning at the firebox end. With no fewer than sixty engines of the class available in the last years of the war, their use was considerably extended and engines of the class were stationed at Carlisle, Preston, and Rugby, in addition to Crewe North, Edge Hill and Camden. The Liverpool engines had a double-home turn to Leeds, on which Claughtons were worked on alternate days by Farnley and Edge Hill men. But although engines of the class had, from the outset, worked into Manchester, none were as yet stationed either at the Patricroft or Longsight sheds. From their early brilliance on pre-war schedules, and their general record of reliability in the later stages of the war, the Claughtons were regarded on the LNWR as an entirely successful design.

During the war years little time had been available to Bowen-Cooke himself, or the Crewe drawing office for any considerations of new locomotive design. Their time was very heavily occupied with the design of special machinery for munitions and other wartime production. The outstanding achievements of Crewe in this respect have been told by G. R. S. Darroch in his stirring book *Deeds of a Great Railway*. Anyone reading this will soon realise why locomotive development stood still at Crewe for several years, and why, in all probability, the London & North Western Railway took no part in the discussions towards new British Standard types that took place during the latter part of the war, and in which Churchward, Fowler, Gresley, Hughes and Maunsell participated. That these discussions proved abortive is beside the point. The LNWR took no part in them. Then, after the war, the LNWR board, anxious to restore normal working on the line as soon as possible, authorised the construction of no fewer than 225 new 4–6–0 locomotives. There was no time to work out new designs. The Prince of Wales class, by its well-proven all round usefulness, was an obvious choice for part of this large authorisation, and orders were placed, sequentially, for engines of this class up to an eventual addition of 155 units, to bring the total strength of the class up to 245. The remaining seventy engines of the authorisation were to be Claughtons.

Now Bowen-Cooke was above all a locomotive man, and although he had been able to devote little or no time to locomotive matters during the war, his wide interests had kept him informed of what was going on elsewhere. Those who were closest to him during the final stages of the war and in the immediate aftermath, knew how anxious he was to develop the Claughton design, particularly now that the outcome of the war had relieved him of any obligations he might have felt towards retaining any, or all of the Schmidt specialities which had come with the original adoption of the Schmidt superheater. But the urgency with which the top management of the LNWR required new engines, left little time for any scientific development, and apart from outward details, such as the adoption of 'pop' safety valves, the new Claughtons that began to take the road from 1920 onwards seemed little different from the originals. Yet internally there was one important and significant difference. The floor of the grate was made continuously sloping from back to front, and this of course required a somewhat different firing technique.

Kenneth Cantlie, who was later to have a distinguished engineering career in China and is today actively concerned with the application of the Giesl ejector in many parts of the world, was then a pupil of Bowen-Cooke at Crewe, and he was given the job of taking the first of the new engines through the final stages of erection, early trials, and introduction in traffic. This was the celebrated war memorial engine No 1914 *Patriot*, and as a matter of prestige it was put on to the afternoon Scotch Corridor express, then leaving Euston at 1.15pm. It was to work the train day in, day out, for many weeks. Cantlie rode on the footplate day after day, and did much of the firing himself. After two days he told me, he 'got the hang' of firing that continuously sloping grate, and then, he added 'What an engine!' Certainly *Patriot*'s work in those early days went far towards rivalling the general reliability of performance that had been shown by the first engines of the class in pre-war days; but the mere fact that the modified firebox did take an engineer—not an ordinary top-link fireman—several days to master tells its own tale.

Traditionally, it would seem, North Western firemen did not adapt themselves readily to different shapes of firebox, as the long period of indifferent performance with the Whale Experiment class showed. With the rapid introduction of many more Claughtons and their utilisation in common user service at many sheds, the running department was faced with a new problem. They had these large and potentially very strong, powerful, and free-running engines with two varieties of firebox. The earlier one was admittedly rather 'touchy' and, unless carefully managed at the start of a run, could land an engine crew in for a dreadful spell of bad steaming; while the later one was a form of grate unlike anything that had previously been used on the LNWR. The earlier form, when expertly handled, had given excellent results; the later form, with a 'Cantlie' at the shovel, did equally well. On the crack workings, like the 1.30pm down Corridor the fireman soon got used to the new grates, but with the general introduction of the class up and down the line the results were not always so happy.

A fine example of the working of the new engines is provided by the accompanying log of a run on the 1.30pm from Euston to Crewe in the summer of 1921 (see Table 7). At the time the important widening works were in progress at Chalk Farm, so that the train got a bad start and took 27¼ minutes to pass Watford; but the 65.1 miles on to Rugby took only 67min 35sec and despite an almost maximum load for a Claughton, 438 tons, the train was brought into Rugby on time. Very fine work continued onwards to Crewe, with a load reduced by 30 tons. Here the colliery workings near Polesworth necessitated a severe slack, and this hindrance became a permanent feature for upwards of twenty years. But, as will be seen from the log, the 2min lost by this check were more than recovered, and the train arrived in Crewe a minute early. In the same summer I had a run on this train that was very similar. One of the newest unnamed Claughtons was on the job, namely No 15, and we also reached Crewe a minute early.

About the same time I had a number of runs on the Perth express then due to arrive in Euston at 7.30pm, and with loads of around 350 tons Claughtons were easily master of a schedule that allowed 93min for the 82.6 miles from Rugby to Euston. With a train of 350 tons gross, for example, engine No 208 passed Tring, 50.9 miles, in 57min 35 sec, and then being ahead of time was eased down so that the last 31.7 miles took 34min 25sec. Downhill speeds at no time exceeded 70mph. On

TABLE 7

1.30pm WEST COAST 'CORRIDOR'
EUSTON—CREWE

Load, to Rugby, 438 tons tare, 475 tons full
to Crewe, 409 tons tare, 445 tons full
Engine: 4–6–0 No 30 *Thalaba* (Claughton class)

Distance Miles		Actual min sec	Speeds mph
0.0	EUSTON	0 00	–
–		pws	–
5.4	WILLESDEN JUNCTION	13 20	–
11.4	Harrow	20 25	–
17.5	Watford Junction	27 15	58
24.5	Boxmoor	34 55	–
31.7	Tring	43 25	50
46.7	BLETCHLEY	57 45	66
54.8	Castlethorpe	65 30	–
59.9	Roade	70 55	53
62.8	Blisworth	74 05	–
69.7	Weedon	80 45	63
75.3	Welton	86 30	53
–		–	67
82.6	RUGBY	94 50	
8.8	Shilton	12 05	–
14.6	NUNEATON	17 55	70
19.8	Atherstone	22 40	70
–		pws	25*
27.5	TAMWORTH	30 35	58
33.7	Lichfield	37 40	52
41.7	Rugeley	46 05	60
44.6	Colwich	49 05	–
51.0	STAFFORD	56 25	40*
56.3	Norton Bridge	63 15	51
65.0	Whitmore	73 20	–
–		–	73 (max)
75.5	CREWE	85 00	

Schedule times:	to Rugby	95min
	to Crewe	86min
Net times:	to Rugby	93min
	to Crewe	83min

* speed restriction

another trip, made on a stormy October evening of wind and rain, engine No 2059 *C. J. Bowen-Cooke*, also with 350 tons, took some time to get going on the ascent to Kilsby Tunnel, and took 12min 20sec to pass Welton, 7.3 miles. But some good running followed. Tring was passed in 56½min at a minimum speed of 50mph, and a fast descent with maximum speeds of 75mph at Kings Langley and 74mph at Wembley, took us through the latter station, 74.5 miles, in 77min 25sec. With a clear road afterwards we could have been at rest in Euston in 87min, but a whole succession of checks delayed the finish, and extended the total time to 92min 5sec. A still better run was made by No 2122 with a load of 370 tons, when Watford Junction, 65.1 miles, was passed in 68min 10sec. The train was then so substantially ahead of time that although there were two permanent way checks to come beyond Willesden the engine was eased right down, and Euston was reached in 91min 50sec.

The impact of grouping had some disastrous effects on train running over the former LNWR lines. The imposition of new methods was carried out in such a way as to cause a deep resentment, and one particular measure was to limit the unpiloted loads for both Prince of Wales and Claughton classes to 360 tons tare—despite the fact that one was a Class 4 and the other a Class 5 group. How this came to be introduced is wrapped in mystery, but it was typical of the muddled situation that developed on the West Coast route. As a result, an enormous amount of piloting became necessary and I have examples in my notebook of such absurdities as a load of 374 tons tare being worked by two 4–6–0s, a Prince of Wales and a Claughton, both apparently in excellent condition, yet not making the slightest attempt to regain any of the lateness with which the train was handed over at Crewe. This was no case of pilots working home either. In the years 1924 and 1925 I logged many runs with Claughtons and when the loads were within the piloted limit much of the old 'sparkle' was evident; indeed some of the work I recorded between Crewe and Preston was quite brilliant. But once the fatal 360 tons was exceeded and pilots were put on, nobody seemed to care what happened. On the up Perth express one night, with a load of 391 tons, Claughton No 119, and a Jumbo No 2180 *Perseverance* as pilot, I thought that for once the drivers had forgotten their new tactics. Leaving Crewe half an hour late we began in great style, passing Armitage, 37 miles, in 40¾ minutes. But a bad signal check sufficed to end this fast spell, and by comparison they dawdled all the rest of the way to Euston. A few years earlier a Claughton driver, with 391 tons tare, would have made much faster times unassisted if running late.

In the North the day Scottish expresses, divided into separate Edinburgh and Glasgow portions at Crewe, were mostly of light formation except in the height of the summer season, and 'Princes' and Claughtons were used indiscriminately. Turning up some of my old notes on train-watching at Grayrigg and Tebay, I find the following relating to a couple of typical days: the first in September and the second in April.

Train	Engine(s)
Liverpool—Glasgow & Edinburgh	Jumbo & Claughton
Edinburgh—Euston	Claughton
Glasgow—Euston	Prince & Claughton
Glasgow—Liverpool & Manchester	Two Princes
Perth—Euston	Prince
Liverpool—Glasgow—Edinburgh	Hughes 4–6–0
Euston—Glasgow	George V & Prince
Euston—Edinburgh	Claughton

Train	Engine
Edinburgh—Euston	Claughton
Glasgow—Euston	Claughton
Glasgow—Liverpool—Manchester	Prince
Perth—Euston	Claughton
Liverpool—Glasgow—Edinburgh	Claughton
Euston—Glasgow	Prince
Euston—Edinburgh	Claughton

In the summer of 1921 I did a considerable amount of train-watching and photography on the Chester and Holyhead line. Two Claughtons were then stationed at Bangor and worked through to Euston daily. At that time however there was some difficulty in turning engines of this class at Holyhead and they were not being used on the Irish Mails. This was, of course, prior to grouping, and then the unpiloted load for a George the Fifth or a Prince of Wales was the pre-war 400 tons. In those days very careful attention was given to the working of all mail trains, and the 400-ton working maximum was rarely exceeded. Just as on the Carlisle road 'Princes' and Claughtons were used indiscriminately in later years, so in 1921 superheater 4–4–0s and 4–6–0s were apparently regarded in much the same way on the Irish Mails. Jumbos, non-superheated Precursors, and even on one occasion a Webb four-cylinder compound 4–4–0, were used as pilots, with the train engines and their pilots working through from Crewe to Holyhead. Between Crewe and Euston the Irish Mails were usually worked by Claughtons.

In the eyes of the new management the reputation of the North Western locomotives was not enhanced by the Interchange Trials on the Settle and Carlisle line conducted in 1923 and 1924; but there again, before condemning the engines concerned on the score of their actual performances, one must appreciate the conditions in which the trials came to be held. North Western partisans were very disappointed that a George the Fifth was not included in the first set of trials, which included Midland Class 4 engines of both the compound type and the simple 999 class. In competition with these was a North Western Prince of Wales. Crewe men felt that while a compound might have been a worthy opponent, a 'George' could 'lick the proverbial pants' off a 999, and ought to have been given the chance of doing so! Certainly the 'Georges' were doing splendid work on the two-hour Birmingham expresses, often with loads exceeding 300 tons, and on trains that included one intermediate stop with the overall time of two hours. But by the new reckoning the 'Georges' were Class 3, and thus considered unsuitable to compete with the Midland Class 4 engines.

We sometimes had George the Fifth class engines on the up Perth express south of Crewe, and I had good timekeeping runs with No 305 *Senator* and 238 *F. W. Webb*. But by far the best one was with No 502 *British Empire* and a load of 305 tons. She began by sustaining 50mph up the 1 in 177 of Madeley bank, and despite a signal check at Milford and easy downhill running reached Rugby in 82¾min. Then with a reduced load of 280 tons she passed Bletchley, 35.9 miles in 36min 10sec and cleared Tring summit in 51min 25sec. We were then so far ahead of time

THE CREWE TRADITION

(above) *a Precursor 4–4–0, No 1419* Tamerlane *as rebuilt with piston valves, superheater, and George V type bogie;* (centre) *the last Prince of Wales 4–6–0 to remain in service; No 25752, withdrawn October 1949;* (below) *one of the 19-inch Goods 4–6–0s, No 8812 as fitted with Belpaire firebox*

EARLY GROUPING DAYS: LNW LINE

(above) *The Royal Train near Bushey, hauled by Claughton No 5944 resplendent in* LMS *red;* (below) *the 1.30pm Euston—Glasgow Corridor leaving Oxenholme after attaching pilot. A 2–4–0 Jumbo* Henry Pease *assisting a* LYR *4–6–0 No 10462, with an 11 coach train*

that speed never exceeded 60mph anywhere on the descent to Euston. Willesden Junction, 77.2 miles, was passed in 79¾min and we crawled on, killing time, to arrive 4min early in exactly 89min from Rugby. Between Rugby and Tring however, with such spirited running, the work was fully up to the best standards of the two-hour Birmingham trains. On another occasion in 1926, authority 'must have slipped up' because another 'George', No 2577 *Etna*, was allowed to take a 13-coach train of 410 tons unassisted from Preston to Crewe. Three checks prevented the schedule of 61min for the 51-mile run being kept, but the net time was exactly 61min. The engine was nevertheless worked pretty hard to achieve this time, but no harder than one expected in LNWR days. This run, although made in 1926, was before the General Strike. The prolonged period of the coal strike afterwards saw an end of all piloting for a time, and I had one run with engine No 1311 *Napoleon*, also of the George the Fifth class, on which we took a train of 439 tons tare. With a very crowded passenger complement the gross load was at least 485 tons, and the loss of time amounted to seconds rather than minutes. A Class 3 engine indeed!

Later that same year I waited half an hour on St Albans station for the 6.37pm semi-fast to St Pancras. The driver of a Class 2 superheater 4–4–0 had been given 270 tons tare from Bedford, and had refused to start until a pilot was found. He explained that to work such a load would have knocked the engine to pieces! On another occasion in that same year 'authority' was evidently forewarned of an overload, and the 4.43pm from St Albans had a Johnson 2–4–0 coupled ahead of another Class 2 superheater 4–4–0 for a tare load of 198 tons—certainly 18 tons over the limit! I fear that this concluding paragraph shows evidence of partisanship, at any rate in respect of events of the early grouping period. But on the LMS of those days what was sauce for the goose was evidently *not* sauce for the gander.

CHAPTER 5

Dynamometer Car Tests: 1923-6

FROM an early stage in LMS history it was clear that the influential position of Derby, as ordained by the high management, was to be justified in the practical working of the railway by the supremacy of Midland locomotives over all others. In view of what I have written in the preceding chapters this may seem a rather extraordinary statement, but the briefest reference to the locomotives that took part in the various trials carried out in those eventful four years makes it appear pretty obvious that those trials formed part of a definite plan to establish the Midland superheater compound as the most generally useful and most economical express passenger locomotive class in the entire group. Although Hughes was chief mechanical engineer for the greater part of this period, the drive and initiative came from Derby and not from Horwich. This could probably be connected with the early operating policy of the LMS, which was directed towards the reduction of train loads on the former LNWR lines, and the eventual recasting of the timetable on Midland precepts. For such a timetable nothing larger than Class 4 engines would be needed. The position of J. E. Anderson, as superintendent of motive power, must also be remembered. In the early days of grouping he had not a good word to say of any save Midland engines, and he would have been as keen as anyone to see them established in a position of pre-eminence technically.

The first group of trials was conducted entirely with Class 4 locomotives, a North Western 'Prince', a 999 class 4-4-0, and a superheated compound. The details of this famous series have many times been discussed at length* both from the technical angle, and equally from that of railway politics; but from every

* *The Midland Compounds, The Precursor Family, The Caledonian Dunalastairs,* all by O. S. Nock

viewpoint Derby were exceptionally fortunate in their choice of an engine to represent the compounds. In earlier references to these trials it was generally understood that Carlisle men were involved in that the round trips were made from Carlisle to Leeds and back. There was talk also of the rival engine crews being relatively near neighbours, and of the affair gradually developing into a 'local Derby'—though in this case not the Derby where the Midland engines were built! It is surprising how little was known about these trials at the time. Logs were published in *The Railway Magazine*, but these were compiled with skill by one of the young engineers engaged on the work, not by direct recording, but from the actual dynamometer car charts. A good deal of further information has come to hand more recently, and the most important point to me is that the driver of the compound was the regular Leeds man on No 1008, Heseltine—'Mad Jack' as he was referred to on the shed.

He was the ideal man for a big occasion. There would have been many Midland drivers who would have been horrified at the idea of taking loads of over the normal Class 4 maximum. They would know well enough that far heavier loads could have been taken by engines in first class condition, but would have hesitated, almost to the point of refusal to go over the limit in case they were asked to do it regularly at a later time. Jack Heseltine had no such inhibitions. One had only to put a man of his temperament up against the North Western, and the sky became the limit—certainly so far as the fire thrown from the chimney of No 1008 was concerned. The trials began with loads of 300 tons tare, and continued with the amazing tonnage, for an unpiloted Midland express engine on such schedules, of 350. Engine No 1008 was often referred to as 'the flower of the flock', and at the time of the first set of dynamometer car trials she was just nicely worked in after a general overhaul at Derby. In other words she was in the pink of condition. Certainly driver Heseltine got work out of her that was never equalled, let alone surpassed in many subsequent trials with Midland compounds over that route. This applies not only to load haulage but in economy of working. No difficulty was experienced in hauling the 350-ton trains to time. In fact, on one of the finest runs the 48.3 miles from Carlisle up to Aisgill were covered in 64min 35sec, against a schedule of 68min, with a gross load of 370 tons behind the tender.

The coal consumption figures showed some considerable variations. With loads at a nominal 300 tons tare, the coal per drawbar horsepower hour varied between 3.64 and 4.02lb. On three trips when, for some reason, lighter loads of around 230 tons were taken, the range was from 3.94 to 4.5lb per dhp hour, while on the 350-ton trips the variation was between 3.7 and 4.02lb per dhp hour. In relation to the work done these were truly excellent results. The North Western 'Prince' No 388, which kept good time on all her trips, varied between 4.31 and 5.12lb per dhp hour, averaging 4.60lb over ten runs. The 'Prince' returned a superior power-output characteristic up to about 35 mph, and bore this out by higher minimum speeds on the heaviest gradients; but the compound did by far the best work above a speed of 40mph and drawbar horsepower attainments of slightly over 1,000 at 50 to 65 mph were quite outstanding for a 4-4-0 engine at that period. The 999 class simple 4-4-0, although driven with great determination and skill, was generally outclassed. She kept good time with the 300-ton trains, but failed somewhat with the 350-ton trains. Even so, considering that the normal load for the class was 230 tons it could hardly be called a discreditable failure.

The Midland authorities had every reason to be delighted with the work of the compound, and in November and December of 1924 the process of vindicating the class was carried on a step further. By that time many new compounds had been built, with 6ft 9in instead of 7ft coupled wheels, and having slightly larger cylinders. Derby wished to establish superiority not only above all other Class 4 engines, but also over Class 5. Consequently it was arranged for a Claughton to be included in the tests. At the same time John Barr's strong advocacy of Caledonian engines was put to the test by the inclusion of a Pickersgill 4-4-0, even though the classification of those engines was only 3. The Midland compounds tested in this second series were of the original 7ft variety and of the latest 6ft 9in engines with short chimneys and cut-down boiler mountings. This latter change was to enable them to work over the Scottish routes between Carlisle and Glasgow. At that time however there were very few, if any, Claughtons stationed at Carlisle. Upperby shed had become a home of the Hughes four-cylinder 4–6–0s, and it was necessary to transfer a Claughton to Carlisle specially for the job. Edge Hill shed was instructed to send an engine, on loan.

At that time in LMS history, the situation on the Western Division had much deteriorated. Under the new organisation, repair and maintenance work had entered into a difficult phase of transition from old to new methods and older men were not taking kindly to the Midland infiltration. A shed instructed to send an engine from its most powerful class on loan would naturally send the unit it could best spare, in other words one with a fairly high mileage that had passed from the stage of being allocated to crack duties. I can well believe that no special instructions about the transfer were given. It was part of the Midland philosophy that any engine that could turn a wheel should be regarded as typical of the class, and against such precepts a Claughton was a Claughton, whether good, bad or indifferent. I can hear some readers commenting that such random methods of 'selection' had hardly applied when No 1008 was chosen to represent the compounds in 1923! Fair enough, but random selection was to recoil on the Midland Division in full measure in the 1924-5 trials. The Claughton sent to Carlisle, No 2221 *Sir Francis Dent*, was a high-mileage unit, not in the best of condition; it ran the test trains to time, but at the expense of heavy coal consumption. It gained for the class the reputation of having a poor steaming boiler.

The Midland Division included three different compounds in these trials. The 7ft engine No 1023 put up a shocking performance. She made only two round trips, both with 350-ton trains, and on the up journeys, against a schedule of 67min from Carlisle to Aisgill she took 76min 49sec on the first trip, and 74min 55sec on the second. These efforts make a startling comparison with the 350-ton performances of No 1008—dimensionally an identical engine—when the times on four successive runs were 64min 31sec, 65min 39sec, 67min 32sec, and 67min 19sec, against a schedule of 68min. Engine No 1023 had covered about 14,000 miles since its last general overhaul. The comparison between the work of these two engines amply explains the need for rigid limitation of load for the class as a whole if any engine, rather than specially selected units, was to be put on the hardest turns. From a study of her running it would appear that 230 tons was about the most No 1023 could have comfortably managed at that time. The Claughton on the other hand had a margin of tractive power, as one would expect from a Class 5 engine, and the official report of the trials, which did not have much good to say for the engine, did concede that she was very free-running and the odd minute lost in adverse conditions uphill was easily regained on the downhill stretches.

This is where the unfortunate Caledonian Pickersgill 4–4–0 failed so lamentably. Before the actual dynamometer car trials, some preliminary runs with the normal loads of the trains concerned were made for road-learning purposes, with engine No 96, reputedly a very good one. The unfamiliar condition for a Caledonian driver of those days was the task of running 113 miles non-stop. The long uphill section to Aisgill bore quite a striking resemblance in its overall 'lift' to that from Carlisle to Beattock summit—a distance of 48.3 miles to a summit 1,151ft above sea level, against 49.7 miles to an altitude of 1,014ft. To a locomotive working a tare load of 300 tons the Caledonian run was easier, because almost certainly a stop would be made at Beattock for rear-end banking assistance. It can of course be argued that the Dunalastair I class were taking loads of 200 tons over Beattock summit as far back as 1896, and making much faster start-to-pass average speeds than anything required from Carlisle to Aisgill in 1924. In my book on the Dunalastairs I have analysed the work of the Pickersgill 4–4–0 in some detail. Worked extremely hard she took a 300-ton train over Aisgill summit in 69min 52sec from the start, but regained none of the 2¾min thus lost on the downhill section to Leeds. On the more severe northbound journey she lost 8½min, and her coal consumption of 6.21lb per dhp hour was much higher than that of any competing Midland or North Western engine. After this one round trip the Pickersgill 4–4–0 was dismissed from the scene.

The other Midland compounds involved in the 1924-5 trials between Carlisle and Leeds were the first two of the short-chimneyed series, Nos 1065 and 1066, which were built with right-hand drive in the Midland style. At the time of the trials both were brand new engines each having run around 14,000 miles since construction. Both were fully worked in, and in excellent shape. As with No 1008 a year earlier, both engines did very fine work on the banks; with the 350-ton trains No 1066 on one occasion notably surpassed the best that No 1008 had achieved between Settle Junction and Blea Moor. The work over this section of 14 miles may be compared as shown in Table 8:

TABLE 8

Date		Engine No	Time m	s	Actual load tons tare	Min speed mph
Dec	1923	1008	25	21	343½	26
		1008	25	15	342½	25
Nov	1924	1065	25	47	361	25
		1065	28	28	353	22½
Dec	1924	1066	23	58	347	28½

The last mentioned was indeed a magnificent performance, though in passing it should be said that on her 350-ton runs the North Western 'Prince' No 388 made times of 24min 29sec and 25min 28sec. The most significant feature of the second series of trials over this route was the consistency of the coal consumption figures returned by all of the three compounds, including the unsatisfactory 1023. On eight round trips, two with No 1023, four with No 1065 and two with No 1066 the figures varied only between 4.33 and 4.68lb per dhp hour—an average of 4.45. This figure makes a striking parallel case to that of the North Western 'Prince' in 1923, with its average of 4.60lb per dhp hour, thus indicating that if the somewhat exceptional case of engine No 1008 be omitted, there was very little in it, on coal consumption, between the compounds and the North Western Prince of Wales class.

In the trials of November and December 1924 it was against the Claughton rather than the Prince of Wales class that the compounds were competing, and with engine No 2221 *Sir Francis Dent* in poor form, it proved an easy win for the compounds, on coal consumption at any rate. With the 300-ton trains the figure was no less than 5.56lb per dhp hour, and although this was reduced to 5.03lb on the 350-ton journeys it was sufficiently above the compound's figures to condemn the

Claughtons, for the time being at any rate. That the results were unrepresentative of the class as a whole, even at that undistinguished period in its history, is of no more than passing interest. Another stage in the establishment of the Midland compounds as the pre-eminent LMS engine design had successfully been attained.

The most interesting series of trials in this period, and perhaps the least known, was that conducted in the late spring of 1925 between Preston and Carlisle, and supplemented by a further set in 1926. In these the 'star' Midland compound No 1065, which had done so well in the November-December trials over Aisgill, was pitted against North Western, Lancashire & Yorkshire, and Caledonian engines. This time, also, the engines concerned were all worthy representatives of their respective classes, and taken collectively the tests included some of the finest work performed in the early history of the LMS. As distinct from the earlier tests, all the 1925-6 series were run with special trains timed at the fastest average speeds then booked between Preston and Carlisle. All the tests originated at Carlisle and were operated on specially arranged paths so as to give, as far as possible, a clear road throughout. The Class 4 engines, compound, Prince of Wales, and Pickersgill 60 class 4–6–0, were tested with trains of 300 and 350 tons, while the Class 5 engines Claughton and Hughes 4–6–0s were tested with 350- and 400-ton trains. This did make a reasonable assessment of locomotive capacity. The schedules demanded non-stop runs of 114min over the 90.1 miles between Carlisle and Preston going south, and a sharp 103min on the northbound journey.

A very full analysis of these trials was made in the May 1963 issue of *The Railway Magazine* in my 'Locomotive Practice and Performance' article. The hardest work was naturally required on the northbound journey, and an important stipulation made to all competing engine crews was that the uphill point-to-point times should be maintained. This was clearly the most serious set of competitive trials yet run on the LMS, and there was to be no 'coal-dodging', by going easily uphill and regaining lost time by fast running afterwards. Even so, those who organised the tests could not avoid a degree of variation in the methods of working individual drivers, and both the compound and the Hughes 4–6–0 were subjected to some very hard driving on the

Grayrigg bank. The coal consumption figures again placed the Midland compound in a position of superiority over all others on the basis of coal consumption per drawbar horsepower hour, though in this series the Claughton returned some excellent figures in pounds per train mile. All five classes of locomotives were tested with 350-ton trains, and the overall results are shown in Table 9:

TABLE 9

Engine Class	Coal Consumption lb per train mile
Claughton	42.4
Midland Compound	43.4
Prince of Wales	48.3
LYR Hughes 4–6–0	51.3
Caledonian 4–6–0	51.55

The driver of the Claughton kept his point-to-point times uphill, and regained the time lost by a bad permanent way check by making use of the free-running capacity of his engine between Shap Summit and Carlisle. The compound driver, on the other hand, went extremely hard uphill, gaining time substantially, and ran easily downhill from Shap to Carlisle. In running to the same schedule with 400-ton trains the Claughton required 52.7lb of coal per train mile, and the Hughes 4–6–0 no less than 58.1lb per mile. With 350-ton trains the basic coal consumption in pounds per drawbar horsepower hour favoured the compound, by a considerable margin, but the Claughton on this basis also showed a decided superiority over the LYR 4–6–0 (Table 10).

TABLE 10

Coal Consumption per dhp hour in pounds: 350-ton trains

Engine Class	Coal per dhp hour
Midland Compound	4.25
Claughton	4.78
Pickersgill 4–6–0	4.84
Prince of Wales	5.05
LYR Hughes 4–6–0	5.07

The engines concerned, in order, were No 1065, No 30

TABLE 11
PRESTON—CARLISLE
DYNAMOMETER CAR TEST RUNS IN 1925

Run No			1		2		3	
Engine No			1065		10460		30	
Engine Class			compound		Hughes		Claughton	
Railway			MR		LYR		LNWR	
Load, tons tare			347.9		397		393.6	
Distance		Sch	Actual		Actual		Actual	
Miles		min	min	sec	min	sec	min	sec
0.0	PRESTON	0	0	00	0	00	0	00
1.3	*Oxheys Box*	3	4	24	4	09	4	05
—			pws		pws		pws	
21.0	LANCASTER	23	24	35	25	48	25	53
27.3	CARNFORTH	29	30	49	32	17	32	10
40.1	Oxenholme	43	43	40	46	00	46	28
47.2	Grayrigg	55	53	27	55	41	57	49
53.2	Tebay	61	59	48	61	45	64	42
58.7	*Shap Summit*	71	68	14	70	27	73	39
90.1	CARLISLE	103	100	00	101	04	102	16
Net times		min	98		98		99½	
Engine Working			Reg	Cut-off*%	Reg	Cut-off%	Reg	Cut-off%
Scorton			0.2	7	0.4	25	0.2	22
Carnforth			0.4	6.7	0.4	30	0.2	22
Milnthorpe			0.6	7.2	0.4	30	0.2	22
Oxenholme			Full	7.5	0.5	40	Full	35
Grayrigg			Full	9	0.4	38	Full	30
Tebay			Full	7	0.4	37	0.2	22
Milepost 36			Full	9	0.4	40	Full	40
Shap Summit			Full	10	0.4	40	Full	60
			mph		mph		mph	
Min speed on Shap			25.5		24		28.5	
Max speed to Carlisle			70		74		79	
			tons		tons		tons	
Max drawbar pull			4.75		5.3		5.8	
			mph		mph		mph	
Corresponding speed			25.5		24.0		28.5	

* Notch on reverser, out of maximum of 12

Thalaba, No 90 *Kestrel*, No 14630, and No 10460. No engine failed to keep net times on any trip, and three of the finest individual performances, regardless of the coal consumption, were those of the compound in making a net time from Preston to Carlisle of 98min with a tare load of 347.9 tons; of the LYR 4–6–0, also 98min with 397 tons, and of the Claughton No 30 in making 99½min with 393.6 tons. The logs of these three runs in the detail given in the official report are shown in Table 11, together with the very interesting particulars of the engine working.

All these engines were delayed by the permanent way check before Lancaster, and Carnforth was passed between 2 and 3 minutes late. The drivers of the compound and the LYR 4–6–0 then proceeded to make exceptionally vigorous ascents to Shap, with times of 37min 25sec and 38min 10sec for the 31.4 miles, instead of the 42min scheduled. The Claughton no more than slightly improved on the scheduled point-to-point time—41min 29sec, and was still 2¾min late on passing Shap Summit. The lateness was easily recovered by a swift descent to Carlisle, with a maximum speed of 79mph. The variation in the working between the three drivers makes a truly strict comparison of the work impossible, nor can the coal consumptions be closely related, because they covered the round trip from Carlisle to Preston and back. In studying the details however it will be seen that the very big effort of the LYR engine on Grayrigg was not achieved without a certain mortgaging of the boiler. The pressure was sustained fairly well, but they topped the bank with the gauge glass showing only 0.62 full. The engine had been worked in 40 per cent cut-off from Oxenholme.

On Shap itself the compound put up a remarkable performance. She went really hard from Grayrigg to Tebay to charge the bank, and took those deadly 5½ last miles in no more than 8min 26sec. Speed fell to a minimum of 25½mph and at this speed the drawbar pull was 4.75 tons. The LYR engine, with her 397-ton train, also took the bank in a charge, in 8min 42sec, though falling to 24mph at the summit, and showing a maximum drawbar pull of 5.3 tons. The Claughton driver eased back to his minimum running cut-off of 22 per cent between Grayrigg and Tebay, and commenced the final bank less vigorously; but he gradually opened out, and passing Scout Green with 170psi 'on the clock' and a practically full boiler he advanced cut-off finally to 60 per cent with full regulator, and made the splendid minimum speed of 28½mph over the summit, with a drawbar pull of no less than 5.8 tons. This certainly caused a drop in water level in the boiler, but it was of no consequence at that stage in the run, being readily recovered on the downhill stage to Carlisle. It would have been very interesting to see how the coal consumption of the LYR engine would have compared had her driver adhered to point-to-point times uphill, instead of indulging in such exuberant regaining of lost time. As it is, one can only comment that such efforts resulted in a higher coal consumption, both in pounds per train mile, and in the basic rate per drawbar horsepower hour. The comparative figures for the two Class 5 4–6–0s, with 400-ton trains are shown in Table 12:

TABLE 12

Engine	Coal consumption lb	
	per train mile	per dhp hour
LNWR	52.7	4.75
LYR	58.1	5.13

It is also interesting, in view of the reputed high coal consumption of all Crewe engines, to study the details of the complete round trip with the 350-ton train which the Claughton made on a consumption of only 42.4lb per train mile. It will be noticed from the engine working details that this driver was using a wide-open regulator, and the shortest cut-offs that would maintain point-to-point times. There were stages on which he was using no more than 20 per cent—quite contrary to much of the misleading surmise that has been written about the working of these engines in the past. On the southbound run the train was nearly 5 minutes early on passing Lancaster, despite 2½min lost by the permanent way check near Penrith, and things were justifiably taken easily on the final stage into Preston. In passing it may be noted that the Prince of Wales 4–6–0 No 90 *Kestrel* did almost as well, so far as times were concerned. Unchecked, she passed Lancaster in 84min 33sec, but at the expense of a higher coal consumption. On the down 350-ton journey the Claughton also did very well, gaining 2min on the point-to-point allowance of 42min from Carnforth up to Shap Summit, and passing the latter point practically on time, despite the Lancaster check. I would venture to suggest that there would have been very few other locomotive classes in Great Britain at that time which could have worked a 350-ton train from Carlisle to Preston at a net average speed of 50mph, and taken it back at 54mph on a coal consumption of only 42.4lb per mile.

One gains the impression, studying the report of these trials, that everyone concerned was out to do his very best. That endeavour may have taken different forms and given variations in results, but taken all round those results represented the work of hard-slogging reliable, dividend earning engines. They were all in good shape, and the coal consumption rates of 4¾ to 5¼lb per dhp hour were around the average of good British locomotives of the period—the Great Western Railway alone excepted. On the East Coast route at that time there were engines using more than 6lb of coal per dhp hour. The compound again stood apart from the rest of the LMS stud, and encouraged Derby to persist with their plans for a 'super-compound' for the heaviest main line express work on the West Coast main line. Nevertheless the mastery of the Class 5 4–6–0s in taking 400-ton loads over Shap did not lead to any immediate relaxation of the 360-ton maximum for all 4–6–0s on the West Coast main line in ordinary service. The allocation of engines to duties was still being made on an indiscriminate basis, and one certainly could not have taken any Prince of Wales, or any Claughton and expected them to have repeated the performances of *Kestrel* and *Thalaba* in these most significant trials. The superiority of the Midland compound was proved. That was all that really mattered in 1925.

The full dress trials of the Pickersgill 4–6–0 No 14630, a year later, provided some extremely interesting data. It was unfortunate that this engine did not get so clear a road as prevailed during the earlier series, but she nevertheless did well on the banks, and generally kept the scheduled point-to-point times. This is just what one would have expected from this class. They steamed well, and at relatively low speed the sluggishness arising from the defects in their valve gear would not obtrude into the working. Maximum speeds of 73mph were attained in descending from Shap to Carlisle, and these were certainly most exceptional for these engines; how No 14630 was being worked at these moments is not stated in the report. Emphasis, both in the stipulated test conditions, and in the ensuing comments, is laid upon the work done in climbing the banks. In this connection all the testing work carried out in the earlier days of the LMS probably tended to give one-sided results. These tests were all conducted over mountain roads, and probably stemmed from the fact that in pre-grouping days the Midland Railway had a mountain road at their very back door, as it were, in the late and much-lamented line through the Peak District to Manchester. Many indicator trials were conducted from Derby over this route. It is certainly true that the long grind from Cheadle Heath up to Peak Forest, equally with those from Settle Junction to Blea Moor, and from Carnforth to Shap Summit, provided a stern test of the stamina of any engine—and of its crew! But where express passenger engines are concerned it does not tell the whole story.

For one thing it does not bring out weaknesses in valve gear that can have astonishing effect upon coal consumption, and freedom of running. While a mountain road can be a test of stamina, particularly if it consists of a single 'gable', like those mentioned in the preceding paragraph, a gently undulating, or level road that requires continuous steaming at a high rate of evaporation for hours on end can be much more trying. The North Western carried out nearly all their dynamometer car trials between Crewe and Euston, and of course there is the classic example of the Great Western, which had to provide for long sustained, high speed level running on a minimum of coal consumption. Churchward set his famous target of performance at 70mph not in slogging up to Whiteball Tunnel or Church Stretton at 30mph. On the basis of the 1925 trials over Shap, coming on top of the Leeds—Carlisle trials of 1923 and 1924 the LMS had every justification in assessing the Midland compound 4-4-0 as its most generally useful and most economical engine, and in building large numbers of them for use all over the system. But they were not the 'flyers' some superficial observers made them out to be, as the North Western men learned pretty quickly when they were substituted for George the Fifths on the Euston—Birmingham two-hour expresses.

That there was prejudice against anything Midland was

understandable enough on the West Coast route; but long after the old fires of controversy had died down, and a new generation was on those famous two-hour trains, I recall a most interesting talk with a Bushbury driver at Euston, prior to travelling down by the 4.35pm express. This was a train that in the early 1930s made two stops within the overall two-hour schedule, and with a normal load of eight coaches one had really to step on it to reach Blisworth in 'even time'. The driver in question, a very pleasant and intelligent man, said that the compounds were excellent for getting away, and climbing the banks, but that he would rather have a 'George' once they were over Tring summit. He added, 'We've still got some very good "Georges", and they'd run the legs off these engines once you get on to the fast part of the road. I'll show you what I mean today.' I went back to the train, looking forward to logging an exceptionally interesting run, and it so happened that an unusual opportunity presented itself. We were stopped dead by signal on Camden bank, and although the engine was very carefully handled in getting away we were a minute late past Willesden. A very hard and uniform run followed; but my recollection of it is the way the engine had to be thrashed to do it. All the way up to Tring at 62-60mph the exhaust was a continuous roar, and on the fast stretches that followed, the sound of the beat still remained quite clear even when we were running at 80mph. It would have been interesting to know what the coal consumption was. We reached Blisworth, 62.8 miles, in 61min 4sec.

CHAPTER 6

1926—A Vital Year

FOLLOWING the results of the dynamometer car trials of 1925 between Carlisle and Preston, work went rapidly ahead at Derby with the design of a huge four-cylinder compound Pacific, but in the meantime, despite the success of the Midland compound in the trials, operating opinion was tending to harden against compounds in general. It seemed as though the influence of the North Western faction was becoming stronger, and it only needed the General Strike of May 1926 and the prolonged period of coal shortage that followed while the miners strike dragged on throughout the summer, for the men of the North Western to show what they could do when released from the shackles of the 360-ton limit for all 4–6–0 locomotives. When a restricted train service was put on after the end of the General Strike, Claughtons were set to haul loads of over 500 tons gross without pilots. The drivers and firemen seemed to revel in showing what they could do. I logged timekeeping runs myself with engines 162 and 163—the latter, *Holland Hibbert*, being one of the original batch of 1913, but clearly in first class form in 1926. I have tabulated a remarkable effort logged at about the same time with engine No 808, on the 5.20pm from Liverpool to Euston which, in the emergency timetable, was making intermediate stops at Stafford and Bletchley.

The run I had with engine No 162 was on the 1.30pm Scotsman, at a time when the 11.50am, 2.35 and 2.55pm expresses were cancelled. The number of passengers trying to board the fifteen coaches of the 1.30pm on the Friday before Whitsun of all days, can be better imagined than described. Not only were the corridors packed, but there were people sitting on suitcases in the ordinary compartments. With this 500-ton load the driver kept the point-to-point times to Whitmore, 65 miles in 75min;

THE MIDLAND TRADITION

(above) *a 999 class non-compound 4–4–0 of Class 4;* (centre) *one of the standard* LMS *compounds with left-hand drive;* (below) *one of the new Class 2 standard 6ft 9in 4–4–0s*

TANK ENGINES, OLD AND NEW

(above) *Hughes Superheater 2–4–2 No 1469* LYR; (centre) *Fowler* LMS *Standard Class 3 2–6–2 No 58;* (below) *Furness non-superheater 4–6–4, Sharples design, No 11104*

but although coming smartly down Madeley bank, a long slowing before Crewe and a tortuous run into No 1 platform made us

TABLE 13

STAFFORD—EUSTON

Load: 454 tons tare, 505 tons full
Engine: 4–6–0 No 808 (Claughton class)

Distance Miles		Actual min sec	Average speeds mph
0.0	STAFFORD	0 00	–
6.4	Colwich	9 15	41.5
9.3	Rugeley	12 00	63.3
17.3	Lichfield	20 05	59.4
23.6	TAMWORTH	25 40	67.7
27.1	Polesworth	29 05	61.6
31.3	Atherstone	33 25	58.2
36.5	NUNEATON	38 40	59.4
51.0	RUGBY	53 45	57.7
58.3	Welton	62 45	48.7
63.9	Weedon	67 45	67.2
70.8	Blisworth	74 05	65.4
73.7	Roade	77 05	58.0
78.8	Castlethorpe	81 45	66.9
81.2	Wolverton	83 40	75.2
86.9	BLETCHLEY	89 35	–
6.5	Leighton Buzzard	9 20	41.8
10.6	Cheddington	13 40	56.8
15.0	Tring	19 05	48.7
18.7	Berkhamsted	23 05	55.5
22.2	Boxmoor	26 05	70.0
25.7	King's Langley	29 05	70.0
29.2	WATFORD JUNCTION	32 05	70.0
30.7	Bushey	33 30	63.7
33.4	Hatch End	36 05	62.7
35.3	Harrow	37 55	62.8
38.6	Wembley	40 50	68.0
–		pws	–
41.3	WILLESDEN JUNCTION	45 40	–
46.7	EUSTON	54 35	–

1½ minutes late on arrival. It was nevertheless a fine and refreshing effort, and except on starting from Rugby and in accelerating from the slack through Stafford, the exhaust was inaudible. The friend who logged the companion run on the 5.20pm from Liverpool (Table 13) took no maximum and minimum speeds; but I have worked out the averages from station to station, and they make pretty astonishing reading. The engine was obviously being worked uniformly hard throughout. There was no let up anywhere, and no sign of any shortage of steam. The times were equivalent to a non-stop run of 137 minutes from Stafford to Euston, showing an average speed of 58½mph—with a 505-ton train!

The work done during the emergency period led to something of a breakaway from the Midland operating principle of putting any engine in the particular power class, on to any job and expecting to keep time. It was obvious that Claughtons in good condition could do vastly much better than the 360-ton standard, and a number of them that were 'in good nick' were set aside, with a large letter 'S' fixed on their cab sides, and these engines were in future allocated to the hardest jobs. In passing, those interested in the *personalia* of the locomotive stock, as distinct from its technical achievements, will not fail to have noticed that in 1926 Claughtons, in first class running order and presumably not long out from works, were still carrying their LNWR numbers, more than three years after grouping. Looking through my travelling diaries of the period I find that it was not until December 1926 that I travelled behind a North Western engine that had received its LMS number. That engine happened to be none other than *Patriot*, which was then renumbered 5964, thus losing all its old significance. Numbers apart, however, the work of the Claughtons during the summer of 1926 had led to further considerations upon future motive power for the West Coast route, and was serving to crystallise out the smouldering opposition to the great Derby project of a four-cylinder compound Pacific.

The publication of the *Report of the Bridge Stress Committee*, with its revelations of the injurious effect of hammer blow from some locomotives, and its absence, or minimal value in others, no doubt stirred some old memories. One poignant result was that in 1928 all the River class engines were transferred from the Caledonian on to the Highland line, to take up the work for which they had originally been designed, while at Crewe the drawings of the original Claughton boiler were brought out of the drawing office records and examined afresh. One can almost hear the arguments being put forward to strengthen the case against the Derby Pacific: if the Claughtons as they are can do so well, how much better might they do with the larger boiler originally planned for them? Whether this was actually the case I cannot say, but in view of subsequent developments it seems a most likely surmise. In *The Railway Magazine* for November 1926, Cecil J. Allen in his usual monthly article commented, in respect of the Derby 'Pacific':

> It was to be of the largest dimensions that the loading gauge would permit, including the provision of 23in. or 24in. low-pressure cylinders, between the frames. And the best Continental compounding practice had been closely studied, with a view to producing a locomotive which should be in every way an outstanding British design. But now alas, it appears unlikely that the engine will materialise, and the probability is that recourse will be had to more 'Claughtons', possibly with larger boilers than those at present fitted.

Knowing well the publication schedules of *The Railway Magazine*, that article would have been written not later than the third week in September. We know that the frames had actually been cut for the first Pacific, before the instruction went forth to hold up work, and Cecil J. Allen would have been aware of this when he penned the article in question.

What precisely happened in the inner councils of the LMS at this particular moment must remain a matter of conjecture, but in the very next issue of *The Railway Magazine* Allen was able to refer to the Interchange Trial between the LMS and the Great Western, in which one of the latest Swindon 4–6–0s, No 5000 *Launceston Castle*, was put through a series of tests with maximum load trains between Euston and Carlisle. These took place in late October and early November of 1926. Some of those most closely in touch with events have expressed themselves as mystified as to the manoeuvres by which the Interchange Trial was organised. Certainly it was not initiated by Derby; but it may not be out of place to mention that in January 1926 a major change had been made in the top management of the LMS. Sir Guy Granet was then chairman, and he decided upon an entirely new organisation, which was, in its way, as revolutionary as that he himself had inaugurated on the Midland Railway twenty years earlier. The historic post of general manager was to be abolished, and on 1 January 1926 he brought in, to the new post of 'President of the Executive', a man entirely new to railways—just as he himself had been: Sir Josiah Stamp, a very distinguished economist and statistician. The general manager, H. G. Burgess (LNWR), and the deputy general manager, D. A. Matheson (Caledonian), remained in office until their retiring dates, in March 1927 and December 1926 respectively; but from January 1926 control passed virtually into the hands of Sir Josiah Stamp, with Sir Guy Granet continuing in his position of omnipotence.

It is well known that Stamp very quickly applied himself to the economics and statistics of the locomotive stock and set in motion the beginnings of a far more rigorous programme of standardisation; and there can be little doubt that those responsible for locomotive running pressed their case for a non-compound locomotive for the West Coast main line, and probably precipitated the Interchange Trial with the Great Western. In the autumn of 1926 also there came another event that was to cause some consternation in the chief mechanical engineer's headquarters at Derby. In the programme of the Graduates Section of the Institution of Mechanical Engineers there was a paper to be read by E. L. Diamond, who had recently completed his pupilage at Derby, entitled: 'An Investigation into the Cylinder losses in a Compound Locomotive'. It was to be a young man's occasion, and I well remember the jocular remark of one of my Westinghouse colleagues saying: 'Are you coming to the "Mechanicals" tonight to learn how locomotives lose their cylinders'! But on arrival we found Sir Henry Fowler himself in the audience, and also H. Holcroft of the Southern, while the chair was taken by Loughnan Pendred, the great editor of *The Engineer*.

The paper itself was an analysis of the work of the Midland compound No 1065 in the Leeds—Carlisle trials of 1924-5; but it was the conclusions arising from a very brilliant analysis that had astonishingly far-reaching results. Quoting from the penultimate paragraph of the paper:

> Perhaps the most important fact of all those set forth is that in the cylinders of the locomotive under investigation, which

is known to be of high efficiency, the total losses due to the restricted passages given to the steam admission and exhaust increase from 17.6 per cent at 24 mph to no less than 67.6 per cent at 68 mph, of which probably not more than 15 per cent is necessary for the production of the draught; that is to say, *an amount of power equal to half the work that is actually exerted on the train is wasted in throttling losses at this speed.* In view of this fact the Author unhesitatingly recommends the universal adoption for compounds as well as simple-expansion locomotives of the long-lap valve by means of which the port opening to steam at admission and exhaust can be materially improved.

This was a courageous peroration for a young graduate and it drew the warmest praise from Pendred and Holcroft, together with characteristically benevolent smiles and kind words from Sir Henry Fowler.

Through Pendred's influence the script of the paper was circulated far and wide, which was very unusual for a paper to the Graduates Section of the Institution, and it produced a highly authoritative written discussion which was published in full in the *Proceedings*. Those taking part included Monsieur Bréville of the Northern Railway of France, L. K. Sillcox of the Pennsylvania, Professor Sauvage, Lawford Fry of the Baldwin Locomotive Company, and many distinguished British engineers. But what none of us knew at the time was that Sir Henry Fowler had taken the manuscript of the paper back to Derby with him and completely scrapped the layout of the valve gear on the new 2–6–4 tanks, which were then in an advanced stage on the drawing boards at Derby. Herbert Chambers, the chief draughtsman, had been building up the design on traditional lines; but on the strength of Diamond's recommendation Fowler insisted on having long-travel long-lap valves. I shall tell in a later chapter how those 2–6–4 tanks proved to be some of the fastest engines that had appeared on LMS metals up to that time. But a far greater cataclysm was to hit the Derby drawing office when the results of *Launceston Castle*'s running became known, and Sir Josiah Stamp demanded the production of fifty new 4–6–0s of comparable power to the Castle in time for the summer traffic of 1927! It was then December, and *fifty* engines of a new design were demanded by June!

During the trials, J. E. Anderson broke through his traditional Midland façade to the extent of saying that he would not mind having twenty Castles for the following summer's traffic, though adding guardedly that he wondered how that valve gear would stand up to current LMS standards of maintenance. This comment duly reached Sir Josiah Stamp, and he promptly instructed Fowler to obtain a complete set of drawings of the Castle. Swindon refused to oblige, and so Fowler sent Chambers post-haste to Waterloo to get drawings of the *Lord Nelson* which was also of the same size and capacity. At this stage it is interesting to recall that in all LMS internal correspondence the new engines were at first referred to as Improved Castles. The design, construction and subsequent progress of the new LMS 4–6–0s forms a story in itself, and I must break off at this stage to mention three other new designs, the valve gear of which benefited greatly from that now-famous meeting of the Graduates Section of the Institution of Mechanical Engineers.

There was first of all the 2–6–4 tank, the first examples of which came out from Derby Works in 1927. It had long been established, much to the disgust of Crewe, that Midland red was to be the passenger engine livery for the whole group, and the earliest batches of the new express tank engines, numbered from 2300 upwards, were turned out in red. Their basic dimensions were: cylinders 19in diameter by 26in stroke; coupled wheels 5ft 9in diameter, boiler pressure 200psi. This provided a nominal tractive effort of 23,125lb. With a maximum axle-load of no more than 18¼ tons, they had a high route availability. The boiler was a shortened version of that used on the new Midland compounds, using the same tubeplates and arrangement of superheater; but the distance between the tubeplates was 11ft 4⅝in against 12ft 3⅝in on the compound, and the heating surfaces were reduced accordingly. The grate area was 25sq ft. The comparative boiler dimensions, together with those of the new Class 2 4–4–0 passenger engine are shown in Table 15 on page 99.

The outstanding feature of the new 2–6–4 tanks was of course the use, for the first time in a new LMS design, of long-lap, long-travel valves. It made them extraordinarily free-running engines. Although it is carrying the story several years forward I shall never forget the impact they made on their first arrival on the

Euston—Watford suburban trains. In the early 1930s I was living at Bushey and travelled daily to Euston. Originally we had the Precursor tanks, non-superheated, and by then they were a bunch of very tired old ladies. The periodic overhauls at Crewe which had kept so many of the ex-LNWR 4–4–0s and 4–6–0s in excellent condition, did not seem to have reached the Precursor tanks, and most of them were very poor tools. Occasionally we might get a superheater 4–6–2 tank, but at the period of which I am now writing these were not much better. Then, from the beginning of 1934, we got the 2–6–4 tanks. The 8.53am non-stop from Watford to Euston originated at Bletchley on weekdays, and consisted of a six-coach corridor set, strengthened by three non-corridors at the rear. But on Saturdays it originated at Tring, and was a six-coach suburban set worked by the Watford tank engines, and when Nos 2375, 2378 and 2379 came on to the job we travelled up to Euston on the wings of the wind!

TABLE 14

8.53am WATFORD—EUSTON (Saturdays)
Load: 168 tons tare, 185 tons full
Engine: 2–6–4 tank No 2387

Distance miles		Sch min	Actual min sec	Speeds mph
0.0	WATFORD JUNCTION	0	0 00	–
1.5	Bushey		2 54	–
2.7	Carpenders Park		4 20	55
4.2	Hatch End		5 54	66
6.1	Harrow		7 30	75
7.5	*Milepost 10*		8 36	78
9.4	Wembley		10 02	81
10.5	*Milepost 7*		10 50	83½
12.1	WILLESDEN JUNCTION	13	12 00	80½
13.9	Queens Park		13 21	79½
15.1	South Hampstead		14 19	74
16.5	*Milepost 1*		16 02	–
–			sigs	–
17.5	EUSTON	21	19 00	–

The first record I have of a 2–6–4 on the train is from January 1934, and although it was vastly better than the work of the

Precursor tanks with sustained speeds of 69 to 71mph, it was no more speedy, with 180 tons, than I had come to expect daily with 'Georges' and Prince of Wales 4–6–0s hauling 285 to 315 tons on the weekday trains. But by the early summer of that year the Watford men had fully taken the measure of these splendid engines, and Saturday after Saturday we used to pass South Hampstead, 15.1 miles from the start, in less than 'even time'. A critic might suggest that this stretch is 'all downhill'; in fact it is level for the first 3 miles, then downhill for 7½ miles, and level for the remainder. The maximum speeds, with the engines always travelling bunker first, were around 77 to 78mph, and the exhaust completely silent after the first half-mile or so. The climax, so far as my own recording was concerned, came on 16 February 1935 when engine No 2387 was on the job, with the usual Saturday load of 185 tons (Table 14). The start was a little slower than usual; but we were doing 75mph at Harrow, and then dashed up to a maximum of 83½mph at Brent Junction. A tremendous pace was kept up on the subsequent level track, and we were still doing 79½mph at Queens Park, and 74mph on entering Primrose Hill Tunnel. Passing Milepost 1 in the record time of 16min 2sec from the Watford start we could, with a normal finish, have been at rest in Euston in 18min. But the staff were not quite ready for the arrival of a commuter train 3min early and we were checked outside. A detailed log is shown in Table 14.

The years do not seem to have slowed the paces of these engines, and a friend sent me details of a run with one of the erstwhile Watford engines, made in December 1963 on the 1.15pm from Windermere to Lancaster. On this fairly recent occasion the load was no more than of three coaches, but the old warrior 'flew' to some purpose. The schedule was a fairly sharp one, allowing only 13min to pass Carnforth from Oxenholme, 12.8 miles, and 20min to the stop at Lancaster, 19.1 miles. Engine No 2378 (then numbered 42378) was doing 86mph at Milnthorpe at the foot of the Grayrigg bank, increased this to a full 90mph on the level towards Holme, and passed Carnforth at 85mph almost 2min inside that exiguous point-to-point booking of 13min. With easy running afterwards, Lancaster was reached in 18½min. The load was certainly a featherweight, but a six-coupled tank engine, with 5ft 9in wheels, that can attain

90mph on level track is a very good advertisement for the valve gear recommended by the late E. L. Diamond. There were eventually 125 of these engines, of which the last thirty had side-windowed cabs.

The second engine design to have long-lap, long-travel valves was the standard Class 2 4–4–0. This was an interesting development of the Midland superheater rebuilt Class 2 4–4–0 with 7ft coupled wheels; but the new engines, numbered 563 to 700 had 6ft 9in coupled wheels. In comparison with the original Midland Class 2 engines, the new series had smaller cylinders and higher boiler pressure, and in their case the principle of long-lap valves was applied to the Stephenson link motion inside. The cylinders, as on the 2–6–4 tanks, were 19in diameter by 26in stroke, and the boiler pressure 180psi. They proved excellent small-power units, though some observers questioned why it should have been considered necessary to build new engines of such moderate power in 1928. A number of them were allocated to the Glasgow & South Western line, which was seriously short of reliable engines for intermediate duties. The boiler dimensions are shown in Table 15:

TABLE 15

DERBY BOILERS 1923-8

Type	4–4–0	2–6–4T	4–4–0
Class	4*	4	2
Distance between tubeplates ft in	12-3⅝	11-4⅝	10-10½
Heating surface sq ft			
Tubes	1170	1082	1034
Firebox	147	138	124
Superheater	272	246	246
Combined Total	1589	1466	1404
Large Tubes			
5⅛in o/o No	21	21	21
Small Tubes			
1¾in o/o No	146	146	146
Grate Area sq ft	28.4	25	21.1
Boiler Pressure psi	200	200	180

* Three cylinder compound

The last of these three new 'standard' classes was the 7F general service freight engine, and this also was a development of a pre-grouping design, though not such an obvious development as the new Class 2 4–4–0. More 0–8–0s were needed. The ex-LNWR G2, by then up-graded to Class 7F, was generally considered a very satisfactory engine; but with the experience of recent new designs it was felt that it could be improved by long-lap, long-travel valves, and a higher boiler pressure. As it was to be a direct development of the G2, the Crewe drawing office was given the job of preparing the detail design, under the general direction of the CME's headquarters at Derby, and some amusing tales are told of the noncommittal answers that were received in response to requests for directives. Typical answers were: 'Oh, make it like the compound', or 'Make it like the banker'—the latter, of course the ten-coupled 'Big Bertha' of the Lickey. Apart from the variations in the basic dimensions that contribute to the nominal tractive effort figure, there was a remarkable similarity in dimensions between the G2 and the new engine (see Table 16).

TABLE 16

0–8–0 Freight Engines

	LNWR	LMS
Cylinders diam in	20½	19½
stroke in	24	26
Coupled wheel diam ft in	4-5½	4-8½
Boiler pressure psi	175	200
Dist between tubeplates ft in	14-10½	14-10½
Tubes:		
Large 5in o/o No	24	24
Small No	142-1¾in O/D	120-2in O/D
Heating surfaces sq ft		
Tubes	1432.4	1402.0
Firebox	148	150
Superheater	358.6	342
Combined total	1939	1894
Grate area sq ft	23.6	23.6
Tractive effort lb	28,043	29,747

A total of 175 was constructed between 1929 and 1932, but the new 0–8–0s never superseded the ex-LNWR variety, and in the years after World War II scrapping of the newer engines proceeded rapidly, and the G2 class outlasted them by many years. The G2 had, of course, all the 'guts' and ability to stand thrashing that was so characteristic of the older Crewe designs. Long-lap, long-travel valves, whatever their attributes in a fast passenger engine, were not an unmixed blessing in a heavy freighter.

Before leaving the period of Sir Henry Fowler's chieftainship and returning to the story of the new main line 4–6–0s, there is another important locomotive class to be mentioned. From the very moment of his appointment as president of the executive, Sir Josiah Stamp began to take a keen interest in locomotive matters. It was not that he was interested in locomotives as such; but their maintenance and running costs represented such a large proportion of the total expense of running the railway that he, with the critical mind of an economist and statistician, was at once drawn towards the problems involved. One can readily imagine that he found the methods of working one of the most potentially lucrative traffics on the line—the Toton—Cricklewood coal trains—somewhat archaic, in that practically every load was double-headed, with two ex-Midland 0–6–0s. Whether or not Stamp himself suggested a trial of the Beyer-Garratt type of locomotive I cannot say; but one can be sure that the adoption of a type that would do the work of two existing engines would have received his warm approbation.

The first three engines of this new series were put to work in 1927. They are sometimes referred to as the direct incorporation of two Horwich 2–6–0s into the Garratt principle, but although the coupled wheelbase is the same this is about the only dimensional similarity between the Garratt and the tender engines. On the former the cylinders were 18in diameter by 26in stroke, and coupled wheel diameter 5ft 3in. With a boiler pressure of 190psi this provided a tractive effort of 45,620lb, or roughly the same as a 4F superheater 0–6–0 and a non-superheated pilot. It is nevertheless one thing to provide tractive effort on paper; what the statistician may not always appreciate is that the development of that tractive effort depends upon the man with the shovel! The firing of a Garratt with a grate area of 44.5sq ft was needless to say a vastly different proposition from that on a 4F, the most puissant partner in the previous standard combination on the coal trains between Toton and Cricklewood. It is interesting to compare the boiler proportions of the two locomotives, noting how the inherent features of the Beyer-Garratt make possible a boiler of almost ideal proportions for free steaming at high rates of evaporation (Table 17).

TABLE 17

Boiler Proportions

	4F	Garratt
Distance between tube plates ft in	10-10½	12-5
Tubes:		
Large O/D in	5⅛	5⅛
number	21	36
Small O/D in	1¾	2
number	146	209
Heating surfaces,		
Tubes, sq in	1034	1954
Firebox	124	183
Superheater	246	466
Combined Total	1404	2603
Grate area	21.1	44.5

A study of these dimensions shows that the Garratt had virtually double the steaming capacity of a 4F 0–6–0, but would of course need very careful firing to make such proportions a reality in actual traffic. The firebox was not greatly *longer* than that of the 4F, being 8ft 5in in comparison with 7ft. The 4F boiler was, of course, identical to, and interchangeable with that of the Class 2 standard 4–4–0.

The three original Beyer-Garratt locomotives were subjected to a long period of testing against the double-headed method of working, including coal consumption trials with the dynamometer car, with loaded trains of 1,450 tons in the southbound direction, and 100-wagon trains of empties taken on the return. The log on p. 103 (Table 18) gives details of a typical run from Toton to Brent sidings, Cricklewood. The average speed originally scheduled was 18mph, but this was subsequently increased to 21mph. The test results proved remarkably in favour of the Beyer-Garratt type of locomotive, and in 1930 a further thirty were ordered. At that time Sir Josiah Stamp stated: 'In addition to saving one set of men per train, they will displace 68 old freight tender engines!' On these later engines Messrs Beyer Peacock & Co were able to incorporate their patent self-trimming coal bunker. There had been many cases on overseas railways where the inclusion of this device would have been welcome on Beyer-Garratt locomotives, but where it was impracticable because of strict limitations upon maximum axle load. The use of this device considerably eased the fireman's work, by eliminating the tiresome necessity of getting coal forward manually. This was a very welcome accessory on locomotives having a grate area more than double that of the largest locomotives with

TABLE 18

1.5pm freight train from Toton to Brent
Load: 1,450 tons; Beyer-Garratt locomotive

Distance Miles		Arr pm	Pass pm	Depart pm
0.0	Toton	–	–	1.5
3¼	Ratcliffe Junction		1.17	
10	Loughborough		1.39	
17½	Syston North Junction		2.1	
28¾	Brentingby	2.38	–	2.48
31¼	Saxby		3.0	
36	Ashwell		3.15	
38¾	Oakham		3.24	
42½	Manton		3.35	
43¾	Wing Sidings	3.40	–	3.55
49¾	Gretton		4.13	
53¼	Weldon North		4.30	
58¼	Glendon South Junction		4.46	
60¾	Kettering		4.54	
67½	Wellingborough	5.15	–	5.40
70½	Irchester South		5.57	
81	Oakley Junction		6.29	
82½	Bedford		6.35	
90¾	Ampthill		7.7	
99¾	Leagrave		7.41	
102¼	Luton		7.49	
112¾	St Albans		8.19	
117¼	Radlett		8.32	
123¼	Mill Hill		8.51	
126¾	Brent Sidings	9.5		

which the freight enginemen of the Midland Division had previously been familiar.

In view of this epoch-marking change in the working of the Toton—Cricklewood coal traffic, the design and operating of the self-trimming coal bunker is worth a detailed description. It consisted of a closed container of conical shape, the axis of which was inclined towards the footplate end of the bunker. The top side of the container was thus horizontal, and the floor had a slope sufficiently steep to work the coal forward when revolving. The front end was fitted with suitable doors and a shovel plate to suit the standard footplate practice of the LMS, while the top of the container was provided with a set of double doors, for coaling. Rotation of the bunker was controlled from the footplate through worm gearing from two reversibly-driving steam engines. The bunker could be revolved in 30 seconds, or less, but in actual practice it was found that three or four revolutions sufficed to bring up any amount of coal required on the shovelling plate. With the introduction of these engines into general service it will be appreciated that the working of the coal trains between Toton and Cricklewood was well on the way to modernisation.

CHAPTER 7

Royal Scots

THE extent to which the design of the Southern Lord Nelson influenced that of the new LMS 4–6–0 is strongly contested by Derby men. It is nevertheless beyond question that a crisis had developed in locomotive affairs, and with work on the Fowler compound Pacific halted, and no alternative immediately available other than that of enlarged Claughtons, the CME's department was caught in a cleft stick when the management announced its intention of putting on a fifteen-coach express in the following summer to serve Glasgow and Edinburgh only, with the minimum of intermediate stops, and those only for locomotive purposes. Any development or design work would have to be held up pending the results of the trials with the Great Western Castle class engine. These were not completed until November, and Stamp wanted new engines for June of the following year. The enlarged Claughtons would have been able to manage the new train as it was actually operated in its first months; but it became obvious later that the arrangements concluded were no more than a temporary expedient until much more powerful engines were available.

The immense resources of the British locomotive building industry then became of priceless value to the LMS. The North British Locomotive Company had experience, not only in building but in designing locomotives, that was then probably without parallel the world over. The drawing office staff at Springburn was large and highly qualified, and the company undertook to build fifty 4–6–0 locomotives of an entirely new design in what proved to be almost record time. But the 'North British' did not have by any means a free hand. It has been stated that the use of three cylinders was stipulated by the operating department, and to this extent I can well imagine that J. E. Anderson was anxious to have as little machinery between the frames as possible. Although drawings of the Lord Nelson were made available one can detect little of similarity when it comes to a careful comparison of detailed design. The boiler barrel was much the same, but the wheel spacing was quite different, and against the trapezoidal shape of the Belpaire firebox on the Nelsons, clearly indicating the Swindon influence in that case, the Scot had a very simply shaped box that looked like a straight enlargement of standard Derby practice.

Herbert Chambers did a remarkably successful job in co-ordinating the precepts of Derby with the world-wide experience of Springburn, though the desire to achieve standardisation of detail produced one or two odd results in outward appearance, such as the use of the standard Midland form of tender, which was much narrower than the cab. I shall never forget my first footplate run on one of the original Scots, and how precarious it seemed to look back from the fireman's seat into an airy nothing! Such oddities were no more than superficial. Following Sir Henry Fowler's action after the reading of E. L. Diamond's paper at the Institution of Mechanical Engineers, long-lap, long-travel valves were a 'must'. Such provision was nothing new at Springburn, and the Scots had a steam lap of $1\frac{7}{16}$in and a travel in full gear of $6\frac{3}{16}$in. But more important perhaps was the use of piston valves of 9in diameter in conjunction with cylinders of only 18in diameter. This may be compared with the 8in valves of the Gresley A3 Pacifics on the LNER, which had 19in diameter cylinders; these dimensions alone made the Scots potentially very free running engines. Following Derby standard practice of the time, they had piston valves with the wide Schmidt type of ring that was universally applied also on the LNWR superheater engines. This, when accurately fitted, gave excellent results when the engines were new, but their subsequent deterioration and the effect on coal consumption and general performance had yet to be fully understood at both Derby and Crewe.

Taken all round the Scots, as originally produced, were in every way a Midland design, incorporating the very important feature of long-lap, long-travel valves, and with the high boiler pressure of 250psi. Try as one can, there is little to be discerned of the Southern influence—which was perhaps just as well, for

NOTABLE FREIGHT ENGINES

(above) *the ex-Midland 0–10–0 No 2290, for banking on the Lickey Incline;* (upper centre) *the ex-*LNWR *G2 class 0–8–0, with Belpaire firebox;* (lower centre) *the Fowler standard 0–8–0, originally 7F, developed from the G2;* (below) *Beyer-Garratt 2–6–0 + 0–6–2 with self-trimming coal bunker*

CLAUGHTON DEVELOPMENTS

(above) *engine No 5908* Alfred Fletcher, *fitted with Caprotti valve gear;* (centre) *one of the large-boilered series, retaining Walschaerts valve gear, No 5986;* (below) *engine No 5927* Sir Francis Dent, *with large boiler and Caprotti valve gear*

the Nelsons as originally built were not the most successful of engines. In one respect the following of Midland, rather than of Southern or Great Western practice, proved a disadvantage in later years. The driving axle boxes were designed in the Derby tradition, with solid manganese-bronze boxes, and the white metal confined by strips of bronze dovetailed into the body of the box. This no doubt gave satisfactory results on locomotives habitually driven on a light rein, as in the old Midland style; but no matter how carefully the loose strips were fitted they tended to come adrift at times, and when engines are heavily worked, as the Scots had to be on the West Coast route, complete disintegration could occur. With increasing mileage therefore the Scots became very prone to failures with hot driving boxes. In 1927 however, when they were so urgently needed, such troubles had not begun to reveal themselves, and paying every respect to the hurry in which the order was placed and the work done, the Royal Scots were an outstanding success. The construction was divided between the Hyde Park and Queens Park Works, twenty-five apiece, and although the engines were not ready for the inauguration of the Royal Scot train in June 1927, they were certainly able to undertake the far more onerous task of non-stop running between Euston and Carlisle in the winter service of that year.

Before coming to the first work of the Scots themselves, mention must be made of the train, which of course was nothing more than the historic 10am from Euston to Glasgow and Edinburgh in a new guise. As retimed, from 11 July 1927 onwards, the train made no passenger stops anywhere between London and the Scottish cities. A stop was made at Carnforth, to change engines, and another at Symington for division of the Edinburgh and Glasgow sections. By use of the new lightweight stock the tare load of the fifteen-coach train was no more than 420 tons, but even with the employment of 'S' Claughtons it was considered necessary to double-head throughout, and 4–4–0 engines of the George the Fifth class were used for this purpose. North of Carnforth the train was worked by a pair of Midland compounds from Polmadie shed. The two engines worked through to Glasgow, and the six-coach Edinburgh portion was taken from Symington by a Caledonian superheater 4–4–0. The Euston—Carnforth non-stop run of 236 miles, which was then a record for the LMS, was scheduled to be covered in 265 minutes, an average of 53.3mph. The allowance for the initial 158 miles to Crewe was 175min, and with no more than 418 tons tare the LNWR would have expected such a timing to be kept by a George the Fifth on its own, let alone a Claughton. But times had changed and in 1927 it was deemed necessary to use one of each! For the record, the engines working down on the inaugural day were No 5299 *Vesuvius* and No 5934.

Delivery of the Royal Scot class engines from the North British Locomotive Company began in August 1927, and the earliest members of the class to be delivered were sufficiently worked in for the new schedules to be inaugurated on 26 September. It was a remarkable, if not a venturesome project to start working the longest non-stop run ever made as a daily event, anywhere in the world, with locomotives of a new type barely two months out of shops. Yet such it was, with all the hazards of rough winter weather ahead, and the prospect of working tare loads of 420 tons over Shap and Beattock without assistance. On the down journey the 299.2 miles between Euston and Carlisle were booked to be run in 345min and the up journey in 355min giving average speeds of 52 and 50.7mph respectively. In view of what was done subsequently these average speeds were not heroic, but in the circumstances it was one of the most remarkable ventures into locomotive operation that could possibly have been imagined. There is no doubt that very strong pressure from the top management was put upon all the departments concerned, otherwise one can hardly imagine the innately cautious locomotive department at Derby consenting to such a gruelling duty being imposed on its latest locomotive, without much longer trial. That the Royal Scots stood up to it so well is a fine tribute to all who were concerned in their design and construction.

The maximum of publicity was given to the introduction of the new engines. The name of the revitalised train, Royal Scot, was a very effective counterblast to the rival Flying Scotsman of the East Coast route, as befitting the crack train of the Royal Mail route to Scotland; but Royal Scot was also the name of one of the most famous of Scottish infantry regiments, and the first twenty-five engines of the class all had regimental names. The second group was originally named after celebrated historic locomotives ranging from the *Lancashire Witch* to the *Lady of the*

Lake. In later years these historic engine names were replaced by further regimental names. Like so many instances one could recall, when systematised naming is extended to a degree not originally intended, the 'system' begins to outstrip the suitability of titles as *names*, and while *Scottish Borderer, Cameron Highlander*, and *Royal Ulster Rifleman* are splendid both in association and as names one does rather shy at *The Prince of Wales' Volunteers, South Lancashire* however distinguished that regiment may have been. In outward appearance the Royal Scots were striking, rather than handsome, and their truncated and small-diameter chimney looked out of place on so huge a smokebox. On grounds of aestheticism this seemed a case for putting a false exterior round the basic chimney. The Scots were originally stationed mainly at Camden, Crewe North, Edge Hill and Polmadie, with smaller contingents at Rugby and Carlisle (Upperby).

While those engaged in the working of the Royal Scot train, handled by picked crews, did very well, the same could not at first be said of the class as a whole, and there was a good deal of quite indifferent performance. Engine working on the West Coast route was still in something of a muddle, and on my first trip behind one of the new engines on the Perth express due into Euston at 7.30pm, she was double-headed by a Midland compound from Preston to Crewe. Again, one of the Carlisle engines No 6139 *Ajax* gave me a poor run on the night Highland express from Wigan to Carlisle. Although a division of the train resulted in our having a load of no more than 318 tons tare, speed fell to under 30mph on Grayrigg bank, and to 24½mph on Shap itself. This was well below the best George the Fifth standards of old. The non-stop running of the Royal Scot train lasted for only one winter season. Furthermore, the lavish provision of separate dining car accommodation in the Edinburgh portion ceased, and by the winter of 1928 the combined Glasgow and Edinburgh train was one of under 400 tons tare, and it stopped intermediately at Crewe. I had a run on the train in December 1928, with engine No 6105 *Cameron Highlander* and a gross load of 410 tons behind the tender; we ran the 158.1 miles from Crewe to Euston in 173min 40sec—unchecked throughout. On the down Midday Scot, with a 440-ton load, No 6111 *Royal Fusilier* only just managed to keep the 93min schedule to Rugby,

82.6 miles, and with very poor running and the feeblest of uphill work lost 7min onwards to Crewe.

There was much controversy about the working of the new engines. Many of the North Western men regarded them as yet another Midland intrusion, and I shall always remember the remark of a driver that I congratulated at Crewe on the completion of a particularly fine Claughton run when we had conveyed, well within schedule time, a load well over the official maximum for the class. The date was August 1929, and on the 5.20pm down from Euston, we had 370 tons tare to Rugby, 398 tons on to Stafford, and finally no less than 426 tons. I ventured to suggest that with such a load they ought to have had a Royal Scot. The driver thereupon roared with laughter and replied: 'We shouldn't be at Stafford yet if we'd had one of those things!' Even on the crack double-home turns with the principal West Coast expresses one could record indifferent, if not definitely poor performance, and on long runs one could always note a gradual deterioration as the journey progressed. In that same August of 1929 I travelled from Crewe to Carstairs on the Midday Scot, with engine No 6128 *Meteor*, and a gross load of 475 tons. We began quite brilliantly, passing Preston in 54½min and, despite signal checks, reaching Lancaster, 72 miles, in 81½min—4½min inside schedule. But we barely kept time up to Shap and when we got north of Carlisle the effort was flagging badly. We took 49½min to reach Beattock; took rear-end banking assistance, and drifted down the Clyde Valley with every sign of being short of steam. Travelling south a fortnight later, *Royal Irish Fusilier* to Crewe, and *Lancashire Fusilier* from there on to Euston, both had difficulty in keeping bare time with a load of 480 tons. The schedule of the up Midday Scot was then 175min on both stages of the run from Carlisle to Euston, requiring average speeds of 48.4 and 54.2mph north and south of Crewe respectively.

Initially there had been immense satisfaction in official circles with the performance of the Royal Scots. A series of dynamometer car trials carried out in October and November 1927 with the pioneer engine, not only showed a comfortable mastery over the work, but the basic coal consumption was lower than anything previously recorded on the LMS, even including that of the Great Western 4–6–0 *Launceston Castle* a year earlier. Table 19 gives the results of six runs on the Royal Scot train, three in each direction and all non-stop between Euston and Carlisle. The actual figures of coal consumption per drawbar horsepower hour must be taken with a slight reserve because it was subsequently found that the dynamometer car instruments were registering slightly more work done than was actually the case. Even if the figures quoted in the table—taken from a contribution Sir Henry Fowler made to the Institution of Mechanical Engineers—are low by as much as 10 per cent, values of coal per drawbar horsepower hour of 2.82 to 3.32lb are most impressive. On the third down journey, the last 5 miles up to Grayrigg summit were covered at average speeds of 33.8, 33.4, 34.5, 33.0 and 31.4mph, while the last five half-miles to Shap Summit averaged 32, 28.1, 25.5, 23.1, and 22.7mph. For a locomotive that had hauled 465 tons and been at work for five hours non-stop, such hill-climbing was certainly excellent.

TABLE 19

DYNAMOMETER CAR TEST RUNS: EUSTON—CARLISLE

Engine No 6100 *Royal Scot*

Direction	Down	Down	Down	Up	Up	Up
Date (1927)	Oct 31	Nov 2	Nov 23	Nov 1	Nov 3	Nov 24
Load, tons tare	419½	420½	449½	420½	420½	449½
Average speed mph	52.7	53.0	53.0	50.3	47.2	51.3
Coal per mile, lb	39.2	40.4	38.9	44.7	40.9	38.8
Coal per dhp hr, lb	3.19	2.94	2.92	3.32	2.86	2.82
Water, galls per mile	33.1	33.9	32.0	35.5	34.9	35.6
Water, lb per lb of coal	8.45	8.38	8.26	7.96	8.53	9.14*

* Tender feed connections leaking: figure too high

Gratifying as such results must have been to all concerned, and particularly to Sir Josiah Stamp, the amassing of detailed statistics upon locomotive operation and repair costs, soon began to show that all was not well with the Royal Scots. The indifferent performance that one could so frequently observe when travelling as an ordinary passenger was reflected statistically in an alarmingly rapid decline in working efficiency. Records of individual locomotives showed increases in coal consumption up to nearly 80 per cent above the initial figure as mileage increased to the point when the locomotives were due for shopping. This meant that engines working on coal consumptions of around 3.2

or 3.3lb per dhp hour when newly overhauled were getting into the 5 or 5.5lb range, with all the accompanying deterioration in performance that went with it. This not only cut clean across the former Midland ideas that any engine of a class should be able to do any job, but it made nonsense of Sir Josiah Stamp's tidy marshalling of statistics of locomotive operation. A run I had in December 1929 on the Liverpool express due in Euston at 9.5pm shows a very different kind of performance from that put up by No 6100 in the tests of 1927. With engine No 6140 *Hector*, and a load of 475 tons, we took 92¾min to pass Rugby from Crewe, 75.5 miles, and eventually lost 18min on the schedule of 171min to Euston. The driver told me that the engine was in poor shape and steaming badly.

Careful scientific investigations were initiated to get to the cause of this deterioration, and eventually it was traced to internal leakage of steam past the piston rings. It seemed, from these investigations, that the single broad ring of Schmidt design would be difficult to improve in this respect, and so an entirely new design, using a solid valve-head with six narrow rings, was introduced. This made an almost phenomenal improvement, and valves of this kind became standard on the LMS in all further designs. Not only this, but older locomotives from which important work was required, had valves of the same kind fitted, to the great advantage of the classes concerned. The variation in performance that had so baffled observers of locomotive running on the LNWR was explained almost in a single sentence, and assumptions that other features of design were causing high coal consumption were easily refuted. So far as my own observations went, the great improvement in day to day work of the Royal Scots began to be evident in the year 1931. By then they were ready for the notable accelerations of service that took place in May 1932, and during the five ensuing years some magnificent standards of performance were established. Even when the advent of the Stanier Pacifics had robbed them of some of their most spectacular turns, the Royal Scots continued to do some really fine work from end to end of the West Coast main line.

When the accelerations of the Anglo-Scottish services took place in May 1932, and such schedules as 88min from Euston to Rugby by the Midday Scot, and 63min from Blisworth to Euston were instituted, some observers felt that the limits of the

Royal Scots had been reached, particularly as such schedules had to be observed with loads up to 500 tons. On the basis of their past record this limit might certainly have seemed so; but few actually outside the CME's department were in a position to appreciate the improvement that had been wrought by that relatively simple and inexpensive change to the piston valves. Cecil J. Allen, indeed, referred to the forthcoming acceleration of the 5.25pm from Liverpool to Euston, including the famous Crewe—Willesden stretch done at 64.2mph start to stop, as 'venturesome'. But the Royal Scots and their crews rose splendidly to the occasion. They seemed to get better as the years went by, and all my own finest runs were made from 1934 onwards. To skip the period from 1930-1933 would, however, be to leave a hiatus in the history of the class, and a reference to some of the more significant among the many runs I logged personally in that particular period is necessary.

It was in 1930 that a further twenty of the class were built at Derby. These were, of course, by far the largest and heaviest express passenger engines built at the former Midland works. They were numbered 6150 to 6169, and the majority were originally turned out without names. All except the last two eventually received regimental names, but of Nos 6168 and 6169 a tale is to be told. Sir Henry Fowler was a man of immensely wide and diversified interests, quite apart from his professional associations. I feel sure it was this diversity of interests that enabled him to take what amounted to a gross insult to his office, and carry on, as if nothing had happened. It is odd to speculate how men like Webb, Churchward or Gresley would have reacted if a new locomotive they had actually commenced to build had been vetoed by the top management, and then they had been told to borrow drawings from another company, and make something like a totally alien design! Put bluntly, that is what happened to Fowler in 1926. But Fowler took the whole thing stoically and took responsibility for what eventually turned out to be a very good engine.

Locomotives apart, however, one of Sir Henry's outside interests was the Boy Scout movement, and at one time he had been district scout commissioner for Derbyshire. In recognition of this, engine No 6169 was named *The Boy Scout*, and in full Scout uniform, Sir Henry was duly photographed in front of the engine. While acknowledging the appropriateness of the name, so far as Sir Henry Fowler himself was concerned, engine No 6169 always seemed slightly incongruous amongst the martial array of guardsmen, dragoons, highlanders, fusiliers, and such like that with one exception formed the rest of the class. That one exception was No 6168, which in proper regard for the equality of the sexes was duly named *The Girl Guide*! For a hulking great cart-horse of a locomotive this name always managed to raise a smile. The naming of engines of the Royal Scot class continued to provide food for the publicists; many of the regiments after which the engines were named presented plaques bearing the regimental crests to surmount the actual name plates. The presentation of such plaques was made the occasion of military ceremony, and many were the stirring occasions on which the plaques were unveiled. It is of interest to recall that the first of such presentations, the cost of which had been covered entirely by voluntary contributions, came from a Scottish Highland regiment, the Black Watch, and engine No 6102 was duly adorned, to the skirl of the bagpipes, at Glasgow Central Station on 15 October 1930.

On 22 March 1931, there was a serious accident to the down Royal Scot at Leighton Buzzard. It was a Sunday, and relaying work further north made necessary a diversion from the fast to the slow line over a crossover requiring reduction of speed to 20mph. The diversion was advertised in the weekly notices, and the signalman at Leighton Buzzard kept his signals in the danger position until he thought that the restriction was about to be obeyed. But in one of those inexplicable cases, in which a driver having an exceptionally good record sometimes errs, all signals were ignored, and the train entered upon the fatal crossover at about 60mph. The engine, No 6114 *Coldstream Guardsman*, overturned, both enginemen were killed, and in the general wreck of the leading part of the train three passengers and one of the dining car staff were killed. In the circumstances it was impossible to determine why so experienced and reliable a driver should apparently have forgotten all about the advance notice of the diversion, and also run through a whole group of signals. But as a result of numerous enquiries suspicion fell upon an unwelcome characteristic of the Royal Scot locomotives, namely for the exhaust steam to cling to the boiler barrel and beat down into the driver's view. This was something that had not previously been experienced on the LMS but which was becoming common with locomotives having large boilers, short chimneys, and the soft blast resulting from free exhaust from long-lap, long-travel valves. As a result of the Leighton Buzzard accident all the Royal Scots were fitted with the vertical type of smoke deflector plates.

So far as actual running is concerned, Table 20 gives summary particulars of twelve runs made in 1932-3.

TABLE 20

Train	Engine No	Load tons gross	Comment
10am Euston—Carlisle	6157	480/390	Punctual throughout
3.43pm Carlisle—Crewe	6121	455	Bad weather 2min lost
1.30pm Euston—Rugby	6168	500	2½min gained
5.33pm Rugby—Euston	6113	435	Punctual
5.25pm Liverpool—Willesden	6105	350	Punctual
5.55pm Euston—Liverpool	6105	460	Punctual
1.30pm Euston—Rugby	6115	500	3½min gained
10am Euston—Carlisle	6154	500/400	2min gained
4.3pm Rugby—Euston	6148	500	1min gained
3.43pm Carlisle—Crewe	6122	465*	7½min gained
Crewe—Euston	6165	530	Punctual
Carlisle—Carstairs	6104	445	1min lost

* Piloted Carlisle to Shap Summit

On the two runs with the down Royal Scot, engines 6154 and 6157 put up thoroughly competent displays, although the load was reduced to 400 tons or under, north of Crewe. The up runs on the Midday Scot from Carlisle to Crewe were less successful. Engine No 6121 *H.L.I.* was definitely in trouble with 455 tons, and the net time of 177min for the 158 miles was not brilliant. On the other hand No 6122 *Royal Ulster Rifleman*, had all the 'sting' of the job removed by having a pilot up to Shap Summit; and whereas No 6121 had struggled up to pass the summit in 56min, No 6122 with only ten tons more had shed her pilot and was away again in 48½min. It is true that the latter engine was working to the faster schedule in operation a year later, and possibly deserved greater consideration up the bank from Carlisle. The two runs up from Rugby to Euston included in the table were both excellent. Engine No 6113 *Cameronian* on the up Perth express, ran the 62.8 miles from Blisworth to Euston in 63¾min inclusive of a bad signal check at Boxmoor. The minimum speed over Tring summit was 58mph. The second run was on the up Irish Mail, with the engine working through from Holyhead to Euston. From the Rugby start the train passed South Hampstead, 80.2 miles, in 81¾min, and reached Euston on time, in 87min despite adverse signals at Camden.

The hardest sustained running was made on the two journeys with the down Midday Scot, between Euston and Rugby. Both engines had rear-end banking assistance from Midland compounds up Camden bank, and there was some fairly level pegging until *Scots Guardsman* was stopped briefly by signal at Boxmoor. In consequence this train was nearly 4½min late in passing Tring. Some fine sustained high speed running followed on both journeys, and the 44.5 miles between Tring and Kilsby Tunnel South Box took only 38min 35sec and 39min 17sec, with respective average speeds over this undulating stretch of 69.2 and 68mph. On both journeys the net time was well inside the 88min scheduled, though minimum speeds on the long rise to Tring were not greatly above 50mph. On the runs commented upon in the table the best start up to Tring was by engine No 6154 *The Hussar* on the Royal Scot. There was certainly no question of nursing this engine in the early stages of the long working through to Carlisle, and Tring was passed in 37min 25sec. Without going into too much detail these runs certainly showed very competent performance that was nevertheless to be substantially surpassed in my own experience in later years.

CHAPTER 8

The 'Claughtons' again

VIEWING the LMS motive power stud as a whole, it was evident from the years 1925-6 onwards that, whatever might emerge from the Derby drawing office in the way of a 'super' new main line express locomotive, the existing engines in the No 5 power class would have to carry on as second-line units for many years to come. The Hughes 4–6–0s were largely confined to the Crewe—Carlisle section, and from the year 1926 onwards a sustained attempt was made to improve the all-round performance of the LNWR Claughtons. The dynamometer car trials between Preston and Carlisle in 1925 had shown these engines to be second only to the Midland compounds in basic economy, as represented by the coal consumption per drawbar horsepower hour, and to be considerably superior to the ex-LYR Hughes 4–6–0s in this respect. As mentioned earlier, some consideration had been given to producing a large-boilered edition of the Claughtons when the compound 4–6–2 project was halted in 1926. Before that however the first development of the existing Claughton engines was already under way.

In July 1926, engine No 5908 *Alfred Fletcher*, one of the original batch of Claughtons of 1913, and a noted performer from Edge Hill shed, emerged from Crewe works fitted with the Caprotti valve gear. It was the first British application of this gear, and it was applied experimentally because its design gave promise of greater economy in steam consumption, and reduction of maintenance costs, most of which were for oil. For detailed comparison, a standard Claughton No 5917 *Charles J. Cropper*, which was returned to traffic after general overhaul at the same time as the Caprotti engine was completed, was placed under special observation. The two engines were worked on the same duties; both were subjected to dynamometer tests between Crewe and Carlisle, and their general performance, as regards repair charges, coal and oil consumption, carefully noted. In view of its subsequent workings it is important to emphasise that at this stage the Caprotti engine No 5908 retained the original type of Claughton boiler. It is also remarkable that as turned out from Crewe in July 1926 she was finished in plain unlined black. The only concession in the way of evidence towards the new ownership was the number 5908 on the smokebox, and the LMS coat of arms on the cab-side sheets. The tender was perfectly plain.

Engine No 5908 showed a marked advantage in every way over No 5917. First of all as regards coal consumption (Table 21).

TABLE 21

From 1 January to 18 September 1927

Engine	Mileage Run	Coal used, tons	Coal* per train mile, lb
5908	33,543	692	46.2
5917	31,970	832.3	58.3

* Including lighting up and shed duties

The saving in oil was even more striking. In Table 22 are the figures for the period from 1 August 1926, to 18 September 1927.

TABLE 22

Oil Consumption

Engine	Mileage run	Cylinder pints	Motion pints
5908	48,478	900	1657
5917	42,886	1620	1879

Allowing for the difference in mileage, engine No 5908 showed a saving of 50.8 per cent over No 5917 on cylinder oil, and of 22 per cent on motion oil.

TABLE 23

1.6pm CREWE—CARLISLE: 25 JANUARY 1927

DYNAMOMETER CAR TEST RUN

Load: 316 tons tare, 325 tons full
Engine: 4–6–0 No 5908 *Alfred Fletcher* (small boiler, Caprotti valve gear)

Distance Miles		Sch min	Actual min	Actual sec	Speeds mph
0.0	CREWE	0	0	00	–
4.9	Minshull Vernon		7	30	55
11.8	Hartford		14	43	64
16.2	*Weaver Junction*	18	18	52	55*
21.2	Moore		23	39	65/55
24.1	WARRINGTON	27	26	25	58
31.0	Golborne		32	20	40 (min)
35.8	WIGAN	40	39	35	57/50
39.1	Standish	44	44	13	33
45.5	*Euxton Junction*	52	51	18	68
48.7	Farington		54	06	64
51.0	PRESTON	59	56	54	25*
55.7	Barton		64	33	45
60.5	Garstang		69	30	57/53
67.6	Galgate		77	03	60
72.0	LANCASTER	83	81	18	70
75.1	Hest Bank		84	00	70
78.3	CARNFORTH	90	86	51	60
82.8	Burton		91	44	45 (min)
85.6	Milnthorpe		94	33	58
91.1	OXENHOLME	104	101	34	39
98.2	Grayrigg		112	44	30
104.2	Tebay	121	119	24	61
109.7	*Shap Summit*	130	129	40	22
119.0	Clifton		139	12	70
123.3	PENRITH	144	142	56	60*
128.0	Plumpton		147	31	65
126.2	Wreay		155	42	70
141.1	CARLISLE	163	159	53	–

* speed restriction

The dynamometer car test runs were carried out on 25-6 January with No 5908, and on 8-9 February with No 5917. For strictly comparative purposes it is a little unfortunate that the coal consumption was taken for the complete round from Crewe to Carlisle and back, extending over two days, particularly as in the case of No 5908 climatic conditions were vastly different on the northbound and southbound runs. Going north, calm and fine weather was enjoyed, but on the following day the return was made in the teeth of exceptional gale conditions. This is evident from the dynamometer car records, for although the northbound run of 141 miles was made in 159.9min, at an average speed of 53mph and the return took 177.3 min, or only 47.8mph, the gross work done on the drawbar, in horsepower hours, was 1082.4 going north, and no less than 1378.3 on the much slower southbound run.

For the purpose of the trials the Glasgow portion of the 10am from Euston was made up to 315 tons tare, and the excellent run shown in Table 23 was made on 25 January 1927. It will be seen that sufficient time was in hand for an easy ascent to be made up to Shap. The Caprotti valve gear enabled the engine to be worked in very short cut-offs on the level and easy stages, and between Preston and Lancaster, for example, the engine was working in no more than 11 per cent cut-off, with a fully opened regulator. On the return journey on the following day an excellent climb was made from Carlisle to Shap despite the weather, covering the 31.4 miles to the summit box in 47min 43sec, with a gross trailing load of 335 tons. The standard engine is reported as taking 165min 55sec for the down run, but no intermediate details are available, except that she reached a maximum speed of 87mph descending from Shap Summit to Tebay. This latter engine showed a typically average Claughton figure of coal consumption for the round trip at 4.86lb per dhp hour. The corresponding figure for the Caprotti engine was the good one of 3.82lb. The standard engine returned a coal consumption figure very similar to that of No 30 *Thalaba* in the 1925 trials between Preston and Carlisle, and this can be taken as representative of average performance of these engines with the original form of trick-ported piston valves.

From the time of the Caprotti trials all the attention of the drawing office and testing staff was concentrated for a time upon getting the Royal Scots launched, and it was not until 1928 that further attention was given to the Claughtons. It was then that twenty of them were fitted with enlarged boilers. To what extent the original boiler proposals of 1911 were consulted it is not possible to say; but the standard and the enlarged boiler dimensions were as shown in Table 24.

TABLE 24

CLAUGHTON BOILERS

	Original	Enlarged
Small tubes:		
Number	159	140
outside diam	1⅞in	2⅛in
Superheater flues:		
Number	24	24
Outside diam	5¼in	5¼in
Superheater elements no	24	24
Heating surfaces in sq ft		
Firebox	171.2	183
Tubes	1647.2	1550
Superheater	379.3	365
Total	2197.7	2098
Length between tube plates, ft in	14-10½	14-0
Grate area sq ft	30	30
Working pressure psi	175	200

It will be seen that in evaporative heating surface the new boiler was actually smaller than the old one; but with a shorter distance between tube plates, and larger tubes, the locomotives would tend to be freer steaming. The enlarged boiler added two tons to the total weight of the locomotive, increasing this to 79 tons, with 60 tons adhesion. The increase in boiler pressure brought the nominal tractive effort of the locomotive up to 27,577lb. Ten of the re-boilered engines, of which No 5908 was one, were fitted with Caprotti valve gear, while ten retained the Walschaerts gear (see Table 25).

After rebuilding, most of the Walschaerts engines were allocated to Preston for working the Liverpool and Manchester Scottish expresses. There the whole stud was kept in positively regal condition, and immense pride in them was taken by all the crews

TABLE 25

Walschaerts		Caprotti	
5906	*Ralph Brocklebank*	5908	*Alfred Fletcher*
5910	*J. A. Bright*	5927	*Sir Francis Dent*
5953	*Buckingham*	5946	*Duke of Connaught*
5970	*Patience*	5948	*Baltic*
5972		5957	
5986		5962	
5993		5975	*Talisman*
5999	*Vindictive*	6013	
6004	*Princess Louise*	6023	*Sir Charles Cust*
6017	*Breadalbane*	6029	

concerned. The Caprotti engines were stationed variously and particularly at Longsight and Holyhead. At the former shed they took over most of the Euston—Manchester services, both via Crewe and via Stoke, while those allocated to Holyhead monopolised the Irish Mails. For some time prior to the rebuilding of these twenty engines there had been a general rationalisation of locomotive working on the Western Division. At Holyhead a batch of unaltered Claughtons was working the Irish Mails on a double-home basis throughout, between Holyhead and Euston. This had become a prestige job, and on these the Welsh-based crews were doing very well. These men were naturally delighted when they received the large-boilered Caprotti engines, and the state of cleanliness of the Irish Mail engines began to rival those of Preston. The Longsight men did equally well, though a number of unaltered Claughtons remained on top link working from that shed well into the 1930s.

The rebuilt engines retaining the Walschaerts gear had their original trick-ported piston valves removed, and were fitted instead with new valves having six narrow rings, as adopted for the Royal Scots (see Chapter 7). They proved to be extremely economical engines, not only by past standards but by comparison with the best of most contemporary express passenger locomotives of the day. Dynamometer car trials were conducted between Euston and Manchester, and revealed that the large-boilered engines with the Walschaerts gear were more economical than those with the Caprotti gear (see Table 26).

FREIGHT AND MIXED TRAFFIC TYPES

(above) *the first Horwich Mogul, No 13000, in* LMS *red livery;* (upper centre) *a later Mogul No 42825 of the batch fitted with RC poppet valve gear, in* BR *livery;* (lower centre) *one of the Stanier Moguls of 1934, No 2979;* (below) *a standard 8F 2–8–0, with the later type of boiler, No 8042*

An intriguing 'might have been': H. P. M. Beames' proposed development of the Prince of Wales class 4–6–0 with inside Caprotti valve gear

TABLE 26

LARGE BOILERED CLAUGHTONS : CLASS 5X

Valve gear	Caprotti	Walschaerts
Average weight of train tons tare	418	417
Average running speed mph	52.9	52.7
Coal consumption		
lb per mile	39.9	38.2
lb per dhp hour	3.53	3.25
lb per sq ft of grate per hour	69.1	65.8

It is probably true that the difference between 3.53 and 3.25lb per dhp hour could have been accounted for by variations between individual engines, rather than the valve gear, but such a figure as 3.25lb was getting down to something near Great Western figures, and was an astonishing improvement over the 4¾lb of the original Claughtons with trick-ported valves.

The up-grading of the rebuilt engines from Class 5 to a power classification half way between 5 and 6, and designated 5X enabled the rostered loads to be increased, and between Preston and Carlisle the introduction of these engines obviated a good deal of piloting. The heaviest load I personally saw taken unassisted was 393 tons tare, and curiously enough it proved to be the fastest I noted, on the 10.52am down from Preston. With lighter loads I had good runs with No 5910 *J. A. Bright* and No 5993, but the run tabulated with the celebrated *Ralph Brocklebank*, in the rebuilt form was excellent (Table 27). It will be seen that the brisk start was no more than needed to keep bare schedule time to Lancaster; but fast running on to Carnforth, and a spirited 'attack' on Grayrigg bank had gained us 1¼ minutes by Oxenholme. The engine was not unduly pressed on the bank itself, but Shap Summit was passed dead on time with this heavy train, and with some typically free running afterwards we should have been in Carlisle at least 2 minutes early, but for the final check.

My only experience of the rebuilt engines on the Irish Mail was on the up night train which I joined at Crewe in the early hours of a June morning in 1929. My enthusiasm for train logging was then such that although I had already travelled across from Leeds by the night mail, I kept awake to record the work of a rebuilt Caprotti engine, No 5957 throughout from Crewe to

TABLE 27

PRESTON—CARLISLE

Load: 393 tons tare, 415 tons full
Engine: 4–6–0 No 5906 *Ralph Brocklebank*
(Large boilered 'Claughton' class, piston valves)

Distance Miles		Sch min	Actual min sec	Speeds mph
0.0	PRESTON	0	0 00	–
4.7	Barton		9 02	55½
9.5	Garstang	12	13 38	65
12.7	Scorton		16 35	63½
16.6	Galgate		20 10	67
19.9	*Lancaster Junction*		23 12	62½*
21.0	LANCASTER	24	24 10	70½
24.1	Hest Bank		26 40	74
27.3	CARNFORTH	30	29 20	69/71
31.8	Burton		33 35	55½
34.6	Milnthorpe		36 10	66
40.1	OXENHOLME	44	42 40	42
43.6	*Hay Fell Box*		48 20	32½
47.2	Grayrigg		55 15	30
53.2	Tebay	62	62 00	63
56.2	*Scout Green Box*		66 20	29½
58.7	*Shap Summit*	73	73 02	21½
68.0	Clifton		82 05	77
71.1	*Eamont Junction*		84 48	55*
72.3	PENRITH	87	86 00	58
77.0	Plumpton	92	90 35	67½
82.7	Southwaite		95 25	78
85.2	Wreay		97 25	72/75
88.7	*Carlisle No 13*		100 45	–
–			sig stop	
90.1	CARLISLE	105	105 35	

* Speed restrictions

Euston. Although the load was relatively light and the schedule was easy, there was always the chance, in my youthful expectation, that something interesting would transpire. It was not to be on this occasion however, and after a brisk start, passing Tamworth, 48 miles, in 55min, it was a matter of killing time, and we eventually reached Euston in 187½min. While on the subject of the Irish Mail I have tabulated the Chester—Holyhead section of a run with the down day train to indicate the work of one of the standard engines on the 263-mile through working from Euston. There was nothing exceptional about the run except that the engine appeared to have complete mastery over load and schedule, with no sign of 'flagging' or shortage of steam in the final stages of this long working.

Mr Cecil J. Allen clocked a good run with one of the Caprotti engines, No 6013, on the down Lancastrian express, from Euston to Manchester, which was decidedly brisk by the standards that had prevailed on the West Coast Route since grouping, but which would not have been thought anything very wonderful

TABLE 28

THE IRISH MAIL—CHESTER—HOLYHEAD

Load: 373 tons tare, 390 tons full
Engine: 4-6-0 No 5992 (Claughton class)

Distance Miles		Sch min	Actual min	Actual sec	Speeds mph
0.0	CHESTER	0	0	00	–
2.0	*Saltney Junction*	4	4	20	–
8.9	Connah's Quay		11	50	61
16.7	Holywell Junction	20	19	20	64½
23.0	Talacre		25	25	–
30.0	RHYL	34	32	25	60
34.2	Abergele	39	37	00	–
37.9	Llysfaen		41	35	37½
40.3	Colwyn Bay	46	44	30	53½
44.4	LLANDUDNO JUNCTION	51	48	45	61½
45.4	Conway		50	15	30*
49.7	Penmaenmawr		56	05	–
54.5	Aber		61	40	53½
59.7	BANGOR	69	68	45	41
61.1	Menai Bridge		70	40	38½
66.0	Gaerwen	78	77	00	72½
72.5	Bodorgan		83	10	52½
81.0	Valley		91	35	69
84.4	HOLYHEAD	100	96	30	

* Speed restriction

in the hey-day of the George the Fifth class, before World War I. It was certainly good work to pass Bletchley in 48¾ minutes from Euston, with a 380-ton load, but after that it seemed that the train was close on the tail of the 5.55pm Merseyside Express, which in its turn was probably following block and block behind the 5.50pm to Wolverhampton. There were signal checks at Castlethorpe, Rugby and Brinklow, and a dead stand outside Crewe. Despite this, Crewe was still passed nearly 4min early, in 166¼ minutes from Euston. The net time was almost exactly 'even', 158 minutes for the 158.1 miles. By far the best run I had personally with one of these engines was on the Ulster Express northward from Crewe, but this I am keeping for the collection of specially good performances with various pre-Stanier classes of locomotive detailed in Chapter 10.

In the meantime there were interesting developments on the Leeds—Carlisle route. The allocation of most of the new Royal Scots of the 6150-6169 batch to the West Coast main line released a number of small-boilered Claughtons for other duties, and a batch of them was transferred to the Midland Division. Their use between Leeds and Carlisle, with the consequent increasing of the maximum load limit from Class 4 to that appropriate to Class 5 engines eliminated a good deal of piloting over Aisgill. The Claughtons were allowed a load of 340 tons and, except in the height of the holiday seasons, very few of the Anglo-Scottish expresses exceeded that tonnage. Contrary to some expectations these big LNWR 4–6–0s soon became quite popular at Leeds. Their smooth riding was much appreciated, and on the first-class hard Yorkshire coal that Holbeck shed received for its top-link turns they steamed well. Among engines thus transferred was the pioneer of them all, *Sir Gilbert Claughton* then numbered 5900, and fitted with an ex-ROD Great Central type tender. The state of cleanliness in which these engines were maintained rivalled the Walschaerts-gear 5X rebuilds that worked north from Preston. There was however much more than a mere transfer of locomotives from one division to another in this re-allocation.

Although the grandiose compound Pacific project had been stillborn, the pundits of Derby continued to keep abreast of current French practice, and one device that aroused particular interest was the Kylala form of multiple jet blastpipe. In France itself this was developed by André Chapelon into the well-known Kylchap (Kylala-Chapelon); but on the LMS the original form of the Kylala was fitted experimentally to two Claughtons then working on the Leeds—Carlisle route: No 5912 *Lord Faber* and No 6001. In 1930 a further series of dynamometer car trials was conducted on the usual trains: the 12.5pm up from Carlisle, and the 4.3pm down. Engine No 6001 was tested against a standard engine No 5973. By that time however the latter engine was not 'standard' in the sense of 1922-3. The unrebuilt Claughtons, like the Royal Scots and the twenty rebuilt engines, were being fitted with new piston valves without trick-ports and having six narrow rings, like those of the Royal Scots. This was having a considerable effect upon their coal consumption. The engine with the standard blastpipe and chimney, No 5973, was last out of shops in July 1929, and when the tests started in the middle of May 1930 it had run 35,894 miles. Engine No 6001, with the Kylala blastpipe, had its last general repair in February 1930, and since then it had run 11,111 miles.

It is interesting to discern a rather more objective attitude to locomotive testing over this route than in the highly partisan contests staged in the early days of grouping. Round trips from Carlisle to Leeds and back were made on 12, 13, 14 and 16 May, two with each engine, and it was then observed that No 6001 was in far better mechanical condition than No 5973. The results substantially favoured the Kylala engine but those responsible felt that because of the difference in condition of the two engines one might well be merely comparing one engine with another, and not the effects of working with or without the Kylala blastpipe. The results obtained with the latter were so good as to attract much attention. It was decided therefore to remove the Kylala blastpipe from No 6001 and substitute the standard arrangement, thereafter conducting a further series of tests. To make things as strictly comparable as possible it was arranged for the same set of men who had worked No 6001 in the first series to officiate again in the second series, which took place on 3 and 4 June 1930. On all six round trips the test trains were made up to a nominal 300 tons, though the actual tare weights, including dynamometer car, varied between 304 and 320 tons.

All the test trains were run punctually, but although the Kylala blastpipe made the steaming of engine No 6001 more free, it was at the expense of a higher coal consumption and a lower evaporation. It is however the performance of this engine with the standard blastpipe that fairly makes one sit up and take notice, for the coal consumption on the two round trips came out at 3.61 and 3.64lb per dhp hour. Details of the tests are shown in Table 29.

TABLE 29

TRIALS OF ENGINE 6001 : JUNE 1930

Date	3/6/30	4/6/30
Load, southbound tons	311	311
northbound tons	313	320
Average running speed mph		
southbound	47.1	47.4
northbound	51.0	49.4
Coal per train mile		
round trip lb	35.7	35.5
Coal per dhp hr	3.61	3.64
Max dhp southbound	791	794
„ northbound	822	938
Evaporation :		
lb of water per		
lb of coal	8.37	8.16
Max speed mph		
southbound	70	74
northbound	81	75

By way of a flashback to the trials of 1923-4, when the Midland compound No 1008 put up so outstanding a performance, her coal consumption figures for three runs with 310-ton trains were successively 3.93, 3.64 and 4.02lb per dhp hour, and with 350-ton trains, six trips with figures varying from 3.71 to 4.2lb per dhp hour. On the 1930 tests, the higher mileage Claughton No 5973 returned figures of 4.64 and 4.69lb per dhp hour, while for No 6001 with Kylala blastpipe, the corresponding figures were 4.08 and 3.79lb.

Nearly three months after the conclusion of the tests I travelled north by the 10.18am from Leeds, and we had engine No 6001. She was in tremendous form, making light of the rising gradients, and reaching Skipton, 26.2 miles, in 31min 55sec, with a 320-ton train. On the harder gradients to Milepost 230, including a lengthy stretch at 1 in 130-173-162-150 past Gargrave, we sustained 47½mph, and cleared the last 1¾ miles to the summit, on 1 in 131, at 44mph. At Hellifield, unfortunately, the addition of the Manchester portion brought the tare load up to 352 tons; and 'rules' being 'rules' we had to take a quite-unnecessary pilot up to Aisgill. The situation was made all the more stupid, because all the advantage we gained in a fast climb of the bank was thrown away by stopping at Aisgill to detach the pilot. We took no less than 10min 10sec to cover the 6.6 miles from Garsdale to Mallerstang, whereas on a subsequent run with the same train and a very heavy load which fully justified piloting we did not stop at Aisgill. But although we took 3min longer to pass Garsdale—then known as Hawes Junction—we were actually a minute *ahead* of No 6001 at Mallerstang. On the form displayed between Leeds and Hellifield there is no doubt that this splendid engine could have passed Aisgill in very little more than 37min and made just as good time to Appleby as she did with pilot assistance and the disadvantage of a 2min stand at the summit. On the second run, with the same train and a load of no less than 470 tons, another Claughton, No 5932 *Sir Thomas Williams,* was piloted to Appleby and covered the 46 miles from Hellifield in 54½min start to stop. No 6001, assisted only to Aisgill and hauling 375 tons, took just 5 seconds less. The pilots in both cases were Midland Class 2 7ft superheater 4–4–0s.

From Appleby both Claughtons now unassisted, ran well. This section is sometimes dismissed as 'all downhill'. This is far from the case. It is true that the initial 1¾ miles down at 1 in 121 gives a good start to to Long Marton, but for the next 20 miles, to Milepost 300, the fall is no more than gradual, and averages about 1 in 500. The two engines passed Long Marton at 62½mph and 60mph respectively, and then the average speeds on to Milepost 300 were 71 and 65.4mph by Nos 6001 and 5932 respectively, with maximum speeds of 79 and 75mph at Little Salkeld. To Scotby, then the last station before Carlisle, and 28.1 miles from Appleby, the times were 26¼ and 28¼min respectively; but both trains were delayed in the final approach to Carlisle.

In the summer of 1931 I had an interesting run on the 12.5pm from Carlisle to Leeds, which carried almost exactly the load conveyed in the dynamometer tests of May and June 1930 with engines 5973 and 6001, namely 313 tons. On my trip however, to my great pleasure, we had the pioneer engine *Sir Gilbert Claughton*. It was an excellent performance characterised by good hillclimbing, keeping comfortably within the scheduled point-to-point times, and thereafter requiring no more than moderate downhill speeds to reach Leeds on time. On what is generally the toughest part of the ascent to Aisgill, the long grind at 1 in 100 from Crosby Garrett up to the south end of Birkett Tunnel, speed fell to 31½mph; but the final stage from Mallerstang up to Aisgill summit was taken at a minimum of 34mph. The engine seemed to be working well within its capacity throughout the ascent, and in view of the easy nature of the working afterwards, I can quite well imagine that the coal consumption was little more than that of No 6001 in the tests of June 1930. At the time of these tests the schedule was 5min slower.

Two months previous to the trip with *Sir Gilbert Claughton* I had been a passenger on the same train, and our engine was one of the two Claughtons that had then been recently rebuilt as three-cylinder machines, and became the pioneers of the so-called 'Baby Scot' class. The Crewe rebuilding of some of the Claughtons with larger boilers had been very successful, but at Derby headquarters it was felt that a still better replacement for the original Claughtons would be to put the new Crewe boiler on to the Royal Scot engine, and this simply expresses just what the 'Baby Scots' were. They had the same cylinders and motion as the big Scots, and by using a number of parts of the original Claughtons they could, accountancy-wise, be called a rebuild. From the viewpoint of locomotive design however there was nothing of the original Claughton left. The coupled wheel spacing was the same as that of the Scots, and in order to keep the motion the same, and interchangeable, the distance between the cylinder-centre line and the leading pair of coupled wheels was the same. In the 'Baby Scots' the original Crewe bogies were used with 6ft 3in wheel centres, as compared to the 6ft 6in Derby bogie on the Royal Scots, and in consequence the spacing between the rear bogie wheels and the leading coupled wheels was 5ft 10½in on the 'Baby Scots' against 5ft 8in. The boiler was identical to that of the enlarged Claughton.

The two engines rebuilt for experimental purposes were No 5902 *Sir Frank Ree* and No 5971, which was originally

Royal Scots

(above) *engine No 6126, as originally delivered from North British Locomotive Co Ltd, before naming (subsequently named* Sanspareil); (centre) *one of the Derby-built Scots, as running in the late 1930s with large Stanier tender No 6160* Queen Victoria's Rifleman; (below) *the experimental high-pressure three cylinder compound No 6399* Fury

CLASS 5X DEVELOPMENTS

(above) *first of the 'Baby Scots': No 5902* Sir Frank Ree, *incorporating certain parts, including coupled wheel centres, from the original Claughton;* (centre) *the Stanier 5X (later Class 6) Jubilee class No 5739* Ulster, *in the final* LMS *style of painting;* (below) *renewal of a 'Baby Scot', with converted Scot type boiler, and new internally-streamlined cylinders, No 45526* Morecambe and Heysham

THE PACIFIC SAGA

(above) *one of the two original Stanier Pacifics No 6201* Princess Elizabeth, *as first built;* (upper centre) *engine No 6201, with modified boiler, as running at the time of the 1936 record runs between Euston and Glasgow;* (lower centre) *one of the later streamlined Pacifics No 6244* King George VI; (below) *first of the non-streamlined Duchesses as originally built, without smoke deflectors, No 6230* Duchess of Buccleuch

The Turbomotive, passing Wavertree Junction, with the 5.25pm up Liverpool Flyer

named *Croxteth*, but which in her rebuilt state took the road nameless. The official title used at first for this name class was the rather cumbersome one of 'Three Cylinder Converted Claughton', but the enginemen quickly found a much more appropriate one of 'Baby Scot'. With a boiler pressure of 200psi but all other basic dimensions the same, the nominal tractive effort was 26,520lb, and like the true rebuilt Claughtons which retained their four cylinders, the new engines were classified 5XP. They were an immediate success and authority was given for the construction of a further fifty engines of the class in replacement of an equal number of original Claughtons. They incorporated a few parts from the originals, such as bogies, reversing gear and whistles, and took the same numbers as the engines they replaced. The almost universal reference to these engines as 'Baby Scots' bothered the LMS management. When the celebrated War Memorial engine *Patriot* was withdrawn this name was transferred to No 5971—one of the two original 'Baby Scots'; the engine was renumbered 5500, and the remaining engines of the class numbered consecutively afterwards. The class was thereupon officially named, the Patriots.

I must confess I was never very happy at the use of the old LNWR name in this way. It had so special and poignant an association with the former engine No 1914 that it seemed incongruous on a class of fifty-two hybrid rebuilds that were a cross between Crewe and Derby practice. Nevertheless Patriots they were dubbed, and as Patriots and nothing else they were known to a later generation. But my readers must forgive me if I continue to call them 'Baby Scots'! As a direct derivative from the Royal Scots in their improved form, with the new type of piston valves, it was no more than natural that the 5X version did excellent work from the outset. Dynamometer car test runs were conducted between Euston and Manchester and produced coal consumption figures of 3.12lb per dhp hour, in hauling trains of 409 tons tare at average speeds of 52½mph. But what commended them particularly to the high management of the LMS was their very low repair cost index. This yardstick of maintenance costs is based on the repair costs for the entire class in pence per mile. The new standard Class 2 superheater 4–4–0 was the cheapest to repair of any relatively modern LMS locomotive, and this was rated at 100. A class having the value

150 had a repair cost in pence per mile 50 per cent greater than the Class 2.

The repair cost indices shown in Table 30 were established for the principal 4–6–0 express passenger classes, all over a period of ten years, except for the 'Baby Scot', which was for only eight years.

TABLE 30

Repair Cost Indices

Engine class	Index
Royal Scot	177
Original Claughton	200
Large boilered Claughton	175
'Baby Scot'	118

Why the 'Baby Scot' came out so much lower than the Royal Scot is difficult to understand. The 'engine' was exactly the same, and the boiler that of the large Claughton. One looks to the duties on which the new engines were employed. The Royal Scots were all engaged in heavy work on the West Coast main line, and the large-boilered Claughtons likewise. But as the 'Baby Scots' were introduced, batches of them were sent to the Midland Division to take over jobs previously done by 3-cylinder compound 4–4–0s, while a number of them were put on to the two-hour Birmingham expresses. Both these groups of services were fairly light, albeit sharply timed. It was only on the Euston—Manchester trains that the new engines had to pull really substantial loads. One feels that the unusually low repair cost index was a measure of the duties on which they were employed rather than any features of design. Nevertheless it was an immense feather in their caps, and the engines enjoyed a spell of popularity with all who had any dealings with them.

Their noses were rather thrown out of joint four years later by the advent of the Stanier version of the 5XP class, with the Great Western type of boiler. Although a stud of them working from Bushbury shed Wolverhampton, continued to do very good work on the two-hour Birmingham trains, elsewhere they began to drift into secondary duties. The standards of maintenance on them deteriorated, and from being among the most popular engines on the line their reputation swung in precisely the opposite direction until an experienced Scottish fireman apostrophised them to me as, 'the wor-r-rlds wust'! This was a sad state of affairs, because at their best they were splendid engines and extremely free running. All my best runs with them were on the Euston—Birmingham expresses, but even so, very little of their work was better than I would have expected from a Prince of Wales, in top form, let alone an original Claughton.

The best run was made on a very stormy night with the 6.20pm up from New Street, which in 1938 made three stops within an overall time of 125min from Birmingham to Euston. Details are tabulated of the run from Rugby to Watford on which 2min were lost (Table 31), but the weather was very bad, with a gale-force wind broadside to the line, and heavy rain. It will be noticed that when the train entered the shelter of Tring cutting there was an acceleration, on the continuous 1 in 335 gradient, from 56 to 59mph. With a load of 390 tons this was

TABLE 31

RUGBY—WATFORD JUNCTION

Load: 364 tons tare, 390 tons full
Engine: 4-6-0 No 5522 ('Baby Scot' class)

Distance Miles		Sch min	Actual min	sec	Speeds mph
0.0	RUGBY	0	0	00	
3.8	*Kilsby Tunnel North*		6	41	51½
7.3	Welton		10	35	61½
12.9	Weedon		15	15	75
19.8	BLISWORTH	19	21	11	69
22.7	Roade	22	23	52	63½
27.8	Castlethorpe		28	05	79
30.2	Wolverton		29	59	75
35.9	BLETCHLEY	33	34	56	66/69
42.4	Leighton Buzzard		40	59	63/66
46.5	Cheddington		44	51	63
48.6	*Tring Cutting Box*		46	58	56
50.9	Tring	47	49	23	59
54.6	Berkhamsted		52	56	68½
58.1	Boxmoor		55	50	76
61.6	Kings Langley		58	32	79
65.1	WATFORD JUNCTION	60	61	59	

Weather: westerly gale and heavy rain

a plucky try at a difficult assignment. On the 4.35pm down, with a 13-coach train of 430 tons gross, No 5507 made a poor start, taking 37min 58sec to pass Tring. There was then little chance of keeping the 63min schedule to Blisworth and in fact we lost 2¼min. On a run with the very fast 6.12pm from Crewe to Willesden, engine No 5503 required to be double-headed with

TABLE 32

SYMINGTON—CARLISLE

Load: 383 tons tare, 410 tons full
Engine: 4–6–0 No 5547 ('Baby Scot' class)

Distance Miles		Sch min	Actual min sec		Speeds mph
0.0	SYMINGTON	0	0	00	–
3.7	Lamington		5	50	61
9.1	Abington		11	43	53½
11.6	Crawford		14	34	53½
14.3	Elvanfoot		17	47	48½/56
17.2	*Summit*	22	21	18	40½
21.5	*Greskine*		25	53	77(max)
27.2	BEATTOCK	33	31	20	
5.2	Wamphray		6	27	72½
8.0	Dinwoodie		8	54	65½
11.0	Nethercleugh		11	27	72½
13.9	LOCKERBIE	16	14	37	
5.7	Ecclefechan		9	04	63½
9.1	Kirtlebridge	9	12	01	74/66
12.8	Kirkpatrick		15	13	75
17.2	Gretna Junction	19	18	38	82½
21.7	Rockcliffe		22	13	69
23.8	*Kingmoor*		24	04	64½
25.8	CARLISLE	28	27	18	

a load of 348 tons tare; with a Midland compound to assist, the run of 152.7 miles was made in 136½min start to stop. To conclude, I have tabulated details of a good run with the 5.34pm from Symington to Carlisle in 1935, when No 5547 made short work of a train of 410 tons (Table 32). By contrast, a study of many runs logged over the Settle and Carlisle line reveals no performances that I could describe as more than adequate.

With the 'Baby Scots' one rings down the curtain upon the

pre-Stanier period of LMS locomotive history. The short period during which E. J. H. Lemon was chief mechanical engineer produced no new locomotive designs that got beyond the drawing board stage. Two new designs were actually prepared at Crewe, of which one was a modernised Prince of Wales 4–6–0, with inside cylinders and Caprotti valve gear, while the other was a heavy freight 4–8–0 with enlarged Claughton boiler. The former was an intriguing, but not very handsome 'might-have-been', which would undoubtedly have been the new mixed-traffic general utility locomotive, had not Stanier arrived and brought with him the conception of the ever-famous Black-Five.

CHAPTER 9

Stanier: The First Phase

THE appointment of Sir Henry Fowler as assistant to the vice-president in January 1931, could have marked the end of Midland domination of the locomotive scene on the LMS. His going left H. P. M. Beames as unquestionably the most senior locomotive engineer in the CME's department, and he could have looked forward in some confidence to getting the job. But Sir Josiah Stamp, in the relatively short time he had been on the railway, had sensed clearly enough the deep antagonism that persisted between Derby and Crewe. At the higher levels, with interchange of personnel it had mellowed considerably; but lower down it persisted strongly enough. To North Western men it was still a case of the b . . . . . Midland, while on the other side there was an attitude of disdainful superiority-complex towards anything that emanated from Crewe. Not long before his death Sir William Stanier told me a story that for all its obvious exaggerations aptly sums up the spirit of that particular time.

Many years after his appointment Stanier was having an informal chat with Stamp, and in a jocular mood referring back to his appointment as CME in January 1932, he asked Stamp: 'Why did you pick on me?' 'Oh,' came the reply, 'if I'd put a Midland man in, the North Western would have gone all ca-canny in protest and we should have had the situation of 1924-6 all over again. If I'd put a North Western man in they'd have had a grand celebration dinner at Crewe, and then all gone over to Derby and burnt down the town hall!'

Faced with this antagonism, Stamp compromised temporarily by appointing the former carriage and wagon engineer, E. J. H. Lemon, and making Beames his deputy, Lemon was a very strong character and a man of outstanding organising ability, and although he had no experience of locomotives he was a shrewd enough administrator to hold the reins. As it turned out, his tenure of office as chief mechanical engineer had little more than that of a 'caretaker' function. Stamp had him marked out for higher things, but in the meantime, under the strong influence of Beames, the ascendancy of Crewe towards its old pre-eminence began. Everywhere on British railways the need for general service, fast mixed traffic locomotives was felt, and Beames turned to the ever-faithful North Western Prince of Wales 4–6–0 as the basis for a modern mixed traffic type. The engine schemed out, and as briefly mentioned, at the conclusion of the preceding chapter, was a curious mixture. It had the boiler of the Prince of Wales class, and inside cylinders, though Beames was evidently satisfied enough with the Caprotti valve gear on the large-boilered Claughtons to specify it for the *inside* cylinders of the proposed new 4–6–0. Externally, the engine would have been distinguished by a high raised running plate, clearing the top of the coupled wheels, and continuing straight to the front-end. Such drawings as have been published of this design do not show any details of the framing, but no doubt there would have been access apertures for maintenance of the inside valve gear. Authorisation for building engines of this class was however not forthcoming, and in the meantime Stamp was casting around for a new CME.

In the year 1931 Great Western locomotive practice was pre-eminent in England. The brilliant second phase of Sir Nigel Gresley's career as CME of the LNER was only just beginning, and there was in any case a covert rivalry between the two north-going companies that would have made it somewhat *infra dig* for the LMS to seek assistance from its ancient enemy at Kings Cross. Furthermore there was then on the LNER no personality within a mile of Gresley's stature. Despite the assistance given at the time of the construction of the Royal Scots, the situation was similar on the Southern. The policy of extending the electrified system on that line was tending to push steam locomotive practice into the background. So the Great Western it had to be, and there personalities greatly favoured the invitation Sir Josiah Stamp wished to make. Principal assistant to Collett was William Arthur Stanier, a man of immense experience, outstanding ability in production, and one who by reason of his age could not look forward to suceeding to the chair at Swindon until fairly late in life. With his ability and experience was combined a genial, charming personality—just the man, in Stamp's view, to weld together the rival factions of Crewe and Derby. After some preliminary contacts through E. J. H. Lemon, the approach from the LMS took Stanier completely by surprise. He was happy and contented on the GWR and quite prepared to continue as second in command to Collett, for what was left of his working life. But the offer, from the LMS, when it came officially, was one that could scarcely be resisted, and in January 1932 he took office at Euston as CME of the LMS.

It was an appointment that created intense interest throughout the locomotive world, and somewhat naturally it caused disappointment and resentment in certain quarters on the LMS. Beames, who had most cause for disappointment, was characteristically frank and generous. He wrote personally to Stanier expressing his feelings but saying that there was no one he would prefer more to serve under; and from that moment the massive strength of Crewe was solidly behind Stanier. Things were not so happy elsewhere. The design headquarters at Derby was not so receptive to new ideas, and on the running side, where D. C. Urie, formerly of the Highland Railway, had succeeded J. E. Anderson as superintendent of motive power, there developed a good deal of opposition. More seriously perhaps, Stanier's appointment had not received the unqualified blessing of all members of the executive over which Sir Josiah Stamp presided. There was one member in particular who had felt that a down-to-earth steam locomotive practitioner was not the ideal man for the job, and that a man of more scientific leanings and academic attainments would have been preferable.

However Stanier it was, and his mandate was simple enough. It could be expressed in a single phrase, namely to reduce drastically the overall cost of locomotive construction, maintenance and running. Although Stamp looked at things with the eye of an economist, he saw clearly enough that if the number of different engine classes could be reduced, the stock of spares carried need not be so large, while if better utilisation could be obtained from each individual unit the total number of locomotives needed to work the traffic need not be so great. Added to this, if by good design the running repairs necessary could be reduced,

STANDARD 2–6–4 TANK ENGINES
(above) *the Derby 2300 class, later variety with side-windowed cab;* (centre) *the Stanier three-cylinder type, of 1934;* (below) *the first of the Stanier two-cylinder class, original variety with domeless boiler, No 2537*

Heavy Freight Workings

(above) *a Stanier Black Five No 45412 on up Class D freight approaching Oxenholme;*
(below) *Horwich 2–6–0 No 42872 on express freight, Bristol to the Midlands near Yate*

and the locomotives could work longer mileages between successive visits to shops for general repairs, costs could be further reduced on that account. Examination of the diagrams of locomotive working all over the system indicated that higher weekly mileages could be obtained if individual units worked longer distances on a through run, dispensing with intermediate engine changing. Thus to further the overall policy the CME had to provide locomotives capable of longer through runs, possibly with remanning en route; to work on lower coal consumption; to return a lighter repair bill, and to run longer mileages between successive visits to main works.

To achieve the degree of standardisation and rationalisation Stamp desired, together with substantially improved technical performance, there was nothing for it but to scrap and build anew. The new CME was expected to work fast. He had little of consequence to build upon and he embarked instead upon a range of entirely new designs. In some ways his position was analogous to that of Churchward on the GWR in 1901 except that Churchward had time on his side and could develop his prototypes and eradicate their faults before quantity production was called for. On the LMS Stanier naturally turned to his Great Western experience in formulating the basic requirements for six new designs. These were:

2–6–0 Fast mixed traffic
4–6–0 Fast mixed traffic
4–6–0 Express passenger
4–6–2 Heavy express passenger
2–6–4 Suburban tank
2–8–0 Goods and mineral.

These six classes, together with the Royal Scots, were intended to cover the whole of the main line and heavy suburban traffic from end to end of the line. Modern examples in three out of the six categories already existed in the Horwich Moguls, the 'Baby Scots', and the Derby 2–6–4 tanks. Of these, the financial performance of the 'Baby Scots' was so exceptionally favourable that further engines of this class were built new pending the production of a still further improved design. Priority was given to the new Pacifics. Not only would these be a prestige job for the company, but they would implement the policy of longer through workings by taking Anglo-Scottish expresses throughout between Euston and Glasgow, instead of changing engines either at Crewe or Carlisle.

In adopting the Great Western type of taper boiler with the trapezoidal-shaped Belpaire firebox so assiduously developed by Churchward in his early days at Swindon, Stanier was providing his new company with a gilt-edged security. It was obviously more expensive in first cost, but that extra cost was paid for over and over again in reduced maintenance charges, and freedom from incidental troubles in day to day working. The initial adoption of a moderate degree of superheat, as on the Great Western, has been set down as a major error of judgement: a slavish copying of Swindon practice with little appreciation of the diverse grades of fuel regularly used on the LMS. What is not generally known however is that fuel conditions on the Great Western were not everywhere of the carefully picked Welsh grades that were supposed to be essential to the attainment of the highest standards of performance. In fact, some of the finest locomotive work on the system, and in Great Britain itself at the time, was done by the Wolverhampton No 1 link on the London expresses, using hard Staffordshire coal. What Stanier was in no position to appreciate in his first years on the LMS, and what would probably have not been acknowledged, even if it were known in the drawing office at Derby, was the 'slap-happy' style of firing that prevailed on many sections of the system. I shall never forget a footplate trip with a pair of particularly keen and conscientious Carlisle men on the down Royal Scot. The engine, No 6137, was free steaming and in excellent condition, but the boiler pressure was allowed to see-saw up and down in the most carefree fashion, between 190 and 250psi.

With a high degree of superheat as used on the Scots and on all the Bowen-Cooke express locomotives this did not matter on trains that were not timed or loaded up to the limit of the capacity of the locomotive; but it was a practice totally different from that prevailing everywhere on the Great Western. No matter where one travelled on the latter system, from the heaviest and fastest main line workings down to local trains in the mountains of central Wales on Moguls and Dukedogs and 14XX 0-4-2s on auto-trains, the firemen seemed to make it a point of honour to maintain the pressure gauge needle constantly on the red line, and the Ramsbottom type safety valves just 'sizzling'. Many an express driver would begin to get fidgety if boiler pressure dropped about 10psi below the rated maximum. In maintaining such ideal conditions Great Western enginemen were undoubtedly helped by the characteristics of their safety valves, which permitted of that nicely balanced 'sizzling' condition, without full blowing-off. Against this the 'Pop' safety valve in general use on all modern LMS locomotives goes off with a bang, and lets out such a volume of steam as to cause an appreciable drop in boiler pressure before it closes again. Unless the firing is very carefully managed and pressure kept just below blowing off point, a see-sawing condition is almost inevitable. I am however anticipating the results of Stanier's first locomotives with moderate degree superheat, before describing the locomotives themselves; but I feel it is essential that this aspect of running conditions on the LMS should be emphasised for a proper assessment of the early Stanier locomotives to be made.

While the many problems in connection with the new Pacifics were being resolved, Crewe works was given an interesting preliminary exercise in the building of taper boilers. A further batch of mixed traffic engines of the 2–6–0 type was authorised, and Stanier took the opportunity of Swindonising the design. The cylinders were moved from their high, inclined position and a taper-barrelled, domeless boiler of very similar proportions to that of the Great Western 43XX provided. Although a concession to LMS practice was made in the fitting of 'Pop' safety valves over the firebox, the boiler had top feed, and the original form of cover was precisely in the style of the Great Western polished brass 'milk can'. As such the first engine of the class was turned out from Crewe, and that indefatigable photographer of everything that transpired there, the late W. H. Whitworth, duly 'copped' her. But even higher authority than Stanier felt that this adornment was too obviously Great Western, and it was removed and replaced by a flat 'dome' cover before the official photograph was taken. Whitworth was implored to suppress his negative. It duly went 'underground' but not before a few of his friends had received copies. I was one of the recipients and at this distance of time the original form of the Stanier Mogul can now be revealed.

The first of the Pacifics was completed at Crewe in the early summer of 1933. It was at once noted that the basic dimensions contributing to the nominal tractive effort value were exactly the same as those of the Great Western Kings; but the 'engine' layout included no form of conjugation for the valve motion. The Royal Scots had three sets of valve gear, and so the Pacifics had four. An immense amount of study went into the design of the chassis in which the main frames were the longest yet fitted to any British locomotive. The result was a beautiful riding vehicle which was greatly appreciated by the footplate men. The huge boiler was not so successful. It was designed to meet the needs of through working over the 400 miles between Euston and Glasgow, and it included a firegrate with an area of 45sq ft. The superheater was of no more than moderate size, but in working out its proportions too much regard was paid to Great Western practice in conditions somewhat outside the Great Western context, and the free gas area through the superheater was inadequate on the Pacific. In consequence the two original engines, Nos 6200 and 6201, never really steamed freely, and there was much difficulty with them when they were first put on to the Royal Scot train, working through between Euston and Glasgow.

The train itself was not an unduly difficult one to work at that time, and the Royal Scots could handle it comfortably enough, with engines changed at Carlisle; but those engines were then at the very top of their form, well understood and liked by the men, and those allotted to these important duties were maintained in excellent condition. There is no doubt that the 45sq ft grate on the Pacifics intimidated some of the firemen. Without instructions to the contrary some of them tried to fire 'all round the box', as was needed on the Claughtons and they got pretty well exhausted in the process, particularly on the up journey, non-stop from Carlisle to Euston. As one of the Carlisle men once expressed it to me: 'The Glasgow boys come in, and say "she won't steam", and you've three hundred miles to go'. The front-end was excellent from the outset, and the new engines ran freely and fast; but many months were to pass before the performance of the new engines showed any significant improvement over that of the Royal Scots, and many of the most experienced men in the Anglo-Scottish links openly expressed their preference for a Scot if any really hard work was to be done.

The difficulties with the Pacifics did not displease those in high places who had questioned the choice of Stanier as chief mechanical engineer, while the introduction of three new classes of locomotive in 1934, did not at first do a great deal to improve his 'image'—to use a popular catch word. These three new classes were the taper-boilered 5X express passenger 4–6–0 of the Jubilee class; the ever-famous Black Five mixed traffic 4–6–0 in its original form, and the three-cylinder 2–6–4 tank for the Southend line. All three had small superheaters, and with the Jubilees in particular there was a lot of trouble with steaming. I well remember the comment of an exasperated Midland driver who had lost a lot of time on a down evening express from St Pancras: 'Superheater?' he snorted. 'It wouldn't even heat the bath water!' There was a brush with Alexander Newlands, the chief civil engineer, over the weight-diagram of the three-cylinder 2–6–4 tanks—shades of the Highland River class. Only the Black Fives seemed to escape general criticism, though they were after all mixed-traffic, and not express passenger engines.

At this critical stage Stanier was fortunate in his staff. Open-hearted and quite incapable of any form of intrigue, he had already endeared himself to all his personal entourage, and of these he had no more devoted admirer and assistant than R. A. Riddles. When Stanier went to the LMS Riddles was assistant works superintendent at Crewe. He worked tirelessly on the production problems concerning the Pacifics, and very shortly afterwards he was brought to Euston as locomotive assistant to the CME. As a life long LNWR and LMS man he was keenly aware of the cross-currents that were flowing so strongly in the locomotive department, and in addition to working ceaselessly to overcome the teething troubles with the new engines, he set himself up, to quote his own words to me some years ago, as 'Stanier's political agent'. With shrewd acumen and skilful but restrained use of the publicity department at Euston, he lost no opportunity of advertising the achievements of the new locomotives, and in consequence the railway press was most favourably disposed. What could have been a very difficult phase was thereby successfully tided over. It was at this time that I began to make my first footplate journeys and I remember vividly how very touchy things then were at Euston. In writing of the Princess Royal class I was particularly requested not to refer to them as Pacifics in case they were confused with the Gresley Pacifics of the LNER. They had to be referred to as 4–6–2s.

It is important to recall that publicity for the new engines was not confined to the official 'handouts' and the facilities given to well-established technical journalists like the late Charles S. Lake to visit the various works, and study production methods, and so on. There had to be publicity within the LMS itself for the rank and file, and it was at this stage that the periodical *On Time* was launched. As its name suggested, it was primarily concerned with operating matters, but it contained interesting and chatty articles on locomotives, their construction and operation, and details of particularly good runs. A sustained drive was inaugurated to get more efficient handling of locomotives, and the economic advantages of driving with a wide open regulator and short cut-offs was frequently stressed. The publicity people caught on to this principle with much enthusiasm, though occasionally there were awkward moments when technically accurate reporting was not in line with what the publicists would like to have been said. The details of one of my earliest runs on a Royal Scot took some explaining away, when one of those engines was driven for long periods on the first valve of the regulator and 30 per cent cut-off and did some very good work with a 500-ton train.

So far as driving methods were concerned the truth of the matter was that with a good valve gear, providing ample port openings for both admission and exhaust, the technique of driving, within certain limits, did not matter very much. With the Stanier Black Fives, when they had settled into their stride one rarely saw them worked on short cut-offs. The LMS engines that did essentially need a wide, if not necessarily full open regulator, were of course the Midland compounds. Drivers inevitably find the best method of handling individual engines whatever the theorist or the publicists might say, and generally speaking I found the Jubilees were worked more frequently with a full open regulator than any other LMS class—Pacifics included. Nevertheless, while its preachings on the technicalities of engine driving were often accepted more in the spirit than in the letter, *On Time* fulfilled an invaluable function, and did much to consolidate the position of the Stanier regime.

Some of my own first travelling experiences with the new

engines were characteristic of their early work. I had a run on the up Midday Scot, on which a Jubilee took over at Crewe from the Royal Scot that had worked down from Glasgow. The addition of the through coaches from Stranraer at Carlisle had brought the load up to 535 tons, and we had been piloted up to Shap; but at Crewe fortunately one coach was detached, though nevertheless leaving a gross load of 500 tons. The Jubilees in their original condition always seemed to take a long time to warm up when making a 'cold' start; and on this trip the combination of a 500-ton load, and the Madeley bank to climb meant that we lost time to Whitmore. In any case the engine was considerably overloaded for a 5X on a 'Special Limit' timing. But once over Whitmore summit the engine ran well, though not well enough to recover all the initial loss of time. The ascent of Madeley bank was very laboured, with a minimum speed of 32mph on the 1 in 177 gradient and a time of no less than 20min 48sec to passing Whitmore. After that the 145.2 miles on to South Hampstead were covered at an average speed of 59.5mph, and the inward time of 81min 57sec for the 82.6 miles from Rugby to the stop in Euston was particularly good. The 'Special Limit' loading for the 5X engines was then 415 tons, and with this consideration a loss of only 6½ minutes was certainly excusable. But if the start up to Whitmore had been up to the standard of performance displayed after Stafford there would have been very little time lost at all.

The second run (Table 33) was on the accelerated Birmingham service, whereby certain trains ran from Euston to New Street in 5 minutes under the level 2 hours, inclusive of one intermediate stop. As on the rival Great Western route, most of the Birmingham trains are worked by Wolverhampton engines and men with 'Baby Scots' stationed at Bushbury shed; but the 11.30am down was a Camden turn, and on the run tabulated we had a low-superheat Jubilee. As usual with those engines the start was very slow, taking no less than 11½ minutes to pass Willesden. After that we ran uniformly well the whole way, and with a complete absence of checks reached Birmingham in 12 seconds over the 115-minute allowance. We were standing for 2¼ minutes at Coventry. Good though this run was however, it was not greatly superior in times and speeds to the best one had come to expect from the George the Fifth class 4-4-0s in LNWR days. The loads

TABLE 33

EUSTON—BIRMINGHAM

Load: 291 tons tare, 315 tons full
Engine: 4-6-0 No 5597 *Barbados* (Class 5X)

Distance Miles		Actual min	sec	Speeds mph
0.0	EUSTON	0	00	–
1.0	*Milepost 1*	4	24	–
5.4	WILLESDEN JUNCTION	11	30	53
8.1	Wembley	14	20	58½
13.3	Hatch End	19	37	60
17.5	WATFORD JUNCTION	23	39	69
24.5	Boxmoor	30	09	64
31.7	Tring	37	07	61½
40.2	Leighton Buzzard	44	07	79/75
46.7	BLETCHLEY	49	14	78/75
52.4	Wolverton	53	42	81
59.9	Roade	59	59	67
69.7	Weedon	68	00	75
75.3	Welton	73	04	62
80.3	*Hillmorton Box*	77	39	72½
82.6	RUGBY	79	54	40*
89.1	Brandon	86	42	73
94.0	COVENTRY	91	44	–
3.5	Tile Hill	6	27	53†
8.8	Hampton-in-Arden	11	36	73
17.0	Adderley Park	18	36	68
18.0	*Proof House Junction*	19	55	–
18.9	BIRMINGHAM	21	13	–

* speed restriction
† attained at Beechwood Tunnel

of such trains as the 9.10am from Euston on Monday mornings often topped the 300-ton mark, and it was a common occurrence to gain several minutes between Willesden and New Street, on a schedule that included one stop within the overall allowance of 2 hours.

One of my earliest experiences with the low-superheat Black Fives was on the up Ulster Express one Sunday morning, between Lancaster and Crewe when No 5153 had to handle a train of

454 tons tare, 490 tons gross. She was given no banking assistance either from Lancaster, up to the 'Old' junction, or from the Warrington start up to the viaduct over the Manchester Ship Canal at Acton Grange Junction. With this heavy train the engine did extremely well, making good starts from each intermediate stop, and then running freely. From Lancaster we climbed the 1.1 miles up to the Old Junction in 3min 54sec, and then gradually accelerated to 69½mph on the level between Garstang and Brock. From Preston we made the excellent uphill starting time of 8min 37sec over the 5.5 miles to Euxton Junction, but the best work of all, and the only stage on which the running was not hindered either by signal or permanent way checks, was between Warrington and Crewe. The initial 1.7 miles to Acton Grange Junction, rising at 1 in 135-160 for 1½ miles, were climbed in exactly 4 minutes and then the ensuing 19.7 miles on to Coppenhall Junction, on a generally rising road took only 20min 35sec. With a smart finish the 24.1 miles into Crewe were completed in 28min 33sec start to stop from Warrington. The debut of the Black Fives was generally better than that of the Jubilees, and this run of mine was certainly an excellent and typical example.

Another Sunday experience was on the 4.40pm up Scotsman from Crewe to Euston with engine No 5028 and a load of 380 tons gross. As was often the case on Sundays, there were a number of incidental checks, and the work of the engine itself suggested that all was not well on the footplate. There were times when the running was positively brilliant, and others when a marked falling off in standards suggested shortage of steam. Against a schedule of 170 minutes for the non-stop run of 158.1 miles we took 173½ minutes actual, and 159½ minutes net, clearly showing the potentialities of these famous engines. Once again, as with all Stanier designs, the high-speed running was very free, with a maximum for the whole trip of 79½mph at Norton Bridge, and speeds of 75-6mph on all the major descents south of Stafford.

CHAPTER 10

Running—Pre-Stanier Classes

At a time when the Stanier locomotives were making their shaky and uncertain debut the older engines were doing some of the finest work of their careers. This applied particularly to the Royal Scots which, with the new type of piston valve mentioned in Chapter 6, and the Great Western type of driving axle-box substituted for the standard Midland type, were being driven really hard in the tradition of the former LNWR. In the mid-nineteen thirties it seemed that the harder you drove a Royal Scot the better it liked it. Looking back through my travelling diaries of the period I can turn up run after run of great merit, in which engine crews from all the principal main line sheds participated. Out of this galaxy I have chosen for special mention (Table 34) two on the down Merseyside Express, both, remarkable to relate, made at Bank Holiday weekends when that train, in addition to the Lancastrian and the Ulster Express, was running in duplicate. In the ordinary course of things this was a closely-timed group of expresses, with the Lancastrian leaving at 6pm, ten minutes behind the 5.50pm two-hour Birmingham express. Then came the 6.5pm to Liverpool and the 6.10pm to Heysham. When the 6.0, 6.5, and the 6.10 were divided the departures were:

5.50pm	Birmingham and Wolverhampton
5.55pm	1st portion Lancastrian (relief)
6.00pm	Lancastrian—regular train
6.5pm	Merseyside Express regular train
6.10pm	Ulster Express ” ”
6.15pm	Merseyside Express relief
6.20pm	Ulster Express ”

Very close attention was given to the punctual working of this

TABLE 34
THE MERSEYSIDE EXPRESS

Engine No			6142			6111		
Engine Name			*Lion*			*Royal Fusilier*		
Load tons E/F			473/505			471/510		
Driver			Brooker			Bishop		
Distance		Sch	Actual		Speeds	Actual		Speeds
Miles		min	min	sec	mph	min	sec	mph
0.0	EUSTON	0	0	00	—	0	00	—
5.4	Willesden Junction	9	10	13	54	10	32	56
11.4	Harrow		16	42	56	17	09	53½
—			—	—	58½	sigs		32
17.5	Watford Junction	22	22	48	67	25	22	54½
24.5	Boxmoor		29	39	eased	33	29	49
31.7	Tring	38	38	45	44	41	52	58
40.2	Leighton		46	28	73½	49	02	78
46.7	BLETCHLEY	51	51	49	74/69	54	13	77/72
52.4	Wolverton		56	33	74½	58	51	75½
59.9	Roade	63	63	23	57½	65	35	59
69.7	Weedon		72	42	64½	74	10	74
76.2	*Kilsby Tunnel South*		79	24	54	80	07	60½
82.6	RUGBY	86	85	44	slack	86	08	69/40*
91.3	Shilton		95	34	63½	96	10	60
97.1	NUNEATON	101	100	38	77½	101	41	73½
—			pws		47	pws		
110.0	TAMWORTH	114	112	19	54	114	12	—
116.3	Lichfield	120	118	47	60/54	119	44	50
124.3	Rugeley	128	126	40	68	128	27	—
133.6	STAFFORD	138	136	15	35*	138	45	40*
138.9	Norton Bridge	145	142	28	58	144	30	55
143.4	Standon Bridge		147	02	64	—	—	—
147.6	Whitmore	154	151	05	60½	154	09	51½
153.3	Betley Road		156	07	75	158	41	75
—			sigs			—	—	
158.1	CREWE	164	164	00	25*	164	30	—
166.9	*Winsford Junction*	174	173	38	77½	174	54	68½
174.3	*Weaver Junction*	181	179	45	54*	181	39	63
177.4	Sutton Weaver		183	31	43½	184	50	48
—			—	—	slack	pws		30
182.8	Ditton Junction	191	190	10	58	191	55	53
187.9	Allerton		196	02	—	198	02	—
189.6	Mossley Hill	200	198	37	—	200	38	—

group of trains at Bank Holiday weekends because late running, particularly of the 6.5 and 6.10pm departures with their Irish connections, could have wide repercussions. I may add that on both occasions tabulated I was bound for Ireland myself by steamers sailing from Liverpool. On both these occasions we were fourth in this close procession from Euston, and on both occasions we clocked into Liverpool on time. Quite apart from the locomotive work involved, these were examples of first class operating. Both trains were worked by well-known Camden drivers, though neither knew his work was being logged in full detail until I went up to the engines on arrival in Liverpool. Brooker, who had No 6142 *Lion* on the first of the two runs, did very good work for the London Midland Region in the Interchange Trials in 1948.

On the first of these two runs the gradual acceleration to 58½mph on the 1 in 335 gradient from Wembley and the fine maximum of 67mph were a little too venturesome for the close running of this group of trains and sighting adverse distant signals far ahead the engine was very much eased down on the ascent to Tring. By this means a definite signal check was avoided, and Rugby was passed on time. On the second run there was a check to 32mph at Hatch End, and this put *Royal Fusilier* 4 minutes behind *Lion* at Boxmoor. But after that the Manchester train must have got well away, for some magnificent running followed with this 510-ton train, and Rugby was passed practically on time. Onwards to Stafford *Lion* made the faster times, despite a strengthening westerly wind, which was later to give us a very rough crossing to Ireland! Then came a really brilliant recovery from the Stafford slack to no less than 64mph at Standon Bridge, and a minimum of 60½mph over Whitmore. Here the engine was developing around 1,200 drawbar horse-power. This exuberance on the part of driver Brooker and his fireman unfortunately resulted in signal checks in the approach to Crewe, whereas driver Bishop on No 6111 got through without hindrance. Both trains were on time at the first passenger stop at Mossley Hill, with net times of 195¾ and 196 minutes from Euston, and the overall times to the arrivals at Lime Street were 216min 5sec and 214 min 50sec—two most excellent runs.

Another very fine Royal Scot run was made at a slightly later date on the up Midday Scot, when that train was normally worked by a Pacific. It was a very rough wintry occasion. Earlier in the day I had been at Haweswater in connection with the dam then in course of construction for the Manchester Corporation Waterworks, and there were times when it was difficult to stand in the tearing wind that was sweeping in from the west. The gale had scarcely abated at all when I reached Carlisle in time to catch the London express, and then I was surprised to see it brought in by a Scot instead of the anticipated Pacific. But it arrived dead on time, and as it ran in I caught sight of one of the best Crewe North enginemen of the day in the cab of No 6103 *Royal Scots Fusilier*, Flemington by name. Gale or no gale we went magnificently up to Shap, passing Summit in 43min 17sec, and with fast downhill running to follow we were several minutes early on arrival at Lancaster. The arrival was in 78min 23sec instead of the 81min booked for this 69.1 mile run.

This splendid run unfortunately ended in anti-climax, not with any discredit to the engine or to the driver who took over at Crewe. There had been a breakdown in communications, and no one had thought to tell the locomotive control at Crewe that a Scot was on the train, and not a Pacific, or alternatively in reporting the engine number the significance had not been appreciated by the control clerk concerned. To keep time on this wild day Flemington and his fireman had thrashed No 6103 good and hard, fully expecting that the engine would come off at Crewe, as was usual with the Scots. When no relief was forthcoming, and the engine had to go forward to Euston the coal supply had been greatly depleted, having already worked over 243 miles. The relieving driver and fireman did the best they could in the circumstances but from Stafford there was a steady falling off in the standard of performance, and at Rugby they stopped for a pilot to get them home.

In Chapter 7 I have referred at some length to the improvements made to the original Claughtons by the fitting of new piston valves with six narrow rings in place of the original trick-ported valves. Details of two runs made in the 1930s show the very high standard of performance of which these engines were capable. The first was yet another Bank Holiday weekend when I was bound for Barrow-in-Furness. Usually business commitments did not allow me to catch the 5.20pm from Euston, which had a through portion; but the 6.10pm Ulster Express made an

TABLE 35

EUSTON—CREWE

Load: to Rugby, 370 tons tare, 400 tons full
to Stafford, 398 tons tare, 435 tons full
to Crewe, 426 tons tare, 465 tons full
Engine: 4-6-0 No 6021 *Bevere* (Claughton class)

Distance Miles		Sch min	Actual min sec	Speeds mph
0.0	EUSTON	0	0 00	–
5.4	WILLESDEN JUNCTION	10	9 45	–
17.5	Watford Junction	24	23 00	61
31.7	Tring	41	38 10	53
46.7	BLETCHLEY	55	51 30	72½
52.4	Wolverton		56 40	–
59.9	Roade	68	64 15	52½
–			sigs	15
75.3	Welton		83 40	52½
82.6	RUGBY	92	91 30	
5.5	Brinklow		7 55	58
8.7	Shilton		11 20	–
14.5	NUNEATON	17	17 00	71
19.7	Atherstone		21 35	63½
27.4	TAMWORTH	31	28 20	70½
33.7	Lichfield	37	34 05	54½
41.7	Rugeley	45	42 00	64½
44.6	Colwich		44 50	61
46.9	Milford		47 05	63½
51.0	STAFFORD	56	52 00	
3.3	Great Bridgeford		5 55	50
5.3	Norton Bridge		8 15	53
9.8	Standon Bridge		13 10	58
14.0	Whitmore		17 30	55¼
16.5	Madeley		20 10	63½
22.4	*Milepost 156*		25 05	75
24.5	CREWE	30	28 20	–

advertised connection at Preston, and by this latter train I usually travelled. But at this particular Bank Holiday I did manage to get away in time to catch the 5.20pm, and was rewarded by a magnificent run (Table 35). The Claughton limit of load on 'Special Limit' timings was then 380 tons; with a train just inside this limit we ran to Rugby with easy competence. There an extra coach was added, and our driver could by rights have claimed a pilot; but instead he ran most vigorously to Stafford and arrived there 4min early—in good enough time indeed to permit of the addition of yet another coach, and still for us to get away on time, now with a gross load of 465 tons. The ascent to Whitmore was truly splendid, with a sustained output of 1,020 equivalent drawbar horsepower, and with a brisk descent of Madeley Bank we were into Crewe comfortably ahead of time.

The second Claughton run in this collection was the only one of those described in this chapter that was not of my own recording. For the details of this most interesting and important occasion I am indebted to the late Eric L. Bell (Table 36). After

TABLE 36

HILLMORTON BOX—WILLESDEN JUNCTION

The up Liverpool Flyer

Load: 351 tons tare, 370 tons full

Engine: 4-6-0 No 5967 *L/Corpl J. A. Christie VC*

Distance Miles		Actual min sec		Av Speed mph
0.0	*Hillmorton Box*	0	00	–
5.1	Welton	7	35	–
10.5	Weedon	12	15	69.3
17.4	BLISWORTH	17	45	75.2
20.3	Roade	20	10	72.1
25.4	Castlethorpe	24	10	76.5
27.7	Wolverton	26	13	67.4
33.5	BLETCHLEY	31	11	71.2
40.1	Leighton Buzzard	36	35	73.3
44.2	Cheddington	39	57	73.1
48.5	Tring	44	00	63.7
55.7	Boxmoor	49	53	73.3
62.7	WATFORD JUNCTION	55	00	82.0
66.9	Hatch End	58	15	77.4
68.8	Harrow	59	45	76.0
74.8	WILLESDEN JUNCTION	65	48	–

the introduction of the Liverpool Flyer in 1932, making a non-stop run from Crewe to Willesden at an average speed of 64.2mph start to stop, I used often to go down to the lineside from my home at Bushey on summer evenings to watch her go streaking by. On one occasion, to my surprise the engine was not a Scot but a Claughton. I was too far from the line to catch her number, but she was going very fast, although a few minutes late. It was not until more than thirty years later that I received from Mr Bell details of what had transpired that night. The 6.12pm from Crewe had what was classified as an XL limit of load. With a Royal Scot this meant a maximum of 380 tons. For a Claughton (Class 5 engine) the limit was 300 tons. That night the load was 351 tons, and no Scot being available a Claughton was put on, No 5967 *L/Corpl J. A. Christie VC*, and duly provided with a pilot in the shape of a standard Class 2P 4-4-0.

From Crewe the two engines made running that was barely adequate for this fast timing, and with no more than a slight check en route passed Rugby roughly a minute late. Then the unexpected happened. Immediately south of Rugby something went amiss with the pilot engine. It was serious enough for a stop to be made at Hillmorton Box, 2¼ miles south of Rugby, and for the engine to be detached. The Claughton driver had 51 tons overload, and was fully entitled to a pilot, though it would have been awkward to get another engine to them, near as they were to Rugby. Because of the occupancy of the up road it would have meant 'wrong line working' between Rugby and Hillmorton, with consequent delay in getting the necessary authorisation and delay to down line traffic. But from the promptness with which things were handled at Hillmorton I should imagine that the idea of getting another pilot never entered anyone's head. For the train was standing for no longer than was necessary to get the disabled engine out of the way, and then the Claughton was driven away, unassisted, in the most brilliant style.

The accompanying log gives details of what transpired. Mr Bell did not take any stop watch readings of maximum and minimum speeds, but he was a recorder of long and wide experience, and I have worked out the average speeds from station to station. First of all it will be seen that the 74.8 miles from Hillmorton to Willesden Junction were covered in 65min 48sec start to stop, an average of 68.3mph; and then it is interesting to compare the booked times of this very fast train with those actually achieved (Table 37).

THE ASCENT OF SHAP

(above) *a 'Lizzie No 6207* Princess Arthur of Connaught *on the down Royal Scot, 15-coach train;* (below) *Manchester—Glasgow express just above Tebay, hauled by Jubilee class 4–6–0 No 45712* Victory *in 1954*

DOUBLE-HEADING ON SHAP

(above) *Horwich 2–6–0 No 42864 and Black Five No 45435 on Manchester—Glasgow express (16-coach load);* (centre) *Derby 2–6–4T No 42322 and a converted Scot No 46121* H.L.I. *on Manchester—Glasgow express (15-coach load);* (below) *Stanier 2–6–4T No 42571, and a Black Five No 45099 on a troop special (train includes some ex-*LNER *stock)*

TABLE 37

Section	Schedule min	Actual m s
Roade—Bletchley	11	11 01
Bletchley—Tring	14	12 49
Tring—Watford	12	11 00
Watford—Willesden	11	10 48

The average speed from Welton to Harrow, 63.7 miles, was 73.3mph and I should judge that the maximum speed on the descent from Tring to Watford was around 85mph in view of the average speed of 82mph over the 7 miles from Boxmoor to Watford. The date of this magnificent piece of Claughton performance was 23 June 1933.

Yet another trip to Ireland gave me some fine running, this time on the Ulster Express. This was not a Bank Holiday occasion, but in mid-July traffic was heavy enough, and the 6.10pm took a load of 520 tons out of Euston. The engine was No 6134 *Atlas*, and driver Chesnay of Camden ran easily out to Tring to keep off the tail of the Merseyside Express, which that evening had 'sixteen' on. So Bletchley was passed 1½ minutes late, in 54½ minutes from Euston. But in the tradition of excellent operating of the 'six o'clock group' there were no checks, and Crewe was reached precisely on time in 167 minutes from Euston—an average speed of 56.8mph. This was no more than a typically good run of the period. It was the continuation north of Crewe that included some outstanding features. A slightly reduced load of 439 tons was taken forward by one of the large-boilered Claughtons. The introduction of the Stanier 5X engines resulted in some of the enlarged Claughtons previously stationed at Preston being transferred to Carnforth for working the Heysham trains, and these engines were still maintained in most regal condition. The Claughtons, whether rebuilt, or otherwise, were always excellent starters, but I must say I cannot recall a previous occasion of a 475-ton train being lifted off the mark in such vigour as *Patience* did on this occasion. In my many travelling records of the 1930-9 period I have nothing with Royal Scots that come anywhere near it—nor for that matter with Pacifics! Passing Minshull Vernon, 4.9 miles, at exactly

60mph we were half a minute inside the sharp initial allowance of 11 minutes to Winsford Junction, 8.8 miles, and passed Warrington in the excellent time of 24min 37sec. The check at Winwick Junction was a bad one and could not have come in a more awkward locality for we had to get going again from practically a dead start up the 1 in 132 gradient that immediately follows. Even so, we should have been very little out on arrival at Preston but for the signal stop outside.

The start out of Crewe was a classic example of the tractive power of a locomotive being used to full advantage in accelerating a heavy train from rest, but there have been very few locomotive classes that could be driven in this way without the risk of slipping—apart of course from those of the Great Western. I was reminded of a similarly 'clean' start eastbound from Reading with engine No 4073 *Caerphilly Castle* and a 470-ton load, in which that very celebrated engine was doing 50mph in 3 miles, and passed Twyford, 5.0 miles in 7min 25sec at 57mph. Both tracks are dead level over the first 5 miles, and in this comparison the advantage lies with the Claughton. After Minshull Vernon the gradients begin to favour the latter engine.

No reference to the work of pre-Stanier types of locomotive on the LMS in the period from 1930 to 1939 would be complete without some mention of the Midland compounds. Although a very large and comprehensive collection of data on their performance has been included in my Locomotive Monograph dealing specifically with these engines there is one journey, in positively classic mould, that must be referred to once again in this new gallery of notable running achievements. I was travelling on the morning express from Leeds to Glasgow St Enoch on a Saturday in late summer, and in 1930 the old arrangements for engine working still prevailed in that engines were changed at Carlisle. We had come north from Hellifield with a load of just over 350 tons, and with the detaching of the Edinburgh portion I anticipated a load of about 300 tons to go forward from Carlisle. But it was near the end of the holiday season and on this Saturday large numbers of people were homeward bound. When we reached Carlisle such a crowd of passengers was waiting that the fresh engine, Midland compound No 913, was waiting to back on with two extra coaches. So we had a load of twelve coaches, including one twelve-wheeled dining car, making a tare load of 350 tons. I am not aware of what the loading limits then were over any part of the G & SW line, but a gross load of 375 tons was in any case a nice proposition for a compound, even over the fairly level stretches of line that extend only to Dumfries.

No one who has studied the results of the various trials over the Settle and Carlisle line, or the work of engine No 1065 in the Preston—Carlisle trials of 1925 will have any doubts as to the ability of the Midland compounds to perform outstanding work on adverse gradients. It is nevertheless one thing to do this under carefully observed test conditions, with the stimulus of competition with locomotives of other classes, and the presence of a dynamometer car coupled immediately behind the tender, and quite another when a locomotive crew is called upon to take an overload in ordinary traffic, and on a summer Saturday into the bargain. Yet in the steam era there were enginemen to whom the footplate and all that went with it were the very breath of life; and make no mistake about it, those worthies were to be found as plentifully on the shovel as on the regulator handle. Such a pair were on compound No 913 that day. I did not ascertain the fireman's name, but the driver was George Paterson of Corkerhill, a giant of a man in spirit as in stature. It was such men who positively inspired and carried their firemen along with them—not because they were heavy-handed and thrashed their engines, but because of the artistry with which they could extract maximum power output on a minimum of coal consumption. Many a fireman, in such circumstances, has said to me: 'It was a real education, and a pleasure to fire to old So-and-so'.

This has been a rather long introduction to the actual run. From the roar of the exhaust as we got away from Carlisle it was evident that an all-out effort was going to be made to keep time. We could not dash away to the Solway in Caledonian style because a slight easing of the speed was necessary to take the diverging line at Gretna Junction; but after Gretna Green we got away in grand style, and touched 66mph before the stop at Annan. The engine was driven veritably all-out up Ruthwell bank with its 1 in 150 gradient, but brilliantly as the run from Carlisle had opened I still expected that we should take a pilot from Dumfries for the long climb up to New Cumnock, to say nothing of the even heavier gradients north of Kilmarnock. No pilot was in sight as we rode into Dumfries, and we got away to make a truly magnificent climb up to New Cumnock. To appreciate the merit of this work it is necessary to make comparison with the work of engine No 1008 in the trials of 1923-4. No 1008 was by any method of reckoning a most exceptional engine, and she produced a number of outputs of around 1,000 drawbar horsepower at 50mph. On this run engine No 913 averaged 51mph throughout the 28.4 miles of ascent from Holywood to Milepost 60, and during this period the *average* drawbar horsepower was 950, with a maximum of 1,109 when the engine was sustaining, absolutely, a minimum speed of 43¼mph on the 1 in 150 gradient leading into Drumlanrig tunnel. And this tremendous effort on the part of engine No 913 and her crew was sustained for 33 minutes on end. Thus the hard sectional time of 45 minutes to New Cumnock was practically kept.

The downhill section to Kilmarnock was then subject to several slight restrictions for engineering work, and there was a signal check approaching Hurlford; but the net time for the 58 miles from Dumfries was certainly no more than 67½ minutes. Having come to Kilmarnock I still expected that assistance might be provided over the very severe concluding gradients of the Barrhead Joint Line. Earlier that same year I had travelled on the 12 noon express from Glasgow St Enoch to Carlisle, with a load of 277 tons tare, and our compound was duly piloted between St Enoch and Kilmarnock. I must admit that despite all driver Paterson had got out of No 913 on the run from Carlisle, the prospect of Stewarton bank was rather daunting, with nearly 2 miles of 1 in 87 from Kilmaurs and a final 2 miles at 1 in 75 up to the summit at Milepost 17. I need have had no doubts! Still unpiloted we thundered out of Kilmarnock to reach 36½mph up the initial 1 in 180; the 1 in 87 stretch lowered the speed to only 31mph, and the mile of slightly easier gradient before Stewarton saw an acceleration to 37½mph. Up the final 1 in 75, with an exhaust like gunfire we fell gradually to 26mph —a magnificent climb. After this effort the engine was eased considerably over the tableland to Lugton, and no fast running was attempted down the Barrhead bank. Without the final checks I think we could just have kept the 35-minute timing from Kilmarnock; but even if we had dropped a single minute it would have done nothing to dim the lustre of an outstanding performance.

Almost at the end of the period under review I had yet another remarkable run with a Royal Scot, a class then at the very top of its form, with all the Stanier refinements of design fully consolidated. I was travelling from Oban, and joined the Aberdeen portion of the Royal Scot express at Stirling. In 1939 the train ran in two sections throughout from Symington, with both portions making a 60mph non-stop run from Carlisle to Euston. From Stirling No 6102 *Black Watch* had no difficulty with a five-coach train of 165 tons. We made the regulation stops at Larbert and Coatbridge, and then at Symington attached the six-coach Edinburgh portion, bringing our load up to 339 tons tare, 355 tons full. We made a fast though easily accomplished run down to Carlisle, covering the 66.9 miles in 66min 43sec start to stop. Here we changed engines and found No 6132 *The Kings Regiment (Liverpool)* waiting to back on. I was interested also to recognise driver Brooker of Camden shed, in the cab. I should add however, in view of what transpired, that I had no conversation with him before the start. I will only add that the day was calm and fine, and that the engine itself, polished and gleaming, was certainly turned out in a condition appropriate to the haulage of so celebrated a train (Table 38).

TABLE 38

CARLISLE—EUSTON

The Royal Scot: Edinburgh portion

Load: 339 tons tare, 355 tons full
Engine: 4-6-0 No 6132 *The King's Regiment (Liverpool)*

Distance Miles		Sch min	Actual min sec	Speeds mph
0.0	CARLISLE	0	0 00	–
4.9	Wreay		9 47	40
13.1	Plumpton	19	19 52	–
17.9	PENRITH	24	24 48	62½
26.1	*Milepost 43*		34 45	37
31.4	*Shap Summit*	41	42 32	47/44½
36.9	Tebay	46	47 07	82
50.0	OXENHOLME	58	58 12	77
55.5	Milnthorpe		62 11	86½

Running—Pre-Stanier Classes

Distance Miles		Sch min	Actual min sec	Speeds mph
62.8	CARNFORTH	69	67 39	–
69.1	LANCASTER	74	73 35	–
80.6	Garstang	85	84 45	72½
90.1	PRESTON	95	94 50	15*
–		–	pws	
105.3	WIGAN	113	113 42	
–			prolonged checks	
141.1	CREWE	148	158 32	
148.9	Betley Road		164 51	54
151.6	Whitmore	161	171 06	64/79
–			sigs	50
165.6	STAFFORD	174	183 27	75/45*
175.0	Rugeley	183	192 30	80½
182.9	Lichfield	190	198 30	77
189.2	TAMWORTH	195	203 07	86½
196.8	Atherstone		209 05	73
202.1	NUNEATON	207	213 07	81
205.7	Bulkington		216 09	70½
211.5	Brinklow		220 28	81
216.6	RUGBY	222	225 18	38*
223.9	Welton		233 26	68
229.5	Weedon		237 46	83½
239.3	Roade	243	245 16	72½
244.4	Castlethorpe		248 58	88
252.5	BLETCHLEY	254	255 02	76/79
259.0	Leighton Buzzard		260 12	74
263.1	Cheddington		263 39	69
267.5	Tring	268	267 36	64
274.7	Boxmoor		273 31	82
281.7	WATFORD JUNCTION	280	278 50	77½
287.8	Harrow		284 42	56
293.8	WILLESDEN JUNCTION	291	290 27	69
299.2	EUSTON	299	298 33	

* speed restriction

On so beautiful a summer day the running conditions over Shap were as different as could be imagined from those prevailing on the run with *Royal Scots Fusilier* detailed earlier in this chapter, and we sailed up in the most carefree style, dropping a little on the sectional time to Shap Summit, but easily regaining it by some free running downhill. Below Oxenholme indeed we had an exhilarating spell at 86½mph. The driver was obviously working the engine under relatively easy steam wherever he could, and having passed Carnforth slightly ahead of time he ran easily onwards to Preston keeping the sectional allowances fairly closely. At Wigan, despite the severe pitfall slack between Standish and Boars Head, the train was less than a minute late, but then we found ourselves on the tail of a train that was obviously making very slow progress, and in the relatively short distance between Wigan and Winsford Junction, 26.9 miles, we lost 10 minutes in running. While one could deprecate this as a piece of poor operating, to allow of such hindrance to a 'star' train, it is nevertheless easy to criticise without knowing all the circumstances. In this particular instance it was a blessing in disguise to me at any rate, for it inspired one of the most brilliant pieces of Royal Scot locomotive running I have ever logged. Even so the sequence of delays must not be minimised; with a different engine crew, or a locomotive in less excellent condition, the late passage of the train through Crewe could have led to cumulative delays with widespread reaction later.

I have not shown the run in any great detail north of Crewe, for the reasons already discussed, and even after Winsford Junction we were not entirely free of checks. Although there had been some most vigorous work intermediately we were still running nearly 10 minutes late after the final signal check at Badnall Wharf, just before Norton Bridge. After Stafford however a most resolute and sustained effort to wipe out the arrears began and the lateness was successively reduced to 9½ minutes at Rugeley, 8 minutes at Tamworth, 6 minutes at Nuneaton, 2¼ minutes at Roade, and Tring summit was passed half a minute early. Intermediately there was some magnificently sustained fast running, with such averages as 77mph over the 39 miles from Colwich to Brinklow, and 78mph over the 39.2 miles from Welton to Cheddington. Maximum speeds of over 80mph followed in rapid succession, including 80½mph at the Trent bridge near Armitage, 86½ at Hademore troughs, 81 before Nuneaton, 81 near Brinklow, 83½ at Weedon, and 88mph at Castlethorpe troughs. Once having regained his correct path however driver Brooker did not continue to force the pace; with Watford Junction passed 1¼ minutes early he eased right down, and with a beautifully judged and quite unchecked final approach we stopped in Euston just 27 seconds inside schedule. The outstanding part of the run was of course that between Rugeley and Watford Junction, where the 106.7 miles were covered in 86min 20sec instead of the 97min booked, and practically all the lost time was regained. This involved an average speed, over this stretch of 74.4mph. Other notable timings to which attention may be drawn are the 140min 1sec from Crewe to Euston, 67.7mph; and 73¼min from Rugby to Euston, also 67.7mph—though this latter includes the easy running from Watford Junction inwards. Although the load was below the maximum tonnage conveyed by the Royal Scot locomotives on other duties, the total of 355 tons was nevertheless well above that of other 'high-speed' trains, and the standard of running was generally above that required by the Coronation Scot streamliner which had been introduced some two years earlier. With one exception it was the last main line run I had on the West Coast main line before the outbreak of war, and as such it was for me a finale to be remembered. As it happened, the very last was made under the shadow of war conditions, on the Irish Mail, in mid-August, when precautions against terrorist activities rendered travelling almost as jumpy as that of wartime, and everyone embarking or disembarking at Holyhead was a suspect!

CHAPTER II

The Pacific Saga

THE performance of the two original Pacific engines Nos 6200 and 6201, in the years 1933-4 made it clear to the locomotive department, without any doubt, that they would not do the job for which they had been designed. They rode like limousines; the cylinder performance was excellent, but they could not be relied upon to steam consistently over the 400-mile workings between Euston and Glasgow, particularly on the southbound run. The job was tackled in no half-hearted style. Stanier had the boiler proportions examined from first principles and, quite apart from their Great Western parentage, it soon became apparent that the free gas area through the superheater was inadequate. The original proportions were derived from those of the Kings, and many years later Stanier told me how he had written to Collett and given him the result of his findings. I remember asking Sir William what the reaction was from Swindon. He chuckled and then said: 'Oh, he never replied!' But the work of the LMS was not lost upon Hawksworth, and it is well known that immediately after succeeding Collett he began work towards the use of higher degrees of superheating on Great Western locomotives, culminating in the 4-row superheater on engine No 6022 *King Edward III*.

On the LMS an entirely new boiler was designed and fitted to engine No 6200 *The Princess Royal*. The changes in dimensions were highly significant as will be appreciated from the accompanying table. Not only was the superheater enlarged from 16 to 32 elements, but the distance between the tube plates was reduced and the diameter of the small tubes increased. The firebox heating surface was increased by the provision of a combustion chamber. All these features combined to produce a boiler that steamed freely over the widest possible range of running conditions, and provided what was so urgently needed on the heaviest Anglo-Scottish duties, a handsome margin in reserve. The success of the modified 6200 was amply displayed by what was then regarded as an almost sensational run on the Liverpool Flyer, when with a load of 453 tons tare, 475 tons full, the 152.7 miles from Crewe to Willesden were covered in 129min 33sec start to stop.

TABLE 39

PACIFIC BOILERS

	Original	1935 modification
Tubes, small		
number	170	123
outside diam	2¼in	2⅜in
Superheater flues		
number	16	32
outside diam	5⅛in	5⅛in
Length between tube plates	20ft 9in	19ft 3in
Heating surfaces	sq ft	sq ft
small tubes	2078	1272
superheater flues	445	825
firebox	190	217
superheater elements	390	653
Total	3083	2967

Some further remarkable results were obtained on a dynamometer car trial from Crewe to Glasgow and back, and it was evident that the modified engine was comfortably master of all duties likely to be placed upon the class in the foreseeable future. During the summer and early autumn of 1935 ten more Pacifics having the improved boiler were completed at Crewe, and numbered 6203 to 6212. By the time the winter service came into operation enough Pacifics were available to work the principal Anglo-Scottish expresses throughout between London and Glasgow, and have Pacifics available for the two heaviest turns on the Euston—Liverpool service. On the Scottish trains the first trials of some very ambitious cyclic diagrams were made, aimed at securing maximum utilisation. One such involved taking the down Night Scot from Euston arriving in Glasgow at

9.30am, and then returning with the up Midday Scot at 1.30pm.

By their working on such duties as these, the Princess Royal class, the 'Lizzies' as they affectionately became known, were established as thoroughly reliable engines. What was even more important was that their performance showed little sign of deterioration as mileage after general overhaul increased. This was following the former Midland precepts that any engine in traffic should be capable of performing any duty specified for the class. A remarkable example of this requirement being fulfilled is shown by the results of a dynamometer car trial conducted with engine No 6210 *Lady Patricia* on the down Royal Scot, when that engine had run 98,977 miles since last general overhaul (Table 40).

TABLE 40

Mileage on test	402
Load, tons tare	522
Average speed mph	52.0
Coal consumption:	
lb per train mile	45.0
lb per ton mile (including engine)	0.068
lb per dhp hour	2.98
Water consumption:	
Gallons per mile	37.2
lb per dhp hour	24.7
Evaporation:	
lb of water per lb of coal	8.30
lb per hour (average)	19,400

My own early experiences of the modified Pacifics were on the Liverpool trains. From the details of performance given in Chapter 10 it will be appreciated that the Royal Scots had to be worked hard to keep time with the down Merseyside Express, quite apart from the intricacies of operating when that train, or the preceding one was run in duplicate. But once the Pacifics were on the job the haulage of 500-ton trains was made to look easy, and the load-limit of 380 tons for the Liverpool Flyer, which had entailed regular double-heading from Crewe to Euston on Friday nights, vanished like a dream. The Pacifics took loads of 500 tons on that very fast train without any difficulty.

The late spring of 1936 saw a remarkable acceleration of the down Midday Scot. Up till then the train had been operated in much the same style as the time-honoured West Coast Corridor, calling at Rugby and Crewe and making a stop at Lancaster, instead of the pre-war stop at Preston. Its load north of Crewe was lessened by the detaching of the Aberdeen, Windermere and Whitehaven portions at Crewe, instead of as previously at Preston; but instead the through carriages from Plymouth to Glasgow were attached at Crewe. In May 1936 however the Rugby stop was omitted but an additional one was put in at Penrith. This was something quite new on the midday service from Euston. Previously, passengers for Keswick and the northern resorts in the Lake District had to travel in the Aberdeen portion, which was transferred to the following Liverpool and Manchester Scottish express at Preston. Whatever commercial reasons may have prompted this development it introduced one of the toughest pieces of scheduling that ever regularly featured in LMS timetables. The overall timing of the Midday Scot, as from 4 May 1936, was 7½ hours; this involved a non-stop run from Euston to Crewe in 163min; a run of 79min over the ensuing 72 miles to Lancaster, and then no more than 59min for the 51.2 miles over Shap, from Lancaster to Penrith. Lastly, the 17.9 miles down into Carlisle were allowed no more than 19min. North of Carlisle the load was much reduced, but even so, with the one engine working through from Euston it was no light task in those days to cover the last 102¼ miles non-stop to Glasgow in 116min.

It was, of course, the run of 59min from Lancaster to Penrith that set such a task to engines and their crews, particularly as the load of the train was at its maximum over this section. The minimum load was one of fourteen coaches, weighing about 475 tons gross behind the tender, and the booked allowance was one of 37min pass-to-pass, for the 31.4 miles from Carnforth to Shap Summit. This required an average speed of 51mph over a section where the vertical rise is one of 885ft, or an average gradient of 1 in 187. Although this analysis indicates, in itself, a fairly severe proposition, and requires an average output for 37min of 1,500 equivalent drawbar horsepower, the passage of the line through the wild fell country north of Oxenholme frequently involved the weathering of severe climatic conditions, and made the working of the train much more than a straightforward 'slog'. Furthermore, fourteen coaches did not represent, by any means, the maximum the 'Lizzies' were expected to tackle without assistance on this train, and records are available of magnificent timekeeping performances with sixteen coach trains. In these conditions the minimum power requirement for bare timekeeping was a continuous average output of about 1,650edhp. As customary with the Midday Scot the train was worked by Crewe North and Polmadie men on alternate days, with different Crewe men making the non-stop run down from Euston. This extremely hard booking over Shap inspired drivers to some truly magnificent feats of performance, and the record, so far as I am aware, stands to engine No 6208 *Princess Helena Victoria,* which took a 16-coach train of 515 tons gross from Lancaster to Penrith in 56min 10sec, nearly 3min inside the schedule. The minimum speed on the Grayrigg bank was 42½mph, and at Shap Summit the speed was 28½mph. The time over the 31.4 miles up from Carnforth was 35min 38sec, an average throughout the ascent of 53mph.

I did not manage to contrive a run on this train myself, but I logged an outstanding performance on the corresponding southbound train (Table 41). In the ordinary way this was not such a severe task, as the 69.1 miles from Carlisle to Lancaster were run non-stop in 81min; but on the occasion of this particular journey the addition of the Stranraer portion at Carlisle brought our load up to no less than seventeen coaches, 532 tons. Coming just after a Bank Holiday, with the train crowded from end to end, the gross load was certainly not less than 570 tons. The train was worked through from Glasgow to Euston by engine No 6206 *Princess Marie Louise*, which had come north from Euston on the Night Scot and had a turn round time of less than four hours in Glasgow. We made light work of the Scottish part of the journey, with 330 tons as far as Symington, and fifteen coaches, 515 tons, down to Carlisle. The latter section of 66.9 miles was covered in 71min 41sec, instead of the 73min booked, despite two checks. Then came the magnificent piece of running tabulated herewith. It will be seen that from Penrith we were steadily gaining on booked time, and the absolutely sustained 41mph on the long 1 in 125 gradient south of Clifton involved an output of approximately 1,800edhp. The continua-

TABLE 41

LMS CARLISLE—LANCASTER

'The Mid-day Scot'

Load: 17 coaches, 532 tons tare, 570 tons full

Engine: 6206 *Princess Marie Louise*

Distance Miles		Sch min	Actual min sec		Speeds mph
0.0	CARLISLE	0	0	00	–
4.9	Wreay		9	48	39
7.4	Southwaite		13	14	50
10.8	Calthwaite		17	23	48
13.1	Plumpton	20	20	11	57½/52
17.9	PENRITH	25	25	15	62½
22.1	Clifton		29	37	52
26.1	*Milepost 43*		35	00	41
28.1	,, *41*		37	56	42
29.4	Shap		39	43	48½
31.4	*Shap Summit*	44	42	29	42½
36.9	TEBAY	50	47	20	82
41.2	Low Gill		50	59	67
43.0	Grayrigg		52	37	64
50.0	OXENHOLME	62	58	50	75
			pws		40
53.6	*Hincaster Junction*		63	12	63½
55.5	Milnthorpe		64	54	77
58.3	Burton		67	08	65
62.8	CARNFORTH	74	71	00	76½
67.2	*Morecambe South Junction*		74	48	–
69.1	LANCASTER	81	77	34	

tion from Lancaster to Crewe presented no difficulties, and then, with a fresh driver and fireman there came the final non-stop run from Crewe to Euston, booked in 164min. There were signs, at one or two points, that there might be some shortage of steam, through easings where one would normally have expected acceleration. Even if there had been some falling off one could hardly criticise after so strenuous a round trip as this engine had worked. The most marked easing was between Rugby and Bletchley, where nearly 3min were dropped on the sharp allowance of 34min for this 35.9 miles. Whatever may have been amiss—if indeed anything was—the crew pulled things round splendidly in the end, and we passed Willesden on time, and clocked into Euston just 40sec to the good. On the final stage of the ascent to Tring we were steadily maintaining 60mph on the 1 in 335 gradients, an output of 1,520edhp.

In the course of travelling on the line in the years 1935-7 my records of performance were notably consistent. I travelled at times behind every one of the new engines except No 6203, and on hard schedules did not note a single instance of loss of time. The two original engines, 6200 and 6201 escaped me; but I have written enough of the transformation of the former for it to be appreciated that it was this change that paved the way for the great success of the new engines 6203-6212. Engine No 6201 *Princess Elizabeth* was also modified, but in a different way from No 6200. By the year 1935 Stanier was gradually moving away from the Great Western tradition of the domeless boiler and regulator in the smokebox, and as will be described in detail in a later chapter of this book, new 4–6–0s of both the 5X and 5 classes were being turned out with domed boilers. It was no more than natural that a domed boiler should be tried on a Pacific and the fact that No 6201 needed modification made her an ideal 'guinea-pig'. While of the two original engines No 6200 had an entirely new boiler, that of No 6201 was re-tubed, and fitted with a 32-element superheater. The original distance between the tube plates, 20ft 9in, remained the same. As compared with the modified 6200 and the new engines 6203-6212, the modified 6201 had 119 small tubes, against 123, and the heating surfaces became: tubes 2429sq ft; firebox 190sq ft and superheater elements 594sq ft. As modified, and with the addition of a dome, No 6201 became a thoroughly reliable engine, and took her place in the regular link working of the class. I must confess that I do not think her appearance was improved with the separate top feed mounted on top of the boiler ahead of the dome; but 'handsome is as handsome does', and Stanier and his men had no cause to be dissatisfied with the modified 6201.

How her performance came to compare in the long run with that of the domeless-boilered engines I cannot say, and it may or may not be significant that she was chosen for a very special duty in November 1936. The origin of the celebrated non-stop trial between London and Glasgow in that month can be traced to the age-old rivalry between East Coast and West Coast routes to Scotland. In 1935 the LNER had drawn upon itself a great amount of publicity through the running of the streamlined Silver Jubilee express, and the splendid speed records that were created. The LMS authorities were anxious that it should be known that they were not entering into any speed competitions, and the timetable developments of 1936, including the strenuous work involved with the down Midday Scot, certainly gave every impression that their policy was to continue the improvement of service with their traditionally heavy trains rather than to introduce light-weight trains on which much higher average speeds might be maintained. But by the autumn of 1936 it had become an open secret that the LNER were planning to introduce a second streamlined 'flyer' to provide a six-hour service between London and Edinburgh. While the high-speed activities had been confined, as with Darlington and Newcastle, in territories outside those of the LMS interests, the 'powers that be' at Euston could afford to stand aside; but when it came to Edinburgh it was another matter. The Scottish capital then had equal treatment with Glasgow on the principal day expresses from Euston, and the Edinburgh portions of both Royal and Midday Scots each had their own dining car. The projected introduction of six-hour streamliners from Kings Cross to Edinburgh was a threat against which the LMS could no longer stand aside. The natural reply would be a six-hour service from Euston to Glasgow, which would more than uphold LMS prestige on the Anglo-Scottish service without entering into open competition by involving the Edinburgh service. Stanier was in India at the time as a member of Sir Ralph Wedgwood's committee of enquiry into the working of the Indian railways, and although Symes was acting as chief mechanical engineer in his absence, the responsibility for locomotive matters fell largely upon Riddles. He was confident that with some suitable limitation of the load, the 'Lizzies' could do the job, and a remarkable demonstration of their ability was duly planned.

With a load roughly equal to that of the LNER Silver Jubilee, a round trip from Euston to Glasgow and back was planned, in an overall time of six hours in each direction, but also to be made non-stop. This of course was an added test of locomotive

On The 'Settle And Carlisle'

(above) *Edinburgh—St Pancras express approaching Aisgill summit, hauled by 4–6–0 No 45573* Newfoundland; (below) *the down Thames—Clyde express near Ribblehead, with converted Scot No 46112* Sherwood Forester

Royal Scot Developments

(above) *the first taper-boilered Scot No 6170* British Legion; (centre) *engine No 6133* The Green Howards *(converted) in the final* LMS *livery;* (below) *an original Scot, No 6134* The Cheshire Regiment *in the final* LMS *livery*

capacity, and a test of enginemanship as well. It was, in all probability, contrived in a spirit of 'one-upmanship' over the LNER because a couple of successful runs would provide a high average speed over a greater distance than anything the LNER had been able to do up to then, or indeed was likely to do in the near future. The engine selected for the job was No 6201, and two most brilliant performances were put up. I have told elsewhere how minor defects that developed on the locomotive could have led to the postponement of the trials; but when men of such enthusiasm and determination as Riddles are set upon a project there is practically no difficulty that cannot be overcome, and so it was in the early preparations at Willesden on Sunday evening, 15 November 1936, and at St Rollox on the following night when a minor defect was discovered on arrival in Glasgow. Either could have caused postponement, but instead Riddles ran the 401.4 miles from Euston to Glasgow Central in 353¾min with a load of 225 tons, and returned the next day, with an additional coach on the train in the truly magnificent time of 344¼min. Much comment was made at the time that it did not need a fancy streamlined casing to enable a modern well-designed locomotive to make very fast time with a relatively light train. The engine behaved in exemplary fashion throughout, with perfect steaming despite the severe demands made for such long periods on end. Furthermore it was clear that the modification to the original boiler was as great a success as the new boiler fitted to No 6200.

When the decision of the high management to go ahead with a high speed service from London to Glasgow for the summer of 1937 was made, Stanier was still away and the responsibility for subsequent work on the project fell primarily upon three men. As chief locomotive draughtsman at Derby, Herbert Chambers had been succeeded by T. F. Coleman; at Crewe, R. C. Bond was assistant locomotive manager and very much the 'coming man', and these two, with Riddles, had to consider the provision of engine power for the new service. In view of the splendid results obtained with the trials of engine No 6201 it was confidently expected that a six-hour run from Euston to Glasgow would be stipulated, with one stop. The high speed running of No 6201 as examined from the dynamometer car records, and Riddles' invaluable experience on the footplate during both trials, showed the desirability of making a number of modifications for any special high speed service. The commercial people then decided that the high-speed train should take the place of the Midday Scot, rather than provide an additional service for which the clientele might be doubtful, and the new train would cater for the full regular business of the Glasgow section. This meant a load of around 300 tons, leaving the Edinburgh and Aberdeen sections to form a train of their own, and also to be run to an accelerated timing. While the Princess Royal class engines were considered capable of running the new service with loads of 225 to 250 tons, it would be another matter with 300 tons or more, so a major feature of the new locomotives was a considerably larger boiler. The Princess Royal class was nevertheless practically at the limit of weight that the civil engineer could accept. Greater steaming capacity had hitherto almost invariably involved an increase in weight roughly in proportion to the increased heating surface provided; but by use of modern materials and improved manufacturing methods the total heating surface of the new engines was increased from the 2,967sq ft of the Princess Royals to 3,637sq ft, at the same time increasing the grate area from 45 to 50sq ft. The total weight of the non-streamlined version of the new engines was 105¼ tons, against 104½ tons in the Princess Royal.

In referring to the non-streamlined variety I am however anticipating the story by more than a year. In the fashion of the day it was essential that the engines for the new Glasgow 'flyer' should be streamlined, though of course to see the strict comparative effect of the larger boiler one has to compare like for like, and in this the non-streamlined version has to be used. The form of the streamlining for the new engines of 1937 was of the utmost importance, publicity-wise, for it was by the 'look' of the engine that prestige of the LMS would be judged in this new and exciting 'race to the north'. Obviously it had to be something quite different from the Gresley streamliners of the LNER, and technically that was quite easy to achieve. The latter engines were not truly streamlined at all. They had a form of aerodynamic screening that was extremely effective as a smoke deflector, and it undoubtedly did something to reduce the air resistance of the locomotive at speed; but the Princess-Coronation class, as the new LMS Pacifics were at first known, had a truly streamlined outer casing, fashioned so as to provide the least possible resistance to motion through the air. It gave the new engines a very striking external appearance, but did little in the way of smoke deflection. In conditions of light steaming the exhaust tended to cling to the boiler, and beat down into the driver's view. The finish, in the Prussian blue of the Caledonian in the days of the first Dunalastairs, was highly distinctive.

With locomotives designed so expressly for show purposes one does tend to concentrate on the superficial rather than the technical aspects, and I must now refer to the features, unseen by the outside observer, that have made these engines the great success they were. The internal streamlining was very thoroughly done, through cylinders, admission and exhaust ports, the regulator, steam pipes, superheater header, and, of course, the blast pipe. Although the new engines had a nominal tractive effort roughly the same as that of the Princess Royals the performance was vastly better, even beyond the splendid standards set up by the latter engines in the years 1935-7. There was a slight enlargement of the cylinders to compensate for the larger diameter of coupled wheel considered to be necessary for a high-speed locomotive, but the most important difference at the front end was the increase in piston valve diameter from the 8in of the Princess Royals to 9in. All in all, the LMS had produced a very speedy and powerful locomotive.

Then, to the disappointment of everyone concerned on the LMS, and of all their most ardent supporters the management announced that the overall time between Euston and Glasgow by the new service would not be the expected six hours, but six and a half. It reduced what would have been a real challenge to a mere 'boy's job', as it was once put to me. One can appreciate that the operating department wished to work up to their higher speeds gradually, and that in comparison with the projected new LNER service to Edinburgh, the LMS had 9 miles further to go and a harder road to traverse; but why then, as a dejected partisan put it, could they not have gone to 6¼ hours for a start! Why go to all the advance publicity build-up, and then produce a pedestrian job after all. With a 300-ton train the new schedule between Euston and Carlisle could almost have been achieved with Royal Scots let alone Pacifics. It could well have been asked, why should an operating department that had been positively venturesome in such schedules as the Liverpool Flyer and Birmingham expresses with two intermediate stops within the two-hour schedule, suddenly have developed an attack of 'cold feet'. Nevertheless the approaching inauguration of the Coronation Scot service was a time of much advance publicity, with the completion of the first of the new engines at Crewe, and the inevitable comparison of the external design with that of the Gresley A4 Pacifics of the LNER.

Looking back to those exciting days of June 1937 and the part I was able to play, albeit as no more than a recorder, I can recall vividly the mounting public partisanship either for the LMS or the LNER. Young men engaged in heated argument over the merits of the rival forms of streamlining; older men shook their heads sadly at the publicity that was developing, and one went so far as to say: 'I wonder what old Webb would have thought of all this'. When it became known that both companies were going to stage demonstration runs with the new trains, the Coronation Scot from Euston to Crewe and back on June 29, and the Coronation from Kings Cross to the Barkston triangle on the following day, partisanship rose to immense heights of exciting anticipation. The LNER then held the British speed record with a maximum of 113mph, and while the moderate schedule of the Coronation Scot did not give any prospects of 100mph running in regular service, this invitation run on 9 June 1937 was another matter. My own expectations of something unusual were heightened when I learned that no fewer than four expert 'stop-watchers' would be travelling on the train. We certainly did get something unusual, so unusual that I still wonder by what small margin we were lucky enough to survive to tell the tale!

The bare details of that precipitous entry into Crewe station, wherein the last 10½ miles from Whitmore occupied no more than 7min 6sec to the dead stop, and the maximum speed occurred only 2 miles from the station, have many times been related. Those on the footplate of engine No 6220 *Coronation* had been given definite instructions to beat the LNER record. A moderate speed restriction was in force on the rising gradient from Stafford to Whitmore, but down Madeley bank the sky was the limit. I think that an error of judgement was made in not pressing the engine harder after observing the 60mph restriction through Norton Bridge. If Whitmore summit had been topped at 95mph instead of the 85 actually run it would have made a world of difference. As it was, the speed had mounted to no more than 106mph by the time we passed Betley Road, and although then getting perilously near to Crewe, the engine was still pressed hard. Actually the finish would not have been so hectic had we not been routed into No 3 platform, involving the negotiation of three crossover roads in succession! But we made a perfect stop in the platform; there was no question of an over-run. The maximum speed attained will always be a matter of debate among those of us who were there. Those four stop-watchers all agreed, without the slightest divergency, that the maximum speed clocked was 112½mph; but we were equally unanimous that between the various milepost readings there could have been a peak of 113mph, and when the four of us sat down together at the invitation lunch at the Crewe Arms Hotel we all agreed that by our own measurements the LNER record of 113mph could have been equalled, but not surpassed. The locomotive was however fitted with a recording speedometer, and during the lunch a note was handed to E. J. H. Lemon giving the result of examining the chart on the engine. He broke into the proceedings to announce that the official maximum speed was 114mph. This of course could not be gainsaid, but among the four of us there was always an element of surprise that not one of us actually clocked more than 112½mph.

We came back from Crewe that afternoon in the style of the modern electrics, covering the 158.1 miles in 118min 57sec at an average speed of almost 80mph from start to stop. The load of that special train was one of eight coaches, 263 tons tare, and about 280 tons gross. The finest sustained running was between Welton and Willesden Junction where the 69.9 miles were covered at an average speed of 87.4mph with maximum speeds of 100mph at Castlethorpe, 99 at Kings Langley and 96mph at Wembley. Such was the debut of the so-called Princess Coronation class 4–6–2. In later years, better known as the Duchesses and eventually divested of their streamlined casing, they created a long record of splendid work, which is discussed in Chapter 16.

CHAPTER 12

Experimental Locomotives

IT seems inevitable that an engineer with so scientific a turn of mind as Sir Henry Fowler would have given the most serious attention to improving the thermal efficiency of locomotives by the simple yet fundamental method of increasing the temperature range over which the steam was used. He had inherited the Deeley compounds on the Midland Railway, and when the time came for producing larger engines for general service on the LMS it was to the compound that he turned first. That much success had been achieved by the Royal Scots was an undoubted feather in the cap of his department; but the fitting of a Schmidt high pressure boiler, built by Henschels of Kassel, to an otherwise standard 4–6–0 in Germany, attracted considerable attention, not least from the very high steam pressure generated in one section of the boiler. The very use of such high pressure steam would have deterred the majority of steam locomotive engineers, but Sir Henry Fowler had always taken a great personal interest in the numerous metallurgical problems in boiler performance and maintenance. In recommending the construction of an experimental locomotive for the LMS using the Schmidt type of boiler, he probably looked forward with some relish to problems with the boiler from which the majority of his colleagues would have recoiled. There is a good story told of an eminent technical journalist of more than forty years ago who had an appointment to visit Sir Henry Fowler at Derby works. On arrival he was conducted not to the CME's office but to the boiler shop, and there the visitor was ushered through the fire-hole door into the firebox of a locomotive in which Sir Henry, clad in a boiler suit, was happily engaged in examining stays.

The experimental engine which was authorised in 1929 was

built on the Royal Scot chassis, and was intended eventually to work in the regular links with the standard engines of the class. Its nominal tractive effort was almost exactly the same. This most unusual locomotive required to be considered in two distinct aspects, the boiler—or system of boilers—and the three-cylinder compound engine and its machinery. The designed working pressures were 900psi in the single high-pressure cylinder having a diameter of 11½in and 250psi in the two low-pressure cylinders, which were of standard Royal Scot type, 18in diameter by 26in stroke. The steam at 900psi was generated in a totally enclosed high-pressure steam drum which was not in contact with the fire but which received its heat from a closed-circuit water-tube firebox in which steam was generated at 1,400 to 1,800psi. Heating coils from this system passed to the interior of the 900lb steam drum. At the same time the water-tube firebox system was connected to a large combustion chamber, the hot gases from which were used to raise and maintain steam in the 250lb section of the boiler. This was constructed on orthodox locomotive lines and provided steam for the low-pressure cylinders. It would not have been sufficient in itself to supply the needs of the two outside cylinders, being less than half the length of a standard Royal Scot boiler barrel; but the steam generated in it was intended to reinforce that exhausted from the high pressure cylinder in the ordinary way of compound locomotives.

The feature of this highly unorthodox and complicated system of steam raising that so appealed to Sir Henry Fowler was that the tubes that were in contact with the fire did not contain any of the ordinary feed water, with its inevitable impurities. The closed circuit system of the water tube firebox used only distilled water. In the standard locomotive firebox the feed water is in contact with the stays on the water side, and the impurities in varying degrees give rise to corrosion and consequent leakage. These troubles, and their partial mitigation by the use of water-softening plants, had always been a subject of great interest and concern to Sir Henry, as a metallurgist of high reputation, and he no doubt hoped that the very elaborate and expensive boiler would eventually pay off in reduced maintenance charges. The detailed design of the boiler was largely undertaken by the Superheater Company Ltd, who were British agents for the Schmidt company. They backed the project to the extent of providing the boiler free of charge to the LMS. As might be imagined, the construction of the boiler involved a number of manufacturing difficulties, but the high pressure steam drum which carried steam pressure of 900psi was built by John Brown & Co Ltd, in Sheffield. The experience of that firm in the manufacture of similar drums for marine boilers was invaluable, and rendered that part of the installation relatively free of trouble. It was remarkable that so complicated a steam-raising system could be designed and accommodated in the very neat exterior displayed by engine No 6399, and result in an overall weight so similar to that of the standard Royal Scots. The all-up weight of the engine was only 87.1 tons, with a maximum axle load of 21.1 tons. It carried the name *Fury*, which had previously been borne by a standard Royal Scot, No 6138.

That name, viewed in retrospect, seems to have been an unfortunate choice. The engine was built in Glasgow by the North British Locomotive Company, and after some early steaming trials in the works yard, and the overcoming of one or two rather alarming traits, she was taken for a trial run down the Caledonian main line to the south. In addition to the driver and fireman—a top link Polmadie crew—there was a representative of the chief mechanical engineer's department, and an engineer from the Superheater Company. The engine was run light, as in the normal way of 'first-out' trial trips. Then as they were running into Carstairs a hair-line crack in one of the water-tubes of the firebox caused the tube to burst. With steam at a pressure of at least 1,400psi the dire effects of such failure was that the steam was suddenly released, and shot through the fire-door bringing most of the fire with it. The fireman jumped and landed badly injured on the station platform; the driver and the CME's inspector being out of the direct line of blast escaped with no more than severe scalding of their legs, but it was the unfortunate representative of the Superheater Company who caught the full blast. He was literally buried under the avalanche of blazing coals blown out by the force of the escaping steam, and although he was extricated and rushed to Edinburgh Infirmary with the utmost promptitude he died soon afterwards. Occurring as it did actually in Carstairs station there could be no 'hushing up' of this disaster. The news of it, and its ghastly details, quickly spread from end to end of the line. *Fury* was taken back to Glasgow, and it is greatly to the credit of the Superheater Company that they persisted with the project, and rebuilt the boiler. The engine was subsequently hauled 'dead' to Derby, where it was intended that trials should continue. But by that time Sir Henry Fowler was in process of laying down his office, and becoming assistant to the vice-president for works. No one was very keen to continue the experiments with *Fury*; she was a troublesome engine to manage, even on special trial trips, and never went into revenue-earning service of any kind. Whether the tests would have been pursued with any vigour had Sir Henry Fowler continued as CME is a moot point. The accident at Carstairs was a profound shock and tended to cloud all subsequent proceedings. The frames were used for the first taper-boilered Royal Scot, No 6170 *British Legion*, in 1935, to which reference is made in Chapter 14.

The second experimental locomotive to be mentioned in detail had its origin in precisely the same way as *Fury*, namely an attempt to increase thermal efficiency by increasing the temperature range. The high efficiencies attained in marine propulsion had for many years drawn attention to the merits of turbine drive, but in all attempted applications of turbine drive to locomotives, the use of condensers and their attendant equipment introduced complications in maintenance that far outweighed the increased thermal efficiency in the actual motive power circuit of the steam. How Stanier became attracted to the trial of a non-condensing steam locomotive is an interesting story. Even before he left Swindon he was one of the most popular men in the mechanical engineering profession; a wise and friendly counsellor to young and old alike, with an immense capacity for making friends. As a member of council of the Institution of Mechanical Engineers he was not merely in touch, but through his personal friendships he was in on many of the major engineering problems. His great skill and immense experience in workshop matters made his advice sought in a diversity of problems, and once he had emerged from the monastic seclusion of Swindon so far as railway engineering matters were concerned, his interests broadened very rapidly. Dr H. L. Guy, then chief turbine engineer of the Metropolitan-Vickers Company and a fellow member of council of the Mechanicals', drew his attention to an interesting experimental locomotive put into service in 1932 on the Grangesberg—Oxelosund Railway in Sweden. This was a non-condensing turbine-driven 2–8–0 which was giving very favourable results in comparison with the ordinary reciprocating steam 2–8–0s in service on the same railway. Tests had indicated a saving of 7¼ per cent in coal consumption and 15 per cent in water; but what appealed to Stanier was the extreme simplicity of the machinery. Guy took him over to Sweden to see the engine at work, and his interest developed into keen enthusiasm.

It was not so much the direct saving in coal and water consumption that attracted Stanier towards turbine drive; it was the possibility of eliminating the traditional cylinders, pistons, valves and valve gear. Ever since the remarkable improvement in the performance of all the larger LMS locomotives had been effected by the change in design of piston valves from the previous Crewe and Derby standards to the use of a simple valve with six narrow rings, a very close watch had been kept upon performance, to check how this varied, and deteriorated as mileage increased from the last overhaul. With the Royal Scots the coal consumption increased by roughly 8 per cent after 27,000 to 29,000 miles, and in consequence it was made a matter of routine to call in engines of this class for piston and valve examination every six to eight months. This of course was a charge on maintenance and however expeditiously such examinations were carried out, they resulted in the locomotives being out of traffic in the meantime. With a turbine it was anticipated that this particular loss of availability of the locomotive would be avoided. Another feature that gave promise of a useful advantage in operation was the elimination of hammer-blow. As a consequence the civil engineer was prepared to accept an axle-load up to 24 tons on a turbine driven locomotive as compared with 22½ tons on the reciprocating Pacifics. As Pacifics are inherently more liable to slip than 4–6–0s, the additional adhesion was a worthwhile feature for working in bad weather on the severe inclines of the north country. So designs were schemed out for a non-condensing turbine locomotive of comparable tractive power to the Princess Royal class.

The collaboration of Metropolitan Vickers with Ljungstrom, the manufacturers of the Swedish turbine, was obtained and while the starting tractive effort was made the same as on the

Princess Royals, Dr Guy and his staff estimated that the turbine would show a considerably enhanced power output at higher speeds. The output at the rail forecast showed the interesting comparative horsepowers shown in Table 42.

TABLE 42

OUTPUT AT RAIL—HORSEPOWER

Speed mph	Princess Royal	Turbomotive
30	1,570	2,050
40	1,700	2,270
50	1,770	2,350
60	1,800	2,400
70	1,770	2,350

These figures were of course based on a continuous evaporation rate from the boiler at 30,000lb per hour, and did not take any account of the enhanced capacity possible when for short periods the boiler is mortgaged and steamed at a rate that a single fireman could not sustain for any length of time. The engine, given the running number 6202, was put into service in July 1935, and went into revenue-earning traffic almost at once. At first she was used principally between Euston and Liverpool, so that she was never far away from Crewe works for examination and attention when necessary. She was originally fitted with a boiler similar to that of the 6203-6212 series of Princess Royals, with the same superheater but a slightly reduced number of small tubes. The early results were highly gratifying, and the Turbomotive as she became generally known, could deal with any task allocated to the reciprocating Pacifics. Moreover she became really popular with the footplate crews. At all times she was under fairly close observation and as a result she was fitted with a modified boiler having a 40-element superheater. But although an isolated engine, and one receiving a good deal of individual attention, she established herself as a thoroughly sound traffic machine.

On one of my then periodic journeys to Liverpool by the Merseyside Express, I found No 6202 on the job on a miserable winter's night late in November 1936. We had the usual fifteen-coach train, weighing 480 tons tare, 515 tons gross, but the start was delayed by a relaying slack between Willesden Junction and Wembley. Because of this, Watford was passed nearly 2½min late. By that time we were doing 66mph, and after covering the next 14.2 miles up to Tring in 14min 36sec we had a spell of very fast running, covering the 47.1 miles from Tring to Kilsby Tunnel North Box in 40min 42sec—an average speed of 69.3mph with a maximum of 81mph. So, despite the initial check we passed Rugby in 83min 23sec. North of that junction we ran into a belt of fog and our driver ran very quietly for a time. Once past Tamworth however he began to pile it on again; Stafford was passed in 135½min and with a maximum of 82mph down Madeley bank we passed Basford Sand Sidings Box, 155.8 miles, in 157min 35sec. After that there commenced a very severe series of delays due to the widespread fog that prevailed over north-western England that night, and we were eventually 23min late reaching Mossley Hill. The net time to passing Crewe was only 159min, an excellent performance on such a night, with a 515-ton load.

At various times during the years 1936 and 1937 dynamometer car test runs were carried out with the Turbomotive, in comparison with standard engines of the Princess Royal class, in all cases working throughout over the 401.4 miles between London and Glasgow. In the course of her ordinary running the Turbomotive did not normally work on the Anglo-Scottish services, but in three distinct series of tests, in closely observed conditions the locomotive did some remarkably fine work. During this period three different boilers were carried. The first was the original with 32-element superheater, and generally conforming to the domeless type of the Princess Royal class; the second was a domed boiler, with a 40-element superheater, and the third a second variety of domed boiler, but in which the 40-element superheater had triple-flow elements providing no less than 852sq ft of heating surface. The ordinary Pacifics involved were No 6210 *Lady Patricia* and 6212 *Duchess of Kent*. The tests were conducted on both the Royal and Midday Scot expresses, and on two occasions when the tests were at their height both engines, 6202 and 6210, did the 401-mile run between London and Glasgow four times in three days—a remarkable example of locomotive utilisation. The trains concerned were:

1 10am Euston to Glasgow
2 10.45pm Glasgow to Euston
3 2pm Euston to Glasgow
4 10am Glasgow to Euston

In climbing the heavy banks north of Carnforth the Turbomotive generally performed faster work than the standard engines, and the basic coal consumption was slightly less. With the down Midday Scot the load was normally much reduced over the Scottish part of the journey, but for the purpose of the tests it was specially augmented north of Carlisle so as to provide a load of nearly 500 tons throughout. The overall results of one excellent run on this train with the Turbomotive, when fitted with the earlier of the domed boilers, are shown in the accompanying analysis. It will be seen that the overall coal consumption was the truly excellent figure of 2.78lb per dhp hour. On this run the 13.1 miles from Oxenholme to Tebay were covered in 14min 55sec, and then followed a truly record ascent of Shap—for a 486-ton tare load—of 7min 10sec for the 5.5 miles from Tebay up to Shap Summit. Later in this same run the 10 miles

TABLE 43

Dynamometer Car Test Run: 27 Oct 1936
2pm Euston to Glasgow: Engine No 6202

Load, tons tare	
Euston—Crewe	454
Crewe—Glasgow	486
Length of trip, miles	401.4
Time, actual running, min	454.9
Average speed, mph	53.2
Maximum speed, mph	85.0
Average drawbar horsepower	943.5
Coal consumptions	
per train mile, lb	49.6
per dhp hr lb	2.78
per sq ft of grate area per hr lb	58.5
Water	
gallons per mile	38.5
Evaporation:	
lb of water per lb of coal	7.71
lb per hour (running time)	20,280

from Beattock station up to the summit were climbed in 15¼min. It will be noted also from the tabulated results that the average drawbar horsepower throughout the 401-mile run was as high as 943.5. On five test runs with the Royal Scot the average drawbar horsepowers were 831, 787, 829, 851 and 858, and the corresponding coal consumptions in pounds per drawbar horsepower hour were 2.86, 3.14, 2.91, 2.81 and 2.74 respectively.

Such performances, coupled with the regular work of the locomotive on the Liverpool service, marked the Turbomotive as not only the most successful unorthodox unit that had ever run on British railways, but a locomotive the basic thermodynamic performance of which could be regarded, in 1936-7, as unquestionably second to none. Her working was a tremendous credit to Stanier, to Dr Guy and all the engineers who worked with them. Many of the top link Camden drivers of the day considered No 6202 without doubt the best engine on the line. It was, nevertheless, almost inevitable that there were troubles and, in view of the special nature of the machinery, some of these took a considerable time to rectify. This meant that the record of availability was not so good as that of the Princess Royal class. Even so, from the time of her construction up to the outbreak of war in September 1939, the Turbomotive had averaged 54,205 miles per annum. This would have been considered excellent in itself for many types of locomotive, but the Princess Royal class was setting up standards of its own in those years, and was averaging the remarkable aggregate of 80,000 miles, most of it in very heavy work on the Anglo-Scottish 401-mile through runs. For a time it seemed that the Turbomotive was going to run the 'Lizzies' very close, for in the year 1936 the extremely fine aggregate of 73,268 miles was run. In the pre-war period however such an achievement could not be sustained, though the record from 1935 to 1939 was in itself very notable with a type of propulsion new on the British railways.

While there had been, in this period, failures of parts of the equipment, and periods of inactivity due to changes in the boiler, the performance of No 6202 at its best was so good as to suggest that any amount of effort would be worth while to secure such standards of performance as a regular thing. Then unfortunately the onset of war conditions put an entirely different complexion on the working of the engine. At first, in view of the specialised attention needed by the locomotive, it was taken out of traffic altogether and stored at Crewe works. But when the war effort began to be stepped up to a pitch of intense activity every engine that could turn a wheel was needed, and No 6202 was put back into traffic. Without the special and expert attention devoted to it in pre-war years the engine succumbed to several serious failures, some of which kept her out of service for many months. Indeed, from the time she was taken out of store until the year 1946 the average annual mileage of the locomotive was only 28,500.

It is true that in war conditions the annual mileages of both classes of reciprocating steam Pacifics had dropped considerably below their pre-war standards, the 'Lizzies' to 53,000 and the Duchesses to 73,000; both however were vastly better than the record of No 6202. At the same time a straight comparison of annual mileages is not entirely fair to the Turbomotive. The ordinary running and maintenance staff were not expertly familiar with the engine, and with that innate caution inherent to all good railwaymen where risks may be involved, the engine was sometimes 'stopped' for defects that the more expert attention of pre-war years could have rectified in time for the engine to continue in her booked roster. When it came to requiring spare parts for some of the turbine machinery things were more difficult. It meant obtaining them from Metropolitan Vickers, and with that firm heavily engaged in war production the supplying spares for a locomotive which had in the first place been no more than a 'one-off' job, could not be accorded a very high priority. Consequently No 6202 lay out of traffic awaiting spares for long periods in the war years. The final misfortune was the breaking of the main turbine spindle while running at 60mph. This caused such damage to the machinery that the engine became virtually a permanent casualty, and she was laid up pending consideration of her eventual fate, when the end of the war and a return to normal conditions enabled the necessary consideration to be given.

The rebuilding of the main turbine would have been a very costly job, and the point at issue became whether a single, unorthodox, though basically vastly successful locomotive was worth perpetuating. The economic climate in 1946-7 was very different from that in which the engine had first been built.

Standardisation and extreme simplicity were the watchwords, and with the quality of fuel available for railway purposes, the ability of a locomotive to steam reliably was more important than the prospect of marginal improvements in coal consumption. It was however not until after the LMS had ceased to exist that the decision was taken to scrap the turbine drive and rebuild the engine as a reciprocating unit. All in all the Turbomotive must go down in history as a great and successful experiment. The circumstances that brought the days of great promise to an end and prevented the consolidation of the notable position obtained were, to quote the old wartime cliché 'beyond the control' of Stanier and his successors.

(above) *a Duchess in the form immediately after removal of the streamlining, No 46240* City of Coventry, *on the 8.40am Perth to Euston near Lancaster;* (below) *engine No 46227* Duchess of Devonshire *arriving at Law Junction with the Glasgow portion of the up West Coast Postal Special*

(above) *a Black Five No 44994 on Glasgow—Inverness express near Bridge of Allan;*
(below) *a down fast freight topping Grayrigg summit, hauled by Black Five No 45329*

CHAPTER 13

Scrap and Build

By the year 1935 the policy of rationalising the locomotive stock of the LMS was getting rapidly under way. Troubles with the earliest examples of the new Stanier classes had been overcome, and all was ready for the replacement of pre-grouping and other non-standard classes by new engines, the quality of which was already being warmly appreciated. Apart from the Pacifics, there were only five new classes involved, namely:

1. Jubilee 3-cylinder 4–6–0 express passenger
2. The Black Five 4–6–0 mixed traffic
3. 2–8–0 standard goods Class 8F
4. 2–6–4 suburban passenger tank
5. 2–6–2 small passenger tank

The early difficulties with the Jubilee class 4–6–0s were corrected by an adjustment to the draughting, though the later examples of both this class and of the Black Five 4–6–0s with 24-element, instead of the original 14-element superheaters, were considerably better in all-round performance, with the sluggishness in starting completely eradicated. Difficulties or not however, 113 new engines of the Jubilee class were ordered straight off the drawing boards as follows:

Nos 5552–5556	Crewe Works
Nos 5557–5606	North British Locomotive Company
Nos 5607–5654	Crewe Works
Nos 5655–5664	Derby Works

In the case of the Black Fives the first order, completed in 1934, was for seventy locomotives as follows:

Nos 5000–5019	Crewe Works
Nos 5020–5069	Vulcan Foundy

Further large orders for both 5X and 5 classes were placed in 1935, and in these later batches the domeless boiler and small superheater was discarded for ever on the LMS. The 5X engines put into service in 1935-6 were numbered 5665 to 5742, while so far as the Black Fives were concerned, following a pilot batch of five engines with domed boilers and 24-element superheaters built at Crewe, orders for no fewer than 377 further engines of the class were placed with contractors and put into traffic in 1935-7. These later engines were built as follows:

Nos 5075–5124 by the Vulcan Foundry
Nos 5125–5451 by Armstrong Whitworth & Co

Thus by the end of 1937 the LMS had 191 new three-cylinder 4–6–0 express passenger locomotives and a fleet of no less than 452 mixed traffic 4–6–0s. To these could be added the 52 three-cylinder 5X 4–6–0s of the 'Baby Scot' class, and the 40 Stanier 2–6–0s of 1933 having tapered domeless boilers. Thus, since the beginning of 1933 a total of 733 new locomotives having a capacity of Class 5 and upwards had been added to the stock. Before referring to the technical features of the two more important classes, the other side of the modernisation programme must be described.

With these new locomotives available it was intended to dispense completely with a large number of pre-grouping types by the end of 1938. These included the entire passenger locomotive stock of the former LNWR; the remaining Lancashire & Yorkshire passenger engines, and most of the Scottish passenger engines other than superheater 4–4–0s of the Caledonian. The Midland compounds, and the Class 2 superheater 4–4–0s were, for the time being, exempt from the slaughter. Of the North Western stud, the non-superheated Experiment class 4–6–0s can be quickly dismissed. Only nine out of the original 105 remained in January 1935, and those were scrapped in the course of the year. Of the 466 engines belonging to the Precursor, George the Fifth and Prince of Wales classes, considerable inroads had already been made by the end of 1934. At that time 66 out of the original 130 Precursors remained; the George the Fifth class, 90 strong, was still intact, but it is a little surprising to find that by then, no fewer than 53 engines of the Prince of Wales class had been scrapped. Of the Claughtons, 52 had already been replaced by new engines of the 'Baby Scot' class; a further 20 had been rebuilt with larger boilers, and by the end of 1935 all the remaining unrebuilt engines had been withdrawn. The large-boilered variety, despite their good work, were included in the extensive scrapping programme and were down for elimination by the end of 1938, together with all the remaining Crewe passenger engines of pre-grouping vintage. As will be told later, the programme did not progress entirely according to plan, and the last three engines were not scrapped until October 1949. This however did not alter the general policy of replacement.

The Lancashire & Yorkshire stud did not represent quite such a major slaughter, because there were fewer locomotives to be dealt with. The programme was no less drastic for all that! The Aspinall Atlantics had all been scrapped by February 1934; the 7ft 3in 4–4–0s had disappeared by 1930, and there remained only the Hughes four-cylinder 4–6–0s. Of these there existed, in January 1935, ten of the original engines of 1908-9, then of course rebuilt and superheated, and 46 of those built new between 1921 and 1925 of which there were originally 55. By the end of 1938 only ten of the entire class remained, and these, like the remaining Crewe engines would undoubtedly have gone to the breaker's yard but for the threat of war which was becoming so apparent from the autumn of 1938 onwards. The passenger 4–6–0s of the former Caledonian and Glasgow and South Western Railways had all been scrapped, but the Pickersgill 4–6–0s of the '60' class managed to survive much longer, and all eight locomotives of the Highland Clan class were still hard at work on the Oban line until 1938. Apart from these 'pockets of resistance' as they could be termed, the Stanier types had, by the end of 1938, virtually taken over the intermediate duties from end to end of the line. The lighter jobs were entrusted to Midland compounds, standard 2P 4–4–0s, and in Scotland to the survivors of the large family of Caledonian 4–4–0s derived from the historic Dunalastairs.

It was a picture that must have gladdened the heart of Sir Josiah Stamp in his campaign to reduce the total number of engine classes, though none of these old diehards could be entirely eliminated by the target date set, namely 31 December 1938. The tender engine stock of the line at that time is shown in Table 44.

TABLE 44

Type	Standard	Non-standard	Total
4–6–2	28	–	28
4–6–0	766	136	902
4–4–0	371	370	741
2–8–0	98	11	109
2–6–0	40	249	289
2–4–0	–	15	15
0–10–0	–	1	1
0–8–0	–	727	727
0–6–0	772	1592	2364

There was still a hard core of non-standard 4–4–0s and 0–6–0s, which would naturally prove an embarrassment to the most ardent disciple of standardisation, and which included many miscellaneous old classes. The Horwich Moguls have been included among the non-standard classes, though these were being retained indefinitely. Similarly none of the various 0–8–0 classes could be considered as standard, though reliance was placed on the ex-LNWR G1 and G2 classes, and the Fowler 9500 class for many years after 1938. The 0–6–0s included as standard are only those of the Midland 4F class and its LMS derivative, while the standard 4–4–0s are the compounds and the 2P 4–4–0s with 6ft 9in wheels. The most gratifying figure to an economist, in the foregoing table, would undoubtedly be the reduction in the number of non-standard 4–6–0s to 136.

So far as freight engines were concerned, the Stanier 2–8–0 came out in the early summer of 1935; but the need for new engines in this category was not so great as for passenger and mixed traffic duties. A total of 96 was built between 1935 and the end of 1937, and construction of further engines of the class began at Crewe at the end of 1938. The 2–8–0s, like the Jubilees and the Black Fives, originally had domeless boilers, but these were later modified. With reference to these engines it is now convenient to consider the technical development of these three important Stanier classes, having regard particularly to details of the boilers. Construction of the Jubilees was completed by 1936, but the Black Fives and the 2–8–0s were to become two of the most important engines ever to run on the railways of this country. Two tables of dimensions are appended herewith. Table 45 shows the basic dimensions on which the tractive effort calculation is based, while Table 46 gives details of the different

TABLE 45
STANIER STANDARD LOCOMOTIVES

Type	4–6–0	4–6–0	2–8–0
Power Class	6P	5P5F	8F
Cylinders:			
Number	3	2	2
Diam in	17	18½	18½
Stroke in	26	28	28
Coupled wheel diam ft in	6–9	6–0	4–8½
Boiler pressure psi	225	225	225

TABLE 46
STANIER BOILER DEVELOPMENT

Engine Class	5P5F			6P		8F	
Boiler type	1	2	3	1	2	1	2
Superheater elements	14	24	28	14	24	14	24
Heating surface	227.5	307	359	227.5	300	235	245
Tubes, hs sq ft	1460	1460	1479	1462.5	1460	1308	1479
Firebox, hs sq ft	156	171.3	171	162.4	181	156	171
Total, hs sq ft	1843.5	1938.3	2009	1852.4	1941	1698	1895
Grate area, sq ft	27.8	28.65	28.65	29.5	31	27.8	28.65

varieties of boiler—two each on the Jubilee and 8F, and three on the Black Five. In their final form there is no doubt that all three were outstandingly successful classes of locomotive. None could be placed among the aesthetic 'top ten' of British designs, but for hard, reliable work, trouble-free service and light repair costs they would have taken some beating. As time went on the need for an engine in the 5X power class receded. The Black Fives were so versatile as to be able to do practically anything originally allocated to a 5X, and in the scheme of locomotive standardisation propounded after the war, the Jubilee was not considered for further development. I may add that the old power classification 5X was later changed to 6, and at the same time the previous Class 6, including the Royal Scots became Class 7, and the Pacifics became Class 8. In the post-war scheme of standardisation no Class 6 passenger tender engines were envisaged.

From the above table it will be seen that the Black Five boilers underwent two enlargements, whereas the Jubilees and the 8F 2–8–0 had only one. The largest type of boiler on the Black Fives dated from 1938 with the engines numbered from 5452 upwards to 5499, and on all those numbered below 5000.

It is perhaps no exaggeration to say that the Black Five was probably the most generally successful steam locomotive ever produced in this country. From close study of every detail of their construction and constant improvement in detail, they achieved a remarkable record of reliability. In the years 1938 and 1939 the 500-odd engines of the class were averaging 145,000 between general repairs, while in those same two years there were only fifty-four cases of overheated axleboxes. This represented the probability of a hot-box once in fifteen years on any one engine. Considering the variety of work they undertook, ranging from high-speed express passenger jobs on the Midland Division, to fast goods, local passenger, and slow freight all over the system, this was a remarkable record. On the West Coast main line they were occasionally called upon to do heavy express work in deputising for Royal Scots or even Pacifics, and I had an interesting experience of this latter kind when I travelled down one morning on the 7am intermediate express from Euston. I was bound for Birmingham, and joined the train at Watford Junction, but it was not until I had logged the run and had the pleasure of a short conversation with our driver on leaving the train at Rugby, that I fully appreciated the nature of the working.

It was a duty worked by the Edge Hill top link, usually with Royal Scots, but occasionally at that time, with Pacifics. We had a fifteen-coach train of 429 tons tare, and fully 460 tons gross, and the best that Camden shed could provide on this particular morning was a Black Five, No 5378. The driver, L. Walls of Edge Hill was, however, an extremely capable man, and he got some magnificent work out of the engine, as will be seen from the accompanying log (Table 47). From the Watford start speed was worked up to a sustained 56mph on the rise to Tring, and then going very hard throughout, the ensuing 15 miles were covered in 12min 55sec to the dead stop at Bletchley. Even so, with a maximum speed of 80mph we could not keep the very

TABLE 47

7.26am WATFORD—RUGBY

Load: 15 coaches, 429 tons tare, 460 tons full
Engine: Class 5 4–6–0 No 5378

Distance Miles		Sch min	Actual min sec	Speeds mph
0.0	WATFORD JUNCTION	0	0 00	
3.5	King's Langley		6 56	49
7.0	Hemel Hempstead		10 57	55¼
10.5	Berkhamsted		14 46	56
12.6	*Northchurch Box*		17 01	56
14.2	Tring	17	18 42	61
18.6	Cheddington		22 30	77½
20.6	*Sears Crossing*		24 02	80
22.7	Leighton Buzzard		25 38	78
27.1	*Stoke Hammond*		29 07	75
29.2	BLETCHLEY	31	31 37	–
5.7	Wolverton		8 23	67
8.1	Castlethorpe		10 35	65
10.7	*Hanslope Box*		13 06	61
12.1	*Milepost 58¾*		14 26	60
13.2	ROADE	14	16 00	35 (slack)
17.3	*Milepost 64*		20 40	66½
19.1	NORTHAMPTON	23	23 22	–
4.0	Church Brampton		7 31	44
6.1	Althrop Park	–	10 20	45½
9.7	Long Buckby	14	14 56	47
–			–	52
12.2	*Milepost 78*		17 59	51
15.2	Kilsby		20 57	68
16.8	*Hillmorton Box*		22 23	71½
			sigs	
19.1	RUGBY	25	26 41	–

sharp 31 minute allowance. This was nevertheless up to the very highest standards of Royal Scot performance, with a Class 5 engine instead of a Class 7. Magnificent work followed, with a fine start to Wolverton and speed finely sustained on the ascent to Roade until the crossover slack was necessary to take the Northampton line. The restart from the latter station was perhaps the finest feat of all, with a gradual acceleration up a continuous gradient of 1 in 230, to 47½mph at Long Buckby.

After no more than half a mile of level had secured a rapid rise in speed to 52 mph, the last 2 miles at 1 in 230 to the summit point at Milepost 78 were cleared at 51mph. This climb, and that from Watford to Tring, involved an output of about 1,150edhp.

Over the years I rode many thousands of miles on the footplate of these engines, in all the variety of conditions in which they worked, and I think the most abiding impression of their performance is the way they responded to almost any kind of driving. There were no particular refinements in handling needed; you just stepped on board and drove away. The method of working most favoured was to use about 25-30 per cent cut-off and vary the regulator opening to suit the job. On level tracks they would streak away to 75 or 80mph with loads of 300-400 tons, while in heavy working conditions, as on the Highland line in Scotland, and on the much-lamented Somerset & Dorset Joint line, they could be pounded almost to their limit with a constancy in steaming that made them immense favourites with their crews, as well as with those who had the management of their working. On one occasion only in my experience did a Black Five fail in her allocated duty, and even then it was nothing more than a moderate failure to keep time. This occurred just after the war when a common-use engine, obviously taken indiscriminately from the 'pool', was put on to the evening mail from Bristol to the north. At one time during the run both injectors had failed, but the crew managed to get one of them working. This incident is mentioned because of its extreme rarity in my experience of the Black Fives.

These engines share with the 8F 2–8–0s the distinction of being very greatly multiplied after Sir William Stanier himself retired from the LMS. I shall refer to the post-war developments of the Black Fives in a later chapter, but now the interesting history of the 8F class must be told. These engines were in the general tradition of British 2–8–0s so far as tractive effort and basic dimensions were concerned. On the basis of tractive effort there was nothing to distinguish them from the 2–8–0s of the Great Western, nor from the various 2–8–0 designs operating on the LNER. What did distinguish them was their extraordinary speediness. One could hardly imagine the Great Central 04 class, or the ex-Great Northern three-cylinder 02s, running at speeds of 60 mph without some pretty venturesome and resolute handling by their crews; but the Stanier 8F class, with a front end similar to that of the Black Five, attained such speeds comfortably. There was, after all, no reason why they should not. If the design of piston valves and motion permitted free running at 80mph with 6ft diameter coupled wheels, the same number of revolutions per minute would give 63mph with 4ft 8½in diameter coupled wheels. By the outbreak of war, however, only 126 of the 8Fs had been built. The developments that brought their numbers up to 719 by the time the war ended are told in the next chapter.

Last among the Stanier ten-wheeled standard engines were the improved Jubilees, and with the domed boilers and larger superheaters these were also excellent engines. My best pre-war runs with them were all on the Midland line though I was never fortunate enough to get one over the Settle and Carlisle route. That however was an experience to come in 1945, and it was an experience not to be readily forgotten. Twice in one week in the summer of 1938 I had occasion to travel on the Thames-Forth Express from St Pancras to Nottingham, and both runs showed splendid quality of work. The variation in the speeds run on different sections of the line, both with 300-ton trains, was a clear indication that both drivers had plenty of time 'up their sleeves' as it were. For example *New Brunswick* made much the harder running as far as Luton and then, being nearly two minutes early, eased right down, to run 15 to 30 seconds behind time from Bedford to Kettering. Then came some fast running from Manton onwards to reach Nottingham comfortably inside schedule time. *Victoria*, an engine for which I was to gain even greater respect in later years, ran magnificently from the Luton check, with such speeds as 87mph at Flitwick, 54½mph over Sharnbrook summit and 83½mph at Irchester. Then, after passing Kettering on time, no more than ordinarily good running was needed to reach Nottingham ¾min early, in 122¼min for the run of 123.5 miles.

All ordinary performances of the Jubilees in pre-war years were surpassed by the special test runs carried out in October 1937, during which engine No 5660 *Rooke* was run successively from Bristol to Leeds, Leeds to Glasgow, Glasgow back to Leeds, and finally to Bristol on four successive days. The purpose was to check accelerated schedules that were planned on these routes, and to ascertain how much time there was likely to be in hand with the 'Jubilee' class engines and a tare load of 300 tons. The two engine crews chosen, namely driver Gardner and fireman Hook of Bristol, and driver North and fireman George of Leeds, were experts and enthusiasts, and the engine was not only worked very hard, but to the best advantage on all four days. The accompanying table (Table 48) gives a summary of the work done, and of the coal and water consumption, and one can only stand amazed that such average speeds as 55·4mph northbound and 55·3mph southbound were made over the difficult route between Bristol and Leeds. On this section intermediate stops were made at Gloucester, Cheltenham, Birmingham, Derby and Sheffield, while on the northbound section the intermediate stops were at Carlisle, Annan, Dumfries and Kilmarnock. In addition, it was of course necessary to stop at Bromsgrove for a bank engine up the Lickey Incline. One of the most spectacular performances was on the southbound run from Glasgow when, from the restart at Carlisle, the 48.4 miles up to Aisgill summit took only 48½ minutes. For those who wish to study the details of these splendid runs in their technical aspects, *The Railway Gazette* of 12 November 1937 carried a very comprehensive account, with charts taken from the dynamometer car record showing the speed throughout all four journeys. From the tabulated details given on page 213 it will be seen that the coal consumption per train mile was much heavier between Bristol and Leeds than on the northern section. This was due to the need to work the engine very hard in recovering from the numerous intermediate slacks. On the other hand, in relation to the actual work done, as represented by the consumption per drawbar horsepower hour, there was very close correspondence between the results obtained on all four runs.

The development of the standard passenger tank engines in the Stanier era, followed the same general pattern as that of the main line express and mixed traffic engines, in that the first examples had domeless boilers and a low degree of superheat. In the Fowler 2–6–4 tanks of the 2300 class, Stanier inherited one of the best designs in the entire LMS stud; but they had the traditional design of Derby boiler, and it was no more than natural that future developments had the tapered variety.

TABLE 48

LMS TEST RUNS, BRISTOL—LEEDS—GLASGOW AND BACK

Engine, 5XP 4–6–0 No 5660 *Rooke*. Weight of engine and tender (with coal and water averaged at 2/3 tender capacity)—121.6 tons

Tare weight of train (including dynamometer car), 302 tons

Date	*12 October*	*13 October*	*14 October*	*15 October*
Journey	*Bristol to Leeds*	*Leeds to Glasgow*	*Glasgow to Leeds*	*Leeds to Bristol*
Distance covered (miles)	205.9	228.5	228.5	205.9
Actual running times (min)	223.0	243.6	241.3	223.4
Average speed (mph)	55.4	56.3	56.8	55.3
Schedule times (min)	229.0	243.0	253.0	226.0
Fastest times then operating (min)	245.0	262.0	270.0	243.0
Coal consumption (excluding shed duties):				
lb per mile	53.7	42.7	43.6	51.1
lb per dbhp per hour	4.16	3.93	3.87	3.81
lb per sq ft of grate per hour	96.4	77.7	80.2	91.3
Water consumption (excluding shed duties):				
gal per mile	33.7	29.7	28.8	35.0
lb per dbhp per hour	26.1	27.3	25.5	26.2
Evaporation:				
lb water per lb coal	6.26	6.94	6.58	6.86

In a relatively short time a further 243 tank engines of the 2–6–4 type had been added to the stock. First of all came thirty-seven engines with three-cylinders specially for the Tilbury line, and introduced in 1934 (see Table 49). These were followed by the new standard two-cylinder variety of which 206 were built. Although the nominal tractive effort of both two- and three-cylinder types was almost the same—24,670 and 24,600lb respectively—the three-cylinder engines were designed for rapid acceleration in the very arduous commuter service between Fenchurch Street and Shoeburyness. The two-cylinder engines had cylinders 19⅝in diameter by 26in stroke. The successive varieties of boiler on the 2–6–4 tank engines are shown in Table 50.

The two-cylinder engines, like their Fowler predecessors, had a high route availability, but when the time came to build more of the class, for the rehabilitation period after the end of World

TABLE 49

Class	Cylinders		Coupled Wheel diam		Boiler Pressure	Nominal TE
	diam	stroke				
	in	in	ft	in	psi	lb
Derby, 1927	19	26	5	9	200	23,125
Stanier, 3-cyl	16	26	5	9	200	24,600
Stanier, 2-cyl	19⅝	26	5	9	200	24,670

TABLE 50

Boiler type	Small Superheater : domeless	Large Superheater : dome
Tubes, number	149	157
small flues	12	21
Heating surfaces, sq ft		
tubes	1,011	1,223
firebox	137	143
superheater	160	230
Total	1,308	1,596
Grate area sq ft	25	26.7

War II, an investigation showed that if the coupled wheel base was reduced, and some reduction in total weight thereby effected, the route availability could be further increased. Another 277 engines having the necessary modification were built from 1945 onwards. The stud of 483 two-cylinder tank engines then available provided a further example of mass-standardisation of locomotive stock, and these engines, like the Black Fives formed the basis for one of the new British Railways standard designs from 1951 onwards.

The Class 3 2–6–2 tank, also introduced in 1935, had exactly the same chassis and cylinder dimensions as the Fowler class of 1930, and the first examples had domeless boilers and small 14-element superheaters. Like their larger counterparts they were speedy and economical engines though the need for the smaller type was not so great. With seventy of the Fowler engines already in existence, a total of 139 more of the Stanier variety was added. As in the case of the 2–6–4s, the later examples had domed boilers. (See Table 51).

TABLE 51

Heating surface	Domeless	Domed
Tubes sq ft	859.1	997.0
Firebox sq ft	106.9	111.0
Superheater sq ft	72.8	138.0
Total sq ft	1038.8	1246.0
Grate area sq ft	19.2	19.2

These smart little engines began to take their places on many branch lines, though of course the 'scrap and build' campaign could not be economically pursued to its most ruthless extent where large numbers of useful engines were still available, and by reason of their light duties still performing over long periods between overhaul, and on light maintenance charges. To sum up this chapter, Stanier and his staff had most successfully fulfilled their mandate and provided the LMS with no more than four designs that were capable of almost indefinite multiplication, if necessary, to operate traffic over practically all the line; these were the 5P5F 4–6–0; the 8F 2–8–0; the 4P 2–6–4 tank and the 3P 2–6–2 tank.

CHAPTER 14

The Years of Change

IN 1937 the directors of the LMS decided to amalgamate the mechanical and electrical engineering departments. There was a growing realisation on railways all over the world that electrical equipment would play an increasing part in traction of the future, even where full electrification of the lines was not undertaken. The development of diesel propulsion was getting under way in many countries, and on the LMS it was felt that by co-ordinating mechanical and electrical engineering in one department, certain overlapping of work could be avoided and economies in staff effected. In 1934 C. E. Fairburn, a man with a brilliant academic career and a record of high achievement in railway electric traction as a contractor, had been appointed electrical engineer of the LMS. His appointment was that of an independent officer, a status that he would lose with the amalgamation of his department with that of the chief mechanical engineer. In 1937 however Fairburn was only fifty years of age, and with the view no doubt of his eventually succeeding Stanier as head of the combined department, he was appointed deputy chief mechanical engineer, while retaining his existing title of electrical engineer. This in turn had further repercussions, because prior to the amalgamation of the two departments Riddles had held the post of principal assistant to the CME. This was analagous to the post Stanier had himself held on the Great Western Railway, and which at Swindon was usually regarded as that of second-in-command of the department, rather than the usual understanding of the title 'assistant to'.

In 1937 a new post was created on the LMS, that of mechanical and electrical engineer, Scotland, and to this Riddles was appointed. Previously there had been a divisional mechanical engineer in Glasgow, but with the amalgamation, a new post embracing responsibility for both sides of the work was essential. At the same time, at headquarters the duties of principal assistant were placed in four categories, namely locomotives, carriages and wagons, electrical engineering, and outdoor machinery. So far as this book is concerned only the first is of significance, and to this post was appointed H. G. Ivatt, son of the former locomotive engineer of the Great Northern Railway. Since 1932 Ivatt had been divisional mechanical engineer, Glasgow, and prior to that his career had been as varied as it was successful. He was trained on the LNWR at Crewe and, until taking up military service in World War I he was concerned almost entirely with locomotive running and experimental work. He took part in the Interchange Trials of 1909, when one of his father's Atlantic engines was making trial runs between Euston and Crewe. On returning from distinguished war service he joined the North Staffordshire Railway, but after grouping he went to Derby, becoming locomotive works superintendent in 1928. With his subsequent responsibilities in Scotland he thus brought to his new post at Euston in 1937 an intimate knowledge of practically all major sections of the LMS. So far as Riddles was concerned, although with the successful inauguration of the Princess-Coronation class engines and the Coronation Scot service his direct responsibility for locomotive development was temporarily halted, it was not without significance that when the LMS board decided to send an engine and train for display at the New York World Fair in 1939, Riddles was chosen to accompany the train.

The period between mid-summer 1937, and the outbreak of war was relatively uneventful so far as locomotive development was concerned. The Stanier classes were well established, and the policy of 'scrap and build' could continue. Remarkable evidence was constantly forthcoming as to the ability of the improved Pacifics. In 1938 when a further ten were built, five of them were without the streamlined casing, and on these Nos 6230-6234, one could appreciate the truly massive proportions. It was with the last of these engines, and notably the only one at that time fitted with a twin-orifice blastpipe and double chimney, that an all-out dynamometer car trial run was conducted on Sunday 26 February 1939, from Crewe to Glasgow and back with a twenty-coach special train weighing 604 tons tare. Before referring to the outstanding results obtained on this special occasion, which gave strong support to the general impression that these engines could lay claim to be the most powerful in Great Britain, I must mention two runs in ordinary service on which I personally recorded work better than any I had previously noted in similar circumstances. One was on the down Merseyside Express just after New Year 1939. The new streamlined engines of 1938 were finished in the same style as those of 1937 except that the colour was standard red instead of the original dark blue. On this trip I was intrigued to see that our engine was No 6229 *Duchess of Hamilton*, yet she was in blue. Examination of some of the motion parts on arrival in Liverpool revealed the figures 6220. This was the original *Coronation* on which the nameplates had been exchanged with those of the new 6229, the engine which was selected to go to New York. It was a dirty winter's night with fog at the start, heavy snow from Nuneaton to Stafford, and a long succession of signal checks in the approach to Crewe which caused the last 4.8 miles from Betley Road to occupy 12¼ minutes. There had in addition been two permanent way checks, and times when the driving snow made slower running than usual imperative. In these conditions I consider it was remarkably fine work to pass Ditton Junction only 2¼min late, in 193¼min for the 182.8 miles from Euston. The net time for the 189.6 miles to Mossley Hill was 188min, no less than 12min inside schedule, with a fifteen-coach train of 520 tons gross behind the tender. Some of the finest running was between Bletchley and Rugby, where we cut the 35min allowance between these two stations to 31min 27sec. On this stretch speed was worked up to 77mph on level track between Weedon and Blisworth. Mention of this particular engine reminds me also that I had run behind her in September 1940 from Crewe to Shrewsbury when she was still in blue, and still carrying the name *Duchess of Hamilton*. The real 6229 was at that time still marooned in the USA.

The second run was a joyous romp on the up Midday Scot on its Saturday schedule in 1938, on which day the Coronation Scot did not run. The work had been good throughout from Edinburgh with Midland compound No 1176, and a 205-ton train, and a Jubilee No 5732 *Sanspareil* down to Carlisle. With a 425-ton train we had passed Gretna Junction 58.3 miles in 58min 52sec. Then, with a load further increased to 453 tons

DEVELOPMENTS UNDER H. G. IVATT

(above) *first of the new Class 4 2–6–0s No 3000;* (centre) *Black Five 4–6–0 No 4758 with roller bearings on all axles;* (below) *the Black Five fitted with Stephenson's link motion No 4767*

(above) *Stranraer—Glasgow express crossing Pinmore Viaduct, hauled by engine No 44799 (Black Five)*; (below) *Liverpool—Glasgow express on the Shap ascent, near Greenholme I.B. signals. A Stanier 2–6–4 tank No 42571 piloting a Jubilee No 45555* Quebec

tare, 490 tons full, a new red streamliner, No 6228 *Duchess of Rutland* came on. The Saturday schedule of the train was made to look ridiculously easy, until signal checks from a preceding Blackpool excursion caused us to lose a considerable amount of time between Preston and Crewe. At the latter place engine No 6228 was remanned, and we left 9min late, on an admittedly ample schedule of 178min for the 158 miles to Euston. We started smartly, though no more so than one had come to expect in 1938, but once over Whitmore summit the engine was allowed to run, so freely indeed that the ensuing 62.6 miles on to Newbold signal box took only 53min 42sec, an average of exactly 70mph and including a maximum speed of 85mph on the descent to Stafford. On this form we should have passed Rugby in a little over 71min, just inside the schedule of the Liverpool Flyer. We were however stopped by signal outside Rugby.

Another very fast spell ensued after we had cleared Kilsby Tunnel, averaging 73mph over the 26.8 miles from Welton to Milepost 48½, before we were stopped by signal a second time, in the approach to Bletchley. On getting away again, the 15 miles from Bletchley station to Tring took 16¼min, and then came another very speedy downhill run, covering the 22.6 miles from Berkhamsted to Willesden Junction in no more than 17min 4sec, an average speed of 79.2mph, with a maximum of 85mph. Eventually we reached Euston 7½min early in a total time of 161min 37sec from Crewe. The net time was 151½min—an average speed of 62.7mph. I was not on the footplate, but it was obvious that the engine was being worked a long way inside her full capacity, and that the very fast running on level and favourable stretches was typical of a very free-running engine making her own pace while being run under relatively easy steam. I had a short conversation with the driver and fireman on arrival at Euston, and far from expressing any suggestion of exertion at having worked a 490-ton train from Crewe to Euston at such speeds, they seemed to regard such tasks as a holiday outing now that they had such competent engines at their command.

How the progress of Stanier's express passenger locomotive development might have further advanced, had circumstances remained normal, we are not to know, except that a design for a 4–6–4 locomotive had been prepared in outline. But the war clouds were gathering even at the time I logged that fast run with the *Duchess of Rutland*; at that very time Neville Chamberlain was in Germany for his ill-starred talks with Hitler. The war, when it did come, not only halted work on the important project of the Rugby locomotive Testing Station, which was being jointly sponsored by the LMS and the LNER, but led to further changes in personnel which were to have important repercussions in after years.

Within a few weeks of the outbreak of war in 1939 the services of Riddles were claimed by the government, to act as director of transportation. R. C. Bond has told me how he was approached to take the vacant post on the LMS in Scotland on an acting basis. At the time there is no doubt that the job of 'Mechanical and Electrical Engineer, Scotland' had a side-tracking ring about it. Its creation, in 1937, solved an awkward situation in London, when the amalgamation of the mechanical and electrical engineering departments would have involved some demotion for Riddles; among some railway men of other companies his move to Scotland was openly referred to as a 'face-saver'. Bond on the other hand had been appointed superintending engineer of the Rugby Testing Station in 1938, an extremely interesting and potentially rewarding job in which he reported jointly to Stanier and Sir Nigel Gresley. While there was every chance that with the outset of war the unfinished work at Rugby would be halted, the prospect of going to Scotland did not seem very attractive. But he was urgently persuaded to do so, and carried on during two very critical years. In London, Stanier's immediate entourage remained unchanged, though naturally there were many tasks other than locomotive engineering to be discharged.

One very important piece of development work was done during the war years, though its outcome was not seen until Stanier himself had been seconded to the Ministry of Production. This development was of course the production of the taper-boilered Royal Scots. The seventy locomotives of this class, though forming a very important section of the motive power of the LMS, lay outside the general scheme of standardisation. They had been greatly improved in many details, and were powerful, fast, and reliable engines; but they had the Derby type of boiler which, so far as maintenance costs were concerned, could not compare with the later ones derived directly from

Swindon practice. As time went on there came plenty of data for making direct comparison between engines doing similar work in the 'Baby Scot' and Jubilee classes of three-cylinder 4–6–0. The first steps towards a taper-boilered Scot had been taken in 1935, when a new 4–6–0 had been built on the frames of the Fowler high-pressure compound, *Fury*. The Stanier tradition was then in process of establishment. The later engines of the Princess Royal class were doing magnificent work, but front-end design had not then reached the stage of such complete internal streamlining as was applied to the later Pacifics of the 'Coronation' series. The opportunity of replacing *Fury* enabled a prototype taper boiler of Royal Scot proportions to be designed, and a fine new engine numbered 6170 and named *British Legion* was completed at Crewe in the autumn of 1935. The basic dimensions contributing to the tractive effort formula were the same as on the original Scots. So far as the boiler proportions are concerned they are discussed in connection with those of the rebuilt 'Scots' which began to appear from 1943 onwards.

From my previous references to the working of the Pacifics it will be recalled that none of them were originally stationed at Longsight. The most powerful engines available for the Manchester trains were the Royal Scots, but as soon as *British Legion* was released for traffic she was sent to Longsight and immediately put on to the down Lancastrian. This train, carrying a tare load of 350 to 380 tons, had a 60mph timing: 176min non-stop for the 176.9 miles from Euston to Wilmslow. *British Legion* quickly made a name as a fast and powerful engine, and the LMS authorities, anxious to publicise this latest development in motive power, offered me a footplate pass on that train. It was late autumn, and I had many commitments, but by arranging to come back from Manchester by a night train a date was settled. Then on the very day I was to travel there came a telephone message from Euston. The engine was not working satisfactorily and they had been compelled to put an inspector on to observe and report. My trip would have to be postponed. At that time LMS regulations permitted only one extra man on the footplate in addition to the driver and fireman, so the presence of an inspector meant that I had to stand down. I gathered that the steaming of the engine was somewhat erratic and it took a little time to get this right, with alterations to the draughting as well. In view of these vagaries my promised footplate trip became indefinitely postponed, and in the end I never rode on *British Legion* at all.

For more than a year, although in revenue-earning service, she remained under fairly close observation, and in January 1937 certain alterations were made to the port sizes and valve dimensions to improve the cylinder performance. These modifications, together with the alterations to draughting made in her early days, put on the finishing touches, and from 1937 onwards *British Legion* was a very fine engine indeed. Of course in that year, and indeed up to the outbreak of war, so much attention was being lavished on the new Pacifics that the working of *British Legion* attracted little attention and received no official publicity. But night after night when on my way home I used to see her come flying through Bushey with the down Lancastrian. Lineside impressions are not always reliable, but the difference between her swift, effortless going and the acoustics when one of the ordinary 'Scots' was occasionally put on in substitution was very marked. In the winter of 1938 a visit to Ireland gave an opportunity of travelling behind her. I went down to Wilmslow on the Lancastrian and then retraced my steps to Crewe in order to pick up the night Irish Mail. Although a somewhat roundabout way of getting to Dublin it certainly brought a rich reward in a record of a truly splendid run by *British Legion*. At that time there was a very bad slack for underline bridge repairs between Kings Langley and Boxmoor, which made us more than 7min late past Tring, and a most resolute effort was made to regain the lost time.

The Lancastrian had a much sharper timing than the Merseyside Express which followed it five minutes later out of Euston. The allowance to passing Crewe was 156min compared with 164min for the Liverpool train. Furthermore, on the night I travelled, the load was one of thirteen coaches, with a gross load of 445 tons behind the tender. Thus, quite apart from any question of making up time, and the use of a 4–6–0, against a Pacific, the Lancastrian had a much harder task than the fifteen-coach Merseyside Express. This train had the advantage over the Merseyside Express of having rear-end banking assistance up to Camden, and the engine showed excellent form at the start with a sustained 60mph up the 1 in 335 past Harrow and Hatch End. But the effect of the two checks was quite devastating and we had not recovered to more than 48mph at Berkhamsted nor 56 at Tring. Then we went like the wind, averaging 75.4mph for 28.4 miles from Cheddington to Banbury Lane, with a maximum of 82½mph near Leighton Buzzard. Before Weedon however we had evidently closed in upon the 5.50pm express to Birmingham as we received a sharp signal check, and on passing Rugby no time had been regained on the stiff point-to-point allowance of 45min for the 50.9 miles from Tring. North of Rugby we continued to run magnificently. The 51 miles to Stafford took only 44min 20sec, and with a speed of 64mph over Whitmore summit, and a well sustained maximum of 85mph down Madeley bank, we were through Crewe less than a minute late in a net time of only 145¾min. This average speed of more than 65mph represented a considerably finer performance than that called for by the schedule of the Liverpool Flyer in the reverse direction, with a load well above the official limit of 380 tons for a Royal Scot on the latter train. On this run the net time between Willesden Junction and Crewe, pass to pass, was 136½ minutes, an average of 67.2mph. North of Crewe time was lost by the severe slowing called for over the section of line subject to the brine subsidence, near Sandbach.

It was quite evident that in this prototype taper-boilered Scot the LMS had a locomotive of outstanding quality, and it seemed no more than a matter of time before the ordinary Scots would be rebuilt with similar boilers as the time came round for boiler replacement. Further developments were to influence the design of the 'rebuilt' engines, and for a few paragraphs I must return to the Pacifics. The last of the non-streamlined engines of 1938, No 6234 *Duchess of Abercorn*, was fitted with a double blastpipe and chimney, and some remarkable results were obtained on the dynamometer car test runs made in February 1939, briefly mentioned earlier in this article. There was no waiting for fine weather to favour the engine performance. That particular Sunday was a wild wintry occasion, and at the moment when the locomotive was putting forth her greatest output of power, in the southbound ascent from Symington to Beattock Summit, they were running through a heavy snow-storm! In view of many subsequent experiences on the footplate of both classes of Stanier Pacifics, on both the Shap and the Beattock ascents, I have often wondered how No 6234 kept her feet so well when the rail conditions were so unfavourable; but keep her feet she did, otherwise such tremendous hill-climbing performances would not have been possible. A very detailed account of the trials, with charts showing speed and power output on the most severe sections, was published in *The Railway Gazette* for 14 April 1939. The quality of the work can be judged from the accompanying extracts from the results, from Carnforth to Shap Summit on

TABLE 52

DYNAMOMETER CAR TEST RUNS
26 FEBRUARY 1939 ENGINE NO 6234

CARNFORTH—SHAP SUMMIT

Section	Carnforth Oxenholme	Oxenholme Tebay	Tebay Summit
Distance miles	12.96	13.08	5.69
Average drawbar horsepower	1870	1668	1830
Maximum drawbar horsepower	2120	1934	2065
Maximum indicated horsepower (calculated)	3209	2806	2963
Average speed mph	68.0	53.0	47.9
Cut-off range %	20-25	25	25-35

MOTHERWELL—BEATTOCK SUMMIT

Section	Motherwell Law Junction	Law Junction Carstairs	Carstairs Symington	Symington Summit
Distance miles	5.42	10.53	6.74	17.28
Average drawbar horsepower	1923	(a)	1520	1860
Maximum drawbar horsepower	1998	1978	1638	2282
Maximum indicated horsepower (calc)	2583	2567	2138	3333
Average speed mph	46.7	48.4	46.1	63.4
Cut-off range %	20-30	30-35	20-25	30-35

(a) Not included, as some coasting was involved.

the one hand, and from Motherwell to Beattock Summit travelling south (Table 52).

In studying these results it is necessary to keep a sense of proportion; while it is true that nothing of a comparable nature, having regard to the power of locomotives and loads, had previously been achieved southbound over the Caledonian line, this is certainly not so in the case of the Shap ascent. The run of No 6234 was an exceptional 'all-out' effort. So was the classic LNWR run with the Claughton class engine No 1159 *Ralph Brocklebank*, on 4 November 1913. The times between Carnforth and Shap Summit on the two runs are shown in Table 53.

TABLE 53

Engine No		1159	6234
Load, tons gross		360	610
Dist		Actual	Actual
miles		m s	m s
0.0	Carnforth pass	0 00	0 00
12.8	Oxenholme	12 45	11 25
–		sig check	–
25.9	Tebay	27 15	26 15
31.4	Shap Summit	34 45	33 20
Speeds:		mph	mph
	Carnforth	71	75
	Hay Fell	47	46
	Tebay	71	76
	Shap Summit	37½	30

I have quoted the speed at Hay Fell rather than Grayrigg because the Claughton was brought down to 18mph by adverse signals at Mosedale Hall Crossing. The ratio of load to the nominal tractive effort of the locomotives was almost identical, namely 34.0 for the Claughton and 34.2 for the Duchess, and the maximum indicated horsepowers were 1,669 and 3,209. In relation to the tabulated details of the performance of engine No 6234, the maximum indicated horsepowers for the Claughton on the three sections concerned were 1,504, 1,669, and 1,606 compared to 3,209, 2,806, and 2,963 respectively for the Duchess. The biggest effort of the entire round trip with the latter engine was in the approach to Beattock Summit in the southbound direction when, at a speed of 64mph, the maximum calculated indicated horsepower was 3,333. This very strenuous trial was conducted with good economy, the coal consumption per drawbar horsepower hour being only 3.12lb.

The design for the new Class 7 4-6-0s to replace the Royal Scots was based upon the experience with *British Legion*, and with the double-chimneyed Duchesses. I have used the word 'new' advisedly because, while the engines are referred to variously as rebuilt or converted, little of the original engines remained save for the frames, wheels, and motion parts. Consideration can first be given to the boilers, of which the comparative dimensions are set out in Table 54. In studying these proportions it must be remembered that the new engines had twin-orifice blastpipes and double chimneys.

TABLE 54

CLASS 7 4-6-0 BOILERS

	Royal Scot	British Legion	6103 class
Heating surface sq ft			
Tubes and flues	1892	1669	1655
Firebox	189	195	195
Superheater	399	360	420
Total	2480	2224	2270
Grate Area	31.2	31.25	31.25

Of course these figures do not mean a great deal in themselves. The principal difference between the two later boiler designs and that of the original Scots was the shaping of the firebox, entirely on Great Western lines, with very careful rounding of the corners, and very great care taken to avoid sharp corners and places where local heating was likely to occur. Again the dimensions of the cylinders were unchanged from those of the original Scots; but all the experience gained with the various Stanier classes since 1933 was put to good purpose in designing the new cylinders for the converted Scots, and the result was a locomotive that used the steam to exceptionally good advantage in the cylinders. To develop 925 indicated horsepower at 62mph using no more than 5 per cent cut-off, was something of a phenomenon. It was one of a series of remarkable results obtained with engine No 6138 *London Irish Rifleman*. In conditions of wartime working no high speed running was practicable on these tests, and nothing higher than 62mph was run while indicator diagrams were being taken. In Table 55 is shown a typical set of results.

TABLE 55

INDICATOR RECORDS: ENGINE NO 6138

Cut-off per-cent	Speed mph	Indicated horsepower
5	62	925
10	60	1070
15	60	1520
18	62	1670
26	52	1820
32	44	1840
46	22	1440

Four of the rebuilt engines were sent to Leeds Holbeck shed for working the double-home turns to Glasgow St Enoch, and early in 1945 I had a footplate pass to ride the down day Scotsman, then a combination of the pre-war Thames-Forth and Thames-Clyde express. With engine No 6117 *Welsh Guardsman*, and a heavy train of 416 tons tare, 450 tons full, we made some excellent climbing on the long 1 in 100 ascent, from Settle Junction to Blea Moor. With the engine working in 30 per cent cut-off and full regulator, we sustained 36mph between Horton and Ribblehead. I estimated that the equivalent drawbar horsepower was approximately 1,555—a magnificently sustained performance with conditions on the footplate quite steady. On the Scottish part of the journey, with load reduced to 320 tons by the detaching of the Edinburgh portion at Carlisle, the engine was working in no more than 10 per cent cut-off throughout from Carronbridge to New Cumnock. Despite this working at very short cut-offs, the new engines showed no more than a slight improvement in coal consumption over the original Scots; but they were far more effective traffic machines, and it is significant of the esteem in which they were held that when the famous series of Locomotive Interchange Trials was organised, shortly after nationalisation, the Scots were allowed to compete with the Class 8 express passenger engines, all of which had a considerably greater nominal tractive effort.

I have reason to believe that the publication of certain test performances with the converted Scots caused no little concern at Swindon! I have no wish to make comparisons that could well be invidious; but in view of Stanier's long association with the Great Western Railway it is no more than natural to look back and see how his latest products compared with those of his earlier days. In the celebrated trials in 1924 with engine No 4074 *Caldicot Castle*, that engine sustained an output of 1,350 indicated horsepower at 65mph working in 22 per cent cut-off with full regulator. Although a straight comparison of cut-offs does not tell the whole story, since it is the amount of steam that enters the cylinders rather than the duration of the admission period that gets the work done, it did seem as though the converted Scots could, in ordinary conditions of steaming, develop a considerably higher indicated horsepower than a Castle. The LMS had every reason to be pleased with the converted Scots, and as the last major design for which Stanier was responsible they were certainly a worthy climax.

In the late summer of 1942, before the first of the converted Scots took the road, Stanier was seconded to the Ministry of Production to form one of a team of three full-time scientific advisers. He continued as chief mechanical engineer of the LMS, but in his absence Fairburn was appointed as acting chief mechanical engineer. Riddles in the meantime had been appointed Deputy Director General of Royal Engineer Equipment, while Bond had been brought south again in 1941 to become works superintendent at Crewe.

The responsibility for steam locomotive work and sponsoring the introduction of the converted Scots fell almost entirely upon H. G. Ivatt. During the war a high honour was paid to the Stanier 8F 2–8–0. The design was first of all chosen for service with the British Expeditionary Force in France, and orders for 240 were placed by the Ministry of Supply in December 1939. Intended for Continental working conditions, the specification included French type wheel profiles, and the Westinghouse air brake. The first deliveries of these engines from British manufacturers began in May 1940, just as the whole pattern of the war was changing by the retreat and evacuation of the BEF from the beaches of Dunkirk. The 2–8–0s were thereupon adapted for oil firing and sent to the Middle East. As the war effort developed and the need for large numbers of additional freight locomotives became urgent, the Wartime Railway Executive Committee selected the Stanier 8F as a national standard, and orders were given for large numbers of these engines to be built in a diversity of railway shops, as well as by the major contractors. Wartime construction is shown in Table 56.

TABLE 56

Numbers (inclusive)	Works
8176–8285	North British Loco Co
8286–8300	Beyer-Peacock & Co
8301–8330	Crewe
8331–8399	Horwich
8400–8479	Swindon
8490–8495	Horwich
8500–8509	Darlington
8510–8539	Doncaster
8540–8559	Darlington
8600–8609	Eastleigh
8610–8612	Ashford
8613–8617	Brighton
8618–8624	Ashford
8625–8649	Brighton
8650–8662	Eastleigh
8663–8670	Brighton
8671–8674	Ashford
8675–8729	Brighton
8730–8752	Darlington
8753–8772	Doncaster

It will be seen that numbers 8480-8489, 8496-8499, and 8560-8599 remained blank. The totals in the various railway shops from engine No 8301 were thus: Ashford 14; Brighton 93; Crewe 30; Darlington 53; Doncaster 50; Eastleigh 23; Horwich 75; Swindon 80.

The war took its toll of leading LMS personalities. Lord Stamp and his wife were killed when their home received a direct hit during the night blitz of 1940-1, and Sir William Wood succeeded him as chairman. In 1942 Symes was due for retirement from the very important post of chief stores superintendent, and at the urgent request of the LMS the release of Riddles from his governmental duties was secured, to take over from Symes. The post of chief stores superintendent may not seem a very suitable job for an able and experienced locomotive engineer, but on the LMS not only did it carry very high status, but it had already proved the stepping stone to still higher things as when W. K. Wallace had proceeded from it to succeed Alexander Newlands as chief civil engineer. So the return of Riddles to Euston was generally considered as a portent of bigger things to come. Stanier was knighted in the New Year Honours of 1943 and a year later he retired, to be succeeded, as had been expected, by C. E. Fairburn. The latter held office however for little more than a year, and his sudden and quite unexpected death took the top management of the LMS somewhat by surprise. Fairburn was only fifty-eight at the time and his passing completely upset the plans that had been laid for continuity in the department after Sir William Stanier's retirement. Fairburn died in October, but it was some little time before a new appointment was made. Ivatt was nominated as acting chief mechanical engineer, while in railway circles it was widely thought that Riddles would get the job.

Nevertheless the whole railway situation in Great Britain had been by then thrown into the melting pot by the result of the General Election of 1945. With a Labour government in power with a large majority in parliament, railway nationalisation was a certainty, and any arrangements that might be made on the LMS at that time, or on any other railway for that matter, were likely to be of no more than an interim character. Early in the New Year Ivatt was appointed chief mechanical engineer, and Riddles received the high honour of appointment as a vice-president of the company, with responsibility for all engineering matters. So, in 1946, ended a period of great stress, anxiety, and much uncertainty. It was followed by one of even greater difficulty.

CHAPTER 15

H. G. Ivatt: 1946-7

THE effect of the immediate aftermath of World War II on the economy and general business life of the country needs some recalling. It is receding into history as one of those periods best forgotten. Unfortunately, so far as railways were concerned, it had the most devastating and lasting effects. So far as the motive power of the LMS was concerned there were two distinct sides to the situation. During the war the reputation of the Stanier locomotives, almost alone among the celebrated British locomotive dynasties, had been greatly enhanced, and in this respect the LMS was perhaps the most favourably placed of all the big four to embark on post-war development. On the other hand, large numbers of locomotives of pre-grouping origin that were due for scrapping in the years 1939-45 had been retained in traffic to meet the exigencies of wartime needs. A very similar situation had developed on the LNER. Somewhat naturally these old engines had been 'patched up' when repairs became necessary, rather than overhauled to pre-war standards, and when the war ended many of them were in in a somewhat parlous condition. The company was faced with an urgent need for large numbers of locomotives of moderate power. The traditional expedient of putting displaced express passenger and main line goods engines on to these light duties could not be generally applied, because many that were suitable from the viewpoint of mechanical condition were precluded because of weight restrictions. Further patching up of still older engines had to continue for a time, resulting in the continued use, for example, of the ex-LNWR 18in goods (Cauliflowers) on certain branch line services.

At the same time a review was made of motive power requirements as a whole over the entire system, and at the end of 1946 it was announced that no more than eleven types of locomotive would be necessary to work the traffic, and of these eleven, three were shunting engines. The main line, and suburban passenger engines were:

1 4–6–2 Express passenger: Duchess class
2 4–6–0 Express passenger: converted Scot
3 4–6–0 Mixed traffic: Black Five
4 2–8–0 Goods and mineral: Stanier 8F
5 2–6–4 tank: suburban passenger
6 2–6–0 mixed traffic (Class 4)
7 2–6–0 mixed traffic (Class 2)
8 2–6–2 tank: light passenger (Class 2)

From this it will be seen that the former 5X class would eventually disappear, and also, perhaps rather surprisingly, the 0–6–0 goods which had been such a faithful maid of all work for countless decades on the railways of Britain. The 2–6–2 tank of Class 3 capacity was also to go and, somewhat naturally, the 4–4–0 express-passenger type. The locomotives in categories 1 to 5 above were all of well-tried Stanier types, but categories 6-8 were still in the design and constructional stage at the time this scheme of standardisation was formulated. It was the consummation of the policy laid down in the late 1920s by Lord Stamp. I may add that of the shunting engines, two were steam 0–6–0s, and the third was the standard diesel which had been carefully developed since pre-war years.

It was soon evident that the locomotive department of post-war years was not going to be content to rest on its laurels of the Stanier era, even though five of its major products had been chosen for future standardisation. The experience of the war years, and the valuable contacts it brought with leading American railwaymen, indicated many ways in which important improvements in detail could be made to the standard classes, such as the use of roller-bearing axleboxes, and roller bearings for motion pins; rocking firegrates; self-cleaning smokeboxes; and the further trial of poppet valve gears. It has sometimes been asserted by those who are always wise after the event, that there was no particular merit in the work done on the LMS in the two years before nationalisation, and that it was merely a case of catching up on what more progressive administrations had done many years previously. Such an attitude is to misunderstand completely the policies followed during the Stanier era. These various refinements in design all cost money—a good deal more money than the simpler details used with complete success in pre-war years. By and large the LMS was well served by its shed staffs, and even if all locomotives were not in pre-grouping Midland state of external cleanliness, they certainly were in good working condition. The war changed everything, and Ivatt and his staff were quick to set out to meet the needs of a very difficult situation.

Early in 1946 the decision was taken to fit all new and rebuilt engines with self-cleaning smokeboxes, rocking grates, and self-cleaning ashpans in order to expedite the disposal of engines after arrival on shed. The process, so far as LMS practice was concerned, involved taking on coal and water, either cleaning or dropping the fire, and clearing the ashpan and smokebox of ashes. These disposal duties usually took about an hour. The apparatus eventually standardised and used on the new British Railways locomotives from 1951 onwards, was so effective that it was usually unnecessary to open the smokebox doors between one boiler wash-out day and the next. It was at first thought that the introduction of self-cleaning plates into the smokeboxes of locomotives of existing designs would not affect the draughting, and thus require minor adjustment to the diameter of the blast-pipe orifice. This however did not turn out to be generally so, and some types from other railways which had the LMS design of self-cleaning plates added, needed considerable attention in this respect. While the self-cleaning plates obviated the need for smokebox clearing at all, except at times of boiler washout, it was found that with locomotives fitted with the rocker-grates and self-emptying ashpan, the time taken to drop the fire and empty the ashpan was no more than five to ten minutes, representing a very great saving in the total time taken for disposal of an engine.

If there was any British locomotive class of the 1940s with which its owners could have cause to be completely satisfied it was the Stanier Black Five; but towards the end of 1947 Ivatt built thirty new engines of the class for special observation, all with experimental modifications to the well-tried standard design. These thirty engines were as shown in Table 57.

TABLE 57

Numbers	Valve gear	Bearings
4738–4747	British Caprotti	Plain
4748–4757	British Caprotti	Roller
4758–4766	Walschaerts	Roller
4767	Stephenson	Roller

Some of these engines had the additional variation of double chimneys. In addition, some further engines of the class constructed to the existing standard design with plain bearings and Walschaerts gear, were built in that same programme for comparative purposes. The object of this large scale experiment was to determine what further increases might be made in availability and in mileage run between shop repairs, and to determine by how much the cost of maintenance and in-shed work might be further reduced. It was not often that devices calculated to save on day-to-day maintenance and to reduce fuel consumption could be incorporated in an otherwise standard design without some increase in prime cost or weight, and the Timken roller-bearing axles on these new Black Fives were a case in point. The driving axles with their special housings for the roller races constituted a massive assembly, and to provide adequate clearance from the front of the ashpan it was necessary to increase the coupled wheelbase by 4in. The distance between the driving and trailing pair of wheels had to be made 8ft 4in. That in turn meant longer frames, and an engine heavier by 3.2 tons.

The use of Caprotti valve gear on a number of these engines was yet another attempt to get away from the conventional type of valve gear, and the layout on the new engines incorporated all those features that the experience of the manufacturers had shown desirable. All was carefully arranged to give quick access to all parts likely to need attention. The cambox was arranged to slide out on to a temporary platform so that the valves might be readily inspected. In the past the Caprotti valve gear had been applied to try and improve the performance of locomotive classes whose work was below standard; but on these experimental Black Fives the valve gear was given a real chance of proving itself on a new and well-designed locomotive. At the same time the engines so fitted were to have no special attention or allocation

The Princess Royal *in 1963, on the down* Perth *express climbing* Beattock *bank*

Pacifics In Fell Country

(above) *the last Duchess built, No 46257* City of Salford *(with roller bearings throughout) on the down Royal Scot near Tebay;* (below) *a 'Lizzie', No 46205* Princess Victoria *on 16-coach Glasgow—Birmingham express just over Shap summit*

in working; they would work in a 'pool' with other Black Fives. The reversing gear in the cab was so arranged as to have the same number of turns from full forward to full reverse gear as with the standard piston valve gear, so as to minimise any confusion on the part of the drivers.

Nevertheless, while the intention behind this design feature was praiseworthy enough, one doubts if it had much value in practice. In the ordinary way the Black Fives were run with a cut-off of 25 to 30 per cent and a fairly narrow regulator opening; this however is about the very last way to drive an engine with Caprotti valve gear, which gives the best results with a full open regulator and the shortest possible cut-off. I must admit that my own experience with the Caprotti Black Fives, whether on the footplate or otherwise, was disappointing. There were several of them working on the West of England line between Derby and Bristol, and while running very freely they never seemed to have the 'guts' of a piston valve engine in getting away or in climbing a gradient. Another of them gave me the worst run I ever experienced over the Settle and Carlisle line, when I had a footplate pass for the down Thames—Forth Express. Her performance was not only far below the average standard of the piston valve Black Fives, but was not to be compared with average Claughton performance over that route in the 1930s. Both engine types were Class 5 and should by rights have been capable of roughly comparable work; but the work of that Caprotti 5 on my footplate trip would have been considered feeble for a Midland compound.

The experimental Black Five that created the most unusual interest was undoubtedly No 4767 fitted with the Stephenson link motion, outside. I have always had the greatest admiration for this gear, with a setting such as that used on the Great Western two-cylinder engines, to which that used on No 4767 was similar. The lead was adequate for fast running when the cut-off was 20 to 25 per cent; it was reduced to nothing at all in 45 to 50 per cent, and with the gear still further forward towards full gear the lead became negative. That setting had the effect of giving enhanced power at slow speeds, very rapid acceleration, and a capacity for hard slogging on heavy gradients that the Walschaerts gear with a constant lead of about $\frac{3}{16}$in did not possess. On the Great Western the Saints were incomparably better engines on a heavy bank than the four-cylinder Stars—in fact, on the North to West route between Shrewsbury and Bristol I have never known even the Castles, let alone the Stars, equal the best hill-climbing performance of the Saints.

The trial of Stephenson's link motion on so well-tried an engine as the Black Five was therefore something of an event. It was perhaps natural on the LMS to have the gear assembled outside, so that all the motion work was accessible; but inside or outside, No 4767 soon gained the reputation of being a very strong engine. She worked mainly on the Lancashire and Yorkshire line, on the rather leisurely duties of the post-war period. It would have been most interesting to see how she compared with the standard Walschaerts gear engines on a line of such grading as the Somerset & Dorset Joint between Bath and Evercreech Junction. No details were ever made public of the respective performances, or of the economics of these experimental locomotives. They took the road just at the time of nationalisation, and while roller bearings were afterwards standardised, the great majority of the BR standard engines had the conventional Walschaerts valve gear.

The claims of diesel-electric traction were at that time so strong that Ivatt felt that a trial must be made on the fairest possible basis of 'steam *versus* diesel'. While inviting the collaboration of the English Electric Company towards the production of two mainline diesel locomotives, for experimental purposes he built two more Pacifics of the Duchess class with all modern improvements incorporated, such as roller bearings throughout, and the standard arrangement of rocking grate, self-emptying ashpan, and self-cleaning smokebox. It was a happy thought to name the first of these new Pacifics, No 6256 *Sir William A. Stanier F.R.S.*, while the second, No 6257, was named *City of Salford*. The extensive trials that Ivatt intended to carry out never materialised. After nationalisation Riddles stopped all work on main line diesels for the time being because, as he so succinctly expressed it, in the economic climate of the day he could get so much more tractive effort per pound sterling from steam than from diesel. The English Electric diesels Nos 10000 and 10001 were completed just in time for them to have the initials LMS on their flanks, but for a few years they became somewhat out of favour. The latest and last of the LMS steam

Pacifics, Nos 6256 and 6257, worked in the ordinary links, and did good work. The former I found exceptionally smooth and free running an engine when I rode her from Glasgow to Carlisle on the up Midday Scot.

In discussing the experimental versions of the Black Fives and the last two Pacifics, I have nevertheless taken the story of the last two years of the LMS as an independent company out of chronological order, for the new standard Class 2 engines, both tender and tank, came out before the modified Black Fives. These two new classes created particular interest, because hitherto it had not been the general practice on any British railway to design locomotives specially for secondary services. At the same time, in the policy that led to the authorisation of the capital costs involved in tooling, pattern making and so on, there seems to have been an over-optimistic view of the continuance of secondary services as they had been known in the past. At the time of their construction it was pointed out that the new engines, although of small size and light weight, would incorporate every modern development that had been found desirable on heavy main line engines. It was considered equally desirable that secondary-service locomotives should also be capable of the highest attainable mileages per year, and between periodic repairs; that they should be capable of quick and easy servicing at sheds, and have a low basic fuel consumption. It was also stressed—and this has a poignant ring about it—that their prospective life could be over thirty years, and therefore they must possess the speed-worthiness and reserve of power to cope with future acceleration of branch line services. Alas for such visions! The new 2–6–0 tender engines and the 2–6–2 tanks were duly equipped with rocker grates, self-emptying ashpans, and self-cleaning smokeboxes, while on the 2–6–0s the tenders were fitted with cabs to afford protection in tender-first running and the coal space was restricted in width so as to give a good lookout ahead when so doing.

As motive-power units they were small, with two cylinders 16in diameter by 24in stroke; 5ft diameter coupled wheels and a boiler with a combined heating surface of only 1,159.5sq ft and a grate area of 17.5sq ft. The boiler pressure was 200psi. The maximum axle load on the 2–6–0, 13.75 tons, was not on the engine at all, but on the leading pair of tender wheels. The maximum load on any of the engine axles was 13.55 tons. It was clear that a free-running engine was aimed at by the use of piston valves of no less than 8in diameter in conjunction with cylinders of only 16in diameter. The tank engine was of identical design, except in respect of the reduced coal and water capacity. The nominal tractive effort at 85 per cent boiler pressure was 17,400lb. In outward appearance, although having a slightly tapered boiler, they had more of a Fowler than of a Stanier appearance, due to the large steam dome extending upwards almost to the same height as the chimney. Despite all the modern appliances built into their design they were neat and compact little things, wholly in the old-style British tradition.

One of the earliest jobs to which the 2–6–0s were allocated was the heavily graded line between Penrith and Workington. In former days the LNWR had been responsible for the passenger train working over the one-time Cockermouth, Keswick & Penrith Railway, and weight restrictions imposed by the light bow-string girder bridges near Keswick precluded the use of any locomotives larger than the Webb 2–4–0 Jumbos and the famous 18-inch Goods. There were Jumbos still in regular passenger service on that line as recently as the year 1931. After they had been withdrawn the entire job was handled by the Cauliflowers until the arrival of the Ivatt 2–6–0s. Indeed when I did some footplate riding over the line in 1950 the passenger service was being handled by Cauliflowers and the new 2–6–0s in about equal numbers. This was, of course, precisely the kind of duty for which the new engines had been designed, and they did it very well. They were less successful when, after nationalisation, they were tried on some duties previously worked by the tough old Dean 0–6–0 goods engines of the Great Western 23XX class. That however is to take the story beyond LMS days. On the Keswick line from the footplate I logged engine No 46456 with a load of four coaches, totalling 120 tons behind the tender, and on the toilsome 1 in 62 gradient between Threlkeld and Troutbeck we sustained 24mph, working in 40 per cent cut-off with the regulator about half-open. The working was strenuous to a degree, but competently done.

The new standard Class 4 mixed traffic engine, to replace the ex-Midland Class 4 0–6–0, did not appear until after nationalisation; but it was wholly an LMS design prepared under the direction of Mr Ivatt, and the first of them, No 3000, took the road early in 1948. If the Class 2 engines that had preceded them had the cosy, traditional look of an old-style British locomotive, the new Class 4 2–6–0s were starkly modern. When the first of them came to Bath to work over the Somerset & Dorset Joint Line, they were immediately christened 'Doodlebugs'! Curiously enough, if one studied the working drawings they did not look anything much out of the ordinary—in fact quite a natural, shortened, 2–6–0 version of the Black Five. But the drawing did not convey the highly unorthodox impression created by the position of the running plate, which was level with the middle of the engine number carried on the cab side. So far as basic dimensions were concerned the two-cylinders were 17½in diameter by 26in stroke; the coupled wheels were 5ft 3in diameter and the boiler pressure 225psi. This provided a nominal tractive effort of 24,172lb at 85 per cent boiler pressure—a potentially powerful little engine with a total weight, engine only, of 59.1 tons. A great deal of thought had been given in design to the layout of the front end. The piston valves, 10in diameter, were exceptionally large in relation to the cylinder volume; the double blastpipe and chimney were of a novel type in which the twin jets, instead of being parallel and vertical, were divergent, in order to give a freer passage to the exhaust steam. Like the Class 2 2–6–0 the tenders had a cab backplate and roof to give protection when running tender first.

On paper the design looked an excellent one, and a fitting conclusion to the story of LMS steam locomotive practice. As is sometimes the case, however, the smokebox and draughting proportions were not quite right, and despite the care put into the design the steaming of the boiler was not up to expectations. Of course the Somerset & Dorset line, with its lengthy stretches of 1 in 50 ascent on both sides of the Mendips, is enough to kill any ailing engine, and I had a very interesting day on engine No 43017, working a busy roster on a summer Saturday. What that involved in the hey-day of weekend holiday railway traffic to Bournemouth is a longer story than I can tell in any detail here. Engine No 43017 had worked down from Bath to Bournemouth during the night, and I joined her on the 8.40am up. We had a ten-coach train of 320 tons gross behind the tender, and we had not proceeded far before it was plain that her steaming was going to be erratic. She would not stand an injector for long without the pressure falling. The fire was in good shape but the fireman was having to 'fiddle' his way along, maintaining boiler pressure by running with spells with both injectors off. It was not so much that the engine was steaming badly, because the moment the regulator was closed the pressure rose rapidly. It was rather that the boiler could not produce steam rapidly enough to keep the cylinders replenished. Over the easier stage of the journey from Bournemouth to Evercreech Junction, the 'on-off, on-off' technique with the injector kept us going, and sectional time was maintained; but we should have been in dire trouble over the Mendips without assistance. In any case our load was well over the maximum for an unpiloted Class 4 engine. Had we attempted to take a maximum load for the class the continuous hard steaming involved in the long climb would have completely beaten the boiler.

From Evercreech Junction we had a Class 2 4–4–0 ahead of us, and our load was well within the combined maximum for two such engines. As we got away it was evident that the pilot was taking more than her fair share. She was hammering away, steaming freely, and showing the white feather at her safety valves all the way up, whereas on No 43017 the pressure at one time fell to 165psi. It was the same on the southbound trip with the same engine on the 2.12pm out of Bath. On that train, with a similar load, we had a particularly good driver and fireman, and the engine exhibited exactly the same characteristics. On the gruelling climb from Radstock up to Masbury Summit it was the pilot engine 4–4–0 No 40564 that 'saved our bacon'. Even though our driver was using no more than 35 per cent cut-off with regulator half-open, and though cut-off was shortened to 20 per cent on the short easier stretch past Binegar we could not maintain pressure, and topped Masbury Summit with no more than 150lb showing on the gauge. Although it is passing beyond LMS days I can add that these engines were subsequently redraughted, with a single-orifice blastpipe, and became the basis for one of the most successful of the BR standard classes.

Before closing the story of LMS steam locomotive development, I must mention the rebuilding of certain engines of the 'Baby Scot' class with tapered Royal Scot boilers. This was a natural counterpart to the rebuilding of the Royal Scots. In 1946 the

'Baby Scots' were about thirteen years old, and were beginning to need new boilers. With the object of bringing them into the general scheme of locomotive standardisation, a plan for rebuilding was worked out that would bring them into the Royal Scot power classification. Originally they had cylinders that were the same as those of the original 'Scots', 18in diameter by 26in stroke. If they had been rebuilt with the original cylinders, or had the redesigned and internally streamlined cylinders of the converted 'Scots', the nominal tractive effort would have been increased from the 26,520lb of the 'Baby Scots' to the 33,150lb of the Royal Scots, a big jump of 25 per cent. This could very likely have led to troubles with the frames. Even the great André Chapelon struck difficulty in this way in the rebuilding of the original small-wheeled Pacifics of the Paris-Orleans Railway into the amazingly powerful 4–8–0s of the PO-Midi. The frames could just transmit the power output, and after an incredibly brilliant début, the 4–8–0s after a time began to develop troubles with their frames. On the LMS the power of the rebuilt 'Baby Scots' was cut back a little by making the new, internally-streamlined cylinders 17in diameter instead of 18in. In consequence the nominal tractive effort of these engines was 29,570lb.

The first engine to be so treated in 1946 was No 5530 *Sir Frank Ree*. By what might have seemed a coincidence the first Claughton to be rebuilt as a 'Baby Scot' was also named *Sir Frank Ree*, and numbered 5902. This latter engine was to a far greater extent a true rebuild of the original LNWR engine No 1191 which, with No 5971, were the two prototypes of the 'Baby Scot' class. When the title of Patriot was officially bestowed on the class, engines 5902 and 5971 were renumbered 5500 and 5501 and renamed *Patriot* and *St Dunstans*. They could be readily distinguished from the remaining fifty engines of the class as they retained the original Claughton driving wheels with circular wheel bosses on the coupled wheels. The name *Croxteth*, which was originally borne by engine No 5971, disappeared but many old Claughton names were used on other engines of the 'Baby Scot' class, long after their significance had passed. One would imagine that there would be very few members of the LMS staff in the late thirties and in post-war years who could recall the identity of *Sir Frederick Harrison, E. Tootal Broadhurst*, and

Sir Robert Turnbull, nor equally the name carried on the first of the engines rebuilt in 1946, *Sir Frank Ree*. Of the fifty 'Baby Scots' built new in 1933, eighteen were rebuilt with taper boiler and new 17in diameter cylinders. They were splendid engines in traffic and their best performances were generally indistinguishable from those of the converted Scots.

CHAPTER 16

LMS to LMR

THE announcement of the major mechanical engineering appointments in the nationalised British Railways was enough to suggest that LMS practice would prevail and continue uninterruptedly. R. A. Riddles was appointed to the key position of member of the railway executive for mechanical and electrical engineering, and at headquarters R. C. Bond became chief officer, locomotive works, and E. S. Cox, executive officer, locomotive design. Cox had not figured prominently in the story of LMS development, but from the early days of the Stanier regime he rose rapidly in the field of design and experimental work, and was one of H. G. Ivatt's principal assistants. The Stanier locomotive stud had, by its proven performance, established a record that was virtually second to none by the end of 1947, and could well have been adopted in its entirety for further requirements of British Railways. Such a course would obviously have incensed regional sentiments and loyalties. As one of the major aims of nationalisation, technically at any rate, was to evolve a practice that was the best from the pre-nationalisation companies, Riddles and his staff embarked on a very difficult course. I need not dwell upon the outcome, except in so far as it reflected the influence of the LMS. Although many details of other regional practice were adopted, the new designs from the Class 5 4–6–0 downwards all had their basis in existing LMS designs, particularly in respect of the boilers. While this was a great compliment to Stanier, and through him to the massive influence of Churchward, one can only comment that if, in the possession of all the evidence to hand, the British Railways staff had *not* followed this course, they could well have been written down as crazy.

Here, of course, I am not concerned with the British standard locomotives, whatever influenced their design, but to continue the story of the LMS types in the closing years of steam in Great Britain. For a variety of reasons the LMS representatives collectively did not do very well in the Interchange Trials of 1948. The converted 'Scots' had their moments, particularly when running on the Southern between Salisbury and Exeter, but the Duchess and the Class 5 4–6–0s disappointed, partly because their crews were attempting a species of 'coal-dodging'. Some of the best work of the Black Fives was between Bristol and Plymouth. The coal consumption figures showed no clear-cut superiority over any of the competing locomotives. By the mid-1950s however, with accelerated schedules and the track on most main lines restored to something like its pre-war excellence, there was a great deal of extremely fine work done on both the West Coast main line, and on the Midland; and an account of some of the finest runs that came to my notice in this period will fitly conclude this story of LMS steam. It is the Scots and the Duchesses that steal the show. I certainly had many very sound runs with Black Fives, ranging from Bristol and Bournemouth in the south-west, to Aberdeen, Wick, and Kyle of Lochalsh; but there was nothing exceptional. The same, with one outstanding exception, applied to the Jubilees, and it is with these latter engines that I can appropriately commence.

The outstanding example of Jubilee performance was, remarkable to relate, a wartime experience early in 1945. I had some engine passes to ride the converted Scots on the double-home turns between Leeds and Glasgow St Enoch, and I had been disappointed when, instead of the expected Scot, a dingy and unkempt Jubilee came backing down for the 10am from St Enoch to St Pancras, piloted into the bargain. But she was a Leeds engine, and while that shed may not have had time to polish their engines as of old, they certainly had the reputation, even in wartime, of maintaining them in good 'nick'. The engine was No 5565 *Victoria,* and on climbing aboard I learned that the pilot was going only as far as Kilmarnock. Furthermore, once we started I realised that she was a grand engine despite all outward appearances. Over the Glasgow & South Western we did some fine work, particularly in the ascent from Kilmarnock to New Cumnock. Through one of the anomalies of wartime operating, the point-to-point times of the express trains over this route had been left practically unchanged from those of 1939, and here we were leaving Kilmarnock with an absolutely packed thirteen-coach train weighing 410 tons behind the tender, with such a timing as 28min for the 21.1 miles to New Cumnock ahead of us. More than that, the initial 9.4 miles to Mauchline were allowed only 14min and of that distance the 5½ miles from Hurlford up to Mossgiel Tunnel are continuously at 1 in 100.

In an attempt to keep these very sharp point-to-point times driver Walker thrashed the engine without mercy, gradually increasing cut-off to no less than 50 per cent, with full regulator! The boiler steamed magnificently, but the injectors could not feed it fast enough, and while pressure was maintained the water level dropped considerably. Regrettably the cut-off had to be shortened, and speed fell from a splendid 34½mph on the gradient, to 30mph. We could not keep time to Mauchline, passed in 16min 38sec and with a permanent way check to follow we were 4¾min late on passing New Cumnock. Without any downhill speed exceeding 75mph we clocked into Dumfries dead on time, in 68 minutes for the 58.1 miles from Kilmarnock. We continued in fine style on to Carlisle, keeping the brisk start to stop allowance of 19 minutes for the 15.5 miles to Annan, and of 22 minutes for the last 17.5 miles into Carlisle, chiefly by very vigorous starts. Our station allowances had been exceeded at each stop—indeed I wondered how it had been possible to pack more passengers into that already jammed train of ours. So it was that we left Carlisle 4 minutes late. Timings over the Midland line had been greatly eased by comparison with pre-war standards, and our driver and fireman took the advantage of this to get the train back to schedule time as quickly as possible. The result was a truly magnificent start out of Carlisle.

From the very outset the engine was pounded with tremendous vigour, and up the 1 in 132 gradient to Scotby driver Walker used 47 per cent cut-off with full regulator. There was absolutely no flagging this time on any account. There was a slight easing of the cut-off to 42 per cent at Cumwhinton, but the boiler, under the careful work of fireman Hudson, supplied all the needs of this tremendous effort, and on the last 3 miles up to Low House Crossing speed was held almost unvaryingly at 44½mph to 45mph, on a gradient of 1 in 132 to 129. The equivalent drawbar horsepower was approximately 1,400, a most remarkable effort for a locomotive of these proportions. Boiler pressure was sustained at 210 to 215psi and the water level dropped roughly 1in in the glass. The full details may be studied from the diagram below, but the effect of it was to wipe out completely

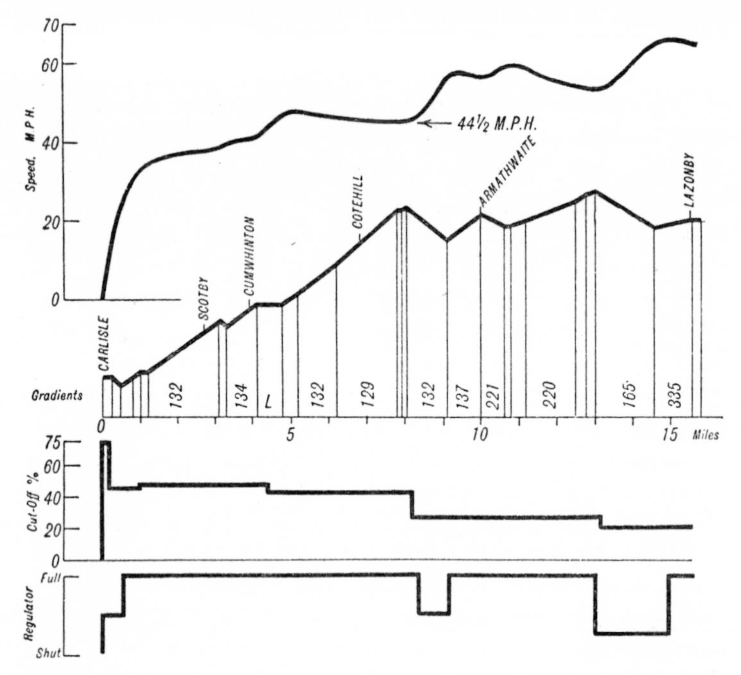

that late start before we reached our first stop at Appleby. The wartime schedule allowed 43 minutes for this first 30.8 miles, and we took only 38¼ minutes, although the engine had been very much eased after passing the summit point just south of Barons Wood Tunnels. We left Appleby on time, yet such was the continuing splendid form of our engine that driver Walker and fireman Hudson treated me to yet another magnificent display of hill-climbing on the final run up to Aisgill. On the long stretches of 1 in 100 gradient, from Ormside viaduct up to Guiseburn Box, and from Smardale viaduct to the south end of Birkett Tunnel, the maximum cut-off used was 37 per cent, with full regulator, as usual. The minimum speed on these two long gradients was 38mph, and after clearing Birkett Tunnel it was evident that we were getting well ahead of time. Actually we passed Aisgill summit, 17.5 miles from Appleby, in 30½ minutes,

4½ minutes early. No fast downhill running was necessary, and we reached Hellifield, 46 miles, in 62¼ minutes from Appleby, nearly 5min early.

This was indeed a very fine example of the working characteristics of the Jubilee class locomotives. I had some interesting correspondence with Mr Ivatt after this run, and he was obviously surprised at the power output of the engine between Carlisle and Lazonby, and again on the final ascent to Aisgill. The celebrated test runs of 1937 with engine No 5660 *Rooke* had been regarded as the optimum performance of the class, and on the southbound journey the average speed between Ormside and Aisgill had been 56mph with a train load of 305 tons. On the long stretches of 1 in 100 ascent the speed was however continuously falling. The maximum actual drawbar horsepower registered in the dynamometer car was 1,113, and the average for the 14.9 miles, 1,054. This would represent an 'equivalent' value of about 1,400. At Birkett Tunnel, No 5565 on my run was developing 1,170 actual, and about 1,450 'equivalent' at, moreover, a lower speed than that of *Rooke*. Of course, on my journey *Victoria* was being worked hard only on certain stretches, whereas *Rooke* was in the midst of a four-day 'endurance test'. In any case however that run with *Victoria* is one of those steam locomotive experiences of which an observer specially treasures the memories.

Turning now to the Euston—Crewe section of the West Coast main line there are a number of notable runs to be recalled. The acceleration of the Royal and Midday Scots to a run of 80 minutes, over the 82.6 miles from Euston to Rugby called forth much fine running on trains frequently loaded to over 500 tons. Looking back through past records however it was the up Red Rose—the post-war equivalent of the famous Liverpool Flyer—that provided the most fruitful results for those seeking details of LMS Pacific performance at its best. Moreover that train was frequently hauled by one of the 'Lizzies', and in their last years on really fast main line jobs those earlier Stanier Pacifics were doing some remarkable work. Before the drastic decelerations that were necessary when the line was being rebuilt in preparation for electrification, the Red Rose was allowed 155 minutes for the 158.1 miles from Crewe to Euston, which would have been equivalent to about 147 minutes to a stop at Willesden, compared to the 142 minutes of the old Liverpool Flyer.

In Table 58 are summary details of four runs with Duchess class engines, and loads varying between 460 and 550 tons. It will be seen that there was no net time greater than 147 minutes, a gain of 8 minutes on schedule.

TABLE 58

CREWE—EUSTON

Run No	1	2	3	4
Engine No	46250	46239	46253	46237
Engine Name	*City of Lichfield*	*City of Chester*	*City of St Albans*	*City of Bristol*
Load, tons E/F	430/460	446/490	457/500	503/550
Actual overall time (min sec)	149 21	152 15	153 25	160 34
Net time (min)	146¼	147	144¾	146¾
Net average speed mph	64.8	64.5	65.5	64.6
Max Speed mph	86	82	90	85

On this train however, within the limit of the numerous logs that have come under my scrutiny, it is the 'Lizzies' that steal the show. The last time I travelled personally by the train was in 1959, on a hot sultry evening in mid-July, when my principal recollections of the earlier part of the journey were those of trying to find a seat in a very crowded train. But the 'music' from the front-end was reassuring, and sure enough No 46203 *Princess Margaret Rose* and her crew certainly gave us a magnificent run. We were taken through the Midlands in the style of the Liverpool Flyer of old, and south of Rugby we were going better still until a very annoying signal check at Bletchley. This was quite a local affair, but it proved no discouragement to the driver and fireman who made a magnificent recovery and passed Tring summit at a sustained 66½mph—an equivalent drawbar horsepower of 1,570. Then the conclusion of the run was spoiled by an emergency stop at Bourne End signal box, to be warned that some children were believed to have put some stones on the line! Nevertheless the net time was certainly no more than 144 minutes. This run is completely eclipsed between Rugby and Euston by two runs in which engines 46208 and 46209 were involved, and on which the net times from Crewe to Euston were 139 and 140½min with average speeds of 68.2 and 67.4mph respectively.

Details of these two superb performances are shown in Table 59 and I must emphasise that the times quoted are those

TABLE 59

RUGBY—EUSTON

Princess Royal class engines

Engine No		46208			46209		
Engine name		*Princess Helena Victoria*			*Princess Beatrice*		
Load tons E/F		449/490			449/490		
Distance Miles		Actual min	sec	Speeds mph	Actual min	sec	Speeds mph
0.0	RUGBY	0	00*	–	0	00*	–
2.3	*Hillmorton Box*	2	37	–	3	23	–
7.3	Welton	7	58	67	8	54	54
12.9	Weedon	12	31	86	13	31	82
22.7	Roade	20	11	72	21	19	70
27.8	Castlethorpe	23	54	88	25	06	90/75
35.9	BLETCHLEY	30	29	70	31	03	80/77
42.4	Leighton Buzzard	35	46	75	36	03	78
50.9	Tring	43	14	63	42	53	71
54.6	Berkhamsted	46	27	77	45	52	80
58.1	Hemel Hempstead	49	04	91	48	19	96
65.1	WATFORD JUNCTION	54	07	80/78	53	03	85
71.2	Harrow	58	37	83	57	11	88
74.5	Wembley	60	56	90	59	24	93
77.2	WILLESDEN JUNCTION	62	51	–	61	10	–
82.6	EUSTON	70	04		68	50	

* Times from passing Rugby

from passing Rugby at about 40mph. On the first of the two runs with engine No 46208 *Princess Helena Victoria*, the recovery from the prescribed slowing through Rugby was vigorous and a maximum of 86mph was attained at Weedon. Hard and sustained running followed throughout to Willesden, with an average speed of 76mph from Welton to Wembley, a minimum speed of 63mph over Tring, and maxima of 88mph at Castlethorpe, 91 at Hemel Hempstead and 90mph at

Wembley. Until I learned of the effort of *Princess Beatrice*, tabulated in the adjoining column, I thought that a time of 70 minutes over the last 82.6 miles into Euston was something of a record, with a 490-ton train. Engine No 46209 was rather slower off the mark after passing through Rugby, and her speeds of 82mph at Weedon and 70mph in Roade cutting, were nothing very much out of the way for those last halcyon days of steam on the West Coast route. But after Roade the driver and fireman of No 46209 must have thrown in all they had! Speeds of 90mph at Castlethorpe, 71 over Tring summit, 96 at Hemel Hempstead and 93mph at Wembley were extraordinary, and contributed to the amazing average speed of 81.8mph over the 46.7 miles from Castlethorpe to Wembley. With details of such a run one can indeed cry *finis* to the saga of steam between Euston and Crewe.

In the meantime some magnificent work was also being done on the Midland line. Dieselisation in East Anglia, and electrification on the Southern had released a number of the Britannia Pacifics; but on the Midland the use of these latter engines on the Manchester expresses, turn and turn about with converted Scots, was producing standards of running that had never been previously seen between St Pancras and Leicester. Two of the finest ever runs over this stretch were made by the first of the 'Baby Scots' to be rebuilt with taper boiler, No 45530 *Sir Frank Ree*, on the up Manchester express at one time leaving Leicester at 4.31pm and allowed 99 minutes for the 99.1 mile run non-stop to St Pancras. I shall always retain particular memories of locomotives bearing this name because of the association of the original LNWR Claughton No 1191 with the working of the famous 2pm West Coast Corridor from Euston, and which was the first long-distance LNWR train on which I ever travelled. As mentioned in the previous chapter however, the LMR engine No 45530 had no connection except in name with LNWR No 1191, or 5902 as she became in LMS days. Connections or not, No 45530 was obviously in top class form in her Midland days, and details of these two runs, as set out in table 60 are worth close study.

The first included an extremely vigorous start with a speed of 67mph over Kibworth summit and a maximum of 86½mph at East Langton. I should mention that on this duty the engine

(above) *relief Euston—Glasgow express (15-coach load) passing Morecambe South Junction: converted 'Baby Scot' class 4–6–0 No 45525* Colwyn Bay; (below) *Manchester—Glasgow express passing Tebay: converted Scot 4–6–0 No 46145* The Duke of Wellington's Regt (West Riding)

(above) *Morecambe—Helensburgh excursion train climbing the Beattock bank, hauled b Jubilee class 4–6–0 No 45716* Swiftsure; (below) *Manchester—Glasgow express climbin Shap, nearing the final cutting. Engine No 45629* Straits Settlements *tackling a 12-coac load unassisted*

TABLE 60

LEICESTER—ST PANCRAS

Rebuilt 3-cylinder 4–6–0 No 45530 *Sir Frank Ree*

Load: tons E/F			304/330	306/330
Distance Miles		Sch min	Actual min sec	Actual min sec
0.0	LEICESTER	0	0 00	0 00
3.7	Wigston		5 56	6 16
9.4	*Kibworth North*		11 27	12 05
12.8	East Langton		14 07	15 00
16.2	MARKET HARBOROUGH	19	16 45	17 51
20.6	*Desborough North*		21 27	22 30
24.5	*Glendon Junction*		24 37	25 50
27.1	KETTERING	31	26 32	27 52
30.9	Finedon		29 33	30 42
34.1	WELLINGBOROUGH	37	32 08	33 00
39.4	*Milepost 59¾*	43	37 16	37 30
42.4	Sharnbrook		39 47	40 03
49.2	*Bedford N Junction*	51	44 42	44 45
57.3	Ampthill		51 34	51 11
61.8	Harlington		55 40	54 56
66.3	Leagrave		59 59	59 00
68.9	LUTON	70	62 02	61 10
74.5	Harpenden		66 18	65 44
79.2	ST ALBANS	79	69 55	69 25
83.9	Radlett		73 22	72 43
86.7	Elstree		75 26	74 48
92.2	Hendon	90	79 38	78 48
			sig stop	sigs
99.1	ST PANCRAS	99	93 48	87 22
	Net times	min	87½	85½

worked through from Manchester to London so that there was no question of starting 'cold' out of Leicester, as was the case on the up Scottish expresses in compound days. There was a marked easing to 60mph through Wellingborough station, after which the engine was driven so hard that the minimum speed up Sharnbrook bank, terminating with 3 miles at 1 in 120, was nothing less than 58mph. There was obviously no sign of steam shortage after this tremendous uphill effort, for the engine was taken full tilt downhill to attain a maximum speed of 91½mph below Sharnbrook station. Up to this stage the second run had fallen slightly behind, though still gaining just over 3 minutes on this fast schedule between Leicester and Kettering. Coming down from Desborough summit the driver on this second run eased from the 'middle-eighties' to 72mph through Kettering, but then opened out to such effect as to reach 90mph at Finedon —a most exceptional speed at that point. This acceleration was the prelude to one of the finest pieces of running I have ever seen on the Midland line.

Sharnbrook summit was cleared at exactly 60mph; a maximum of 91mph followed, but on passing Bedford North Junction, only 6¼ minutes of the 9-minute late start had been recovered. Only 6¼min indeed! This was good enough but by then the second run was only just drawing level with the first. Bedford itself was passed at 75mph, speed increased to 82mph on the level beyond, after which the long 1 in 200 up to Ampthill Tunnel did not bring any reduction below 71mph. The mile of level past Flitwick brought an acceleration to 76mph, and the final 6 miles up to the summit point at Milepost 34 were cleared at a minimum of 65mph. Although the train was practically on time at Luton very fast running continued, with maximum speeds of 90 mph at both Radlett and Hendon; and with a clear road through the outer suburbs Kentish Town, 97.6 miles, was passed in the remarkable time of 83min 10sec, a gain of nearly 13 minutes on schedule.

Nevertheless, while giving every credit with the driver and fireman on this splendid run it must be noted that the companion run was less than a minute behind at Hendon. The latter run was badly checked inwards from this point, though still arriving in St Pancras comfortably inside the fast schedule time. The second run, with no more than a moderate check at the finish, reached St Pancras 2¾ minutes early, after a 9-minute late start. The net time of 85½ minutes represented a start-to-stop average speed of 69.5mph, and had this driver emulated the very vigorous start of his colleague who officiated on the first run, the net time would have been 84 minutes, showing a truly remarkable average over this hilly road of 70.7mph. I should add that there existed then, as now over this route, an overall maximum speed limit of 90mph, which both of these drivers faithfully observed. At that time there were occasions when even faster running was noted by some of my friends, particularly with the Britannias. In *The Railway Magazine* I have set on record one instance of a maximum speed of 98mph and another of 101mph. That the drivers of No 45530 achieved such very fast overall times without indulging in such downhill exuberance adds further merit to these two runs.

For a final survey of the performance of ex-LMS locomotives we can turn, perhaps appropriately, to the West Coast main line north of Crewe. The Crewe—Carlisle section was the vindication and downfall of many a locomotive class famed in the history of Crewe Works, while of its continuation north of the Border one has only to breathe the words *Dunalastair* and *Cardean,* to recall a flood of old memories. Personal experience always has a way of supplanting the most arresting data that arrives, through the post, or which one can study in the rarified atmosphere of the drawing office; but in commencing this final survey with an account of a run of my own it will, I am sure, be agreed that this certainly proved an outstanding occasion. In the early spring of 1960 I had to travel to Glasgow at short notice, and using the Midland line from Cheltenham I caught the 10.55am express from New Street. The journey began badly, with such a succession of checks that we passed Preston 28 minutes late. With the train so much out of its path I feared many more checks, and was resigned to an arrival around an hour late in Glasgow. But then we got an absolutely clear road as far as Symington and had it not been for delays from a local train between there and Law Junction, we should have arrived in Glasgow Central on time. The engine was No 46241 *City of Edinburgh*, manned by driver A. Brown and fireman Lightfoot of Polmadie shed, and it was at Lancaster, having experienced no further checks after Preston, that a really major effort began.

Carnforth was passed at 72mph and then speed averaged just over 60mph throughout the 31.4 miles up to Shap Summit, such speeds as 48½mph at Grayrigg, and 37 at Shap itself being indeed notable with a 405-ton train. We regained 11½ minutes between Lancaster and Shap Summit, but due to the incidence of a relaying slack nothing further could be gained before Carlisle. A tremendous run was made over the Caledonian line. The time to Beattock station is certainly not my record, for on a previous occasion, when I was riding engine No 46252 *City of Leicester* on the down Midday Scot, our time was 35min 10sec. But the *City of Edinburgh* was opened out to a greater extent on Beattock bank, and passed the summit inside 'even time' in 48min 50sec from the Carlisle start, and no less than 14¼ minutes inside schedule. At that stage we were only 4 minutes late and with such a spectacular recovery from our earlier late running, a punctual arrival was now to be hoped for. Unfortunately, checks from local trains from Symington onwards prevented this, but even so we were only 3 minutes late in reaching Glasgow Central. As to the technical details of the engine performance, the average equivalent drawbar horsepower throughout the ascent from Milnthorpe to Grayrigg was 1,800, while on the Beattock bank an output of 1,860edhp was sustained. The steam rate necessary to produce such outputs would have been around 30,000lb per hour, involving a firing rate considerably above that which a single fireman could be expected to maintain continuously.

The work of the Duchess class engines in the North Country frequently provided classic examples of the way in which a skilful and determined engine crew could get a substantial 'extra' out of a steam locomotive, by building up for a big effort in advance, and then drawing upon the reserve of steam accumulated in the boiler. In the last years before dieselisation the load of the Royal Scot express was limited to eight coaches, as was also the Caledonian. The booked time from Lancaster to Carlisle, pass to stop, was then 69 minutes, with 35 minutes from Carnforth up to Shap Summit. Details are tabulated of two runs on which exceptionally high transitory outputs of power were recorded (Table 61). The first of the two runs, with engine No 46221 *Queen Elizabeth*, was on the Caledonian and the major effort followed a signal stop north of Carnforth. Speed was worked up to 75mph at Milnthorpe, and then the entire 12½ miles of the Grayrigg bank were climbed without speed falling below 66½mph. The equivalent drawbar horsepower was 2,150. There was clearly no shortage of steam, or exhaustion of the fireman, for speed was worked up powerfully to no less than 83½mph at Tebay, and Shap itself was climbed at a minimum speed of 51mph. The average edhp between Tebay and Summit was 1,940. Such a grand uphill effort was fitly rounded off by a downhill maximum of 92mph at Southwaite.

TABLE 61

LANCASTER—CARLISLE

Run No			1		2	
Engine No			46221		46247	
Engine Name			*Queen Elizabeth*		*City of Liverpool*	
Load tons E/F			264/280		277/295	
Distance Miles		Sch min	Actual min sec	Speed mph	Actual min sec	Speed mph
0.0	LANCASTER	0	0 00	20	0 00	72
3.1	Hest Bank		3 39	57	–	–
			sigs			
6.3	CARNFORTH	5	7 05	60	4 55	82
			sig stop		–	66
13.6	Milnthorpe		17 32	75	10 48	77
19.1	OXENHOLME	17	22 00	70	15 50	60
26.2	Grayrigg		28 10	66½	23 17	56/57
32.2	Tebay	32	32 47	83½	28 20	77
35.2	*Scout Green*		35 21	–	30 49	63
37.7	*Shap Summit*	40	38 05	51	33 15	60
47.0	*Clifton*		45 52	80	40 37	84
					pws	30
51.2	PENRITH	52	49 33	60*	45 25	–
61.7	Southwaite		57 31	92	–	83max
64.2	*Wreay*		59 30	–	55 45	–
			sigs		–	
69.1	CARLISLE	69	65 42	–	58 32	–
Net time, pass to stop (min)			56½		57½	

* Speed restriction

So far as transitory power was concerned however, this run is far eclipsed by the second, with engine No 46247 *City of Liverpool*, on the Royal Scot. This run was made when engineering delays, in preparation for electrification, were at their worst south of Crewe, and by the time Preston was passed there was much lee-way to be made up. A speed of 82-3mph was sustained on the level before Lancaster, and the tabulated portion of the run was entered upon. The engine was not being steamed particularly hard up Grayrigg bank, though the sustained minimum speed of 57mph on the final stretch at 1 in 106 was very good. The friend who logged this run ascertained that the cut-off was no more than 20 per cent on this section. Then Shap itself was climbed in well-nigh sensational style, for the 5.5 miles up from Tebay took only 4min 55sec. My friend took very complete details of the running, clocking the times at every milepost, and over the last 1¾ miles of ascent on the 1 in 75 the speed was sustained absolutely at 60mph. This gives an output of 2,600 equivalent drawbar horsepower, a completely outstanding transitory effort that has, so far as I am aware, only one recorded counterpart, and that in the middle of World War II.

This latter was one of those flashes of brilliance, so unexpected at the time as to be scarcely believable. It was an extraordinary burst of power output in the middle of a typically delayed wartime run, and could have passed barely noticed had not a railway enthusiast and an expert recorder been travelling on the train in the person of Mr C. M. Furst. It speaks volumes for his sustained interest that he should have continued to log in the fullest detail after so discouraging a start to the ascent of Grayrigg bank as a dead stand for signals at Oxenholme South. From the restart he clocked every milepost and was rewarded by a brief, but outstanding example of Stanier Pacific performance. The train was the wartime 10.5am from Euston to Perth, hauled by engine No 6244 *King George VI* with a load of 475 tons gross behind the tender. From the very moment the signals cleared the driver must have opened well out, for Mr Furst's milepost timings show a perfectly even and rapid acceleration on the continuous ascent. By the time the train crossed the Docker viaduct, then on a steady gradient of 1 in 131 and only 5 miles from the dead start, the speed reached was no less than 59mph, and on the last 2 miles to Grayrigg summit, at 1 in 106, it fell only to 55mph. This was equal to an output of around 2,500edhp. The effort was soon cut short, for the train was almost immediately involved in further severe signal checks.

In this brief period the crew of No 6244 had given a scintillating display of locomotive capacity and superb enginemanship. Some years later I discussed its implications with R. C. Bond, and he very kindly had it analysed by the staff at the Rugby Stationary Testing Plant. It was a power output far beyond anything they had obtained on the full dress trials with engine No 46225 *Duchess of Gloucester* when that engine was tested at Rugby, and again with the dynamometer car between

Skipton and Carlisle. Those trials were of course conducted at rates of evaporation that could be sustained indefinitely, even though it meant using two firemen. On the service run with No 6244 it is clear that the driver and fireman had built up a willing and free-steaming engine for a hard climb to Grayrigg; the enforced stop at Oxenholme South enabled them to harbour their resources still further, so that when they did get away the engine could be worked temporarily at a steam-rate that could not be sustained indefinitely. Fortunately the rail conditions were good, and there was no slipping. In this connection I recall an occasion when with the Midday Scot we were stopped at Sedgwick intermediate block signals, about two miles south of Oxenholme, and slipped so badly at the restart that we stopped again at Oxenholme for rear-end banking assistance. The engine was a Duchess and the load just over 500 tons.

And so, with recollections of both the strength and weakness of its mightiest engines I come to the end of this account of LMS steam. Like everywhere else on the railways of Great Britain, it was a premature end. The Duchesses, the Scots, the Black Fives and the many lesser lights had years of economic life left when their death warrant was signed by the so-called 'Modernisation Plan'. Future historians and future economists may well ponder upon the assets that were thrown away in the early 1960s. By then, of course, the London Midland & Scottish Railway had long since ceased to exist, though its locomotives, as this final chapter has shown, were still in very top form. Their memory remains a monument to Sir William Stanier, and to the team of engineers he gathered around him.

Acknowledgements

The author and publisher wish to thank the following for allowing the use of photographs:

P. M. Alexander for page 148 (lower)
E. D. Bruton for page 148 (upper)
Derek Cross for pages 166, 202 (upper), 220, 237, 238, 255 (lower), 256
M. W. Earley for page 165 (upper)
Ian S. Pearsall for pages 165 (lower), 183 (lower), 201, 255 (upper)
Ivo Peters for page 202 (lower)
Bishop E. Treacy for pages 18, 183 (upper)
Real Photographs Ltd (taken by H. G. Tidey) for pages 53 (upper), 72
Pages 53 (lower) and 90 (upper) are from the author's collection
The remainder are reproduced by courtesy of British Railways, London Midland Region
The coloured frontispiece and dust jacket picture is from a painting by Victor Welch

Index

Index